DURKHEIM'S *SUICIDE*

Durkheim's book on suicide, first published in 1897, is widely regarded as a classic text, and is essential reading for any student of Durkheim's thought and sociological method. While the subject of suicide, the violence of self-destruction, exerts an intrinsic emotional fascination, Durkheim employed an empirical methodology that attempted to build on fact. This book examines the continuing importance of this work for sociologists today, and revisits some of the key issues explored in *Suicide*.

Written by world renowned Durkheim scholars, the wide-ranging chapters in this book cover such issues as:

- the use of statistics
- explanations of suicide
- anomie
- religion and the morality of suicide.

Together, these studies illustrate both the central importance of *Suicide* in the teaching of sociology, and the continuing relevance of Durkheim's focus on the moral base of society and the importance of the social when attempting to understand modern society. This book will therefore be of vital interest to any serious scholar of Durkheim's thought, and to the sociologist looking for a fresh methodological perspective.

W. S. F. Pickering helped to found the British Centre for Durkheimian Studies at the University of Oxford and is currently its General Secretary. His recent publications include *Debating Durkheim*, *On Durkheim's* Elementary Forms of Religious Life, and *Durkheim and Modern Education*.

Geoffrey Walford is Reader in Education Policy and a Fellow of Green College at the University of Oxford. His publications include *Doing Educational Research*, *Doing Research about Education*, and *Durkheim and Modern Education*.

ROUTLEDGE STUDIES IN SOCIAL AND POLITICAL THOUGHT

1 HAYEK AND AFTER
Hayekian liberalism as a research programme
Jeremy Shearmur

2 CONFLICTS IN SOCIAL SCIENCE
Edited by Anton van Harskamp

3 POLITICAL THOUGHT OF ANDRÉ GORZ
Adrian Little

4 CORRUPTION, CAPITALISM AND DEMOCRACY
John Girling

5 FREEDOM AND CULTURE IN WESTERN SOCIETY
Hans Blokland

6 FREEDOM IN ECONOMICS
New perspectives in normative analysis
Edited by Jean-François Laslier, Marc Fleurbaey, Nicolas Gravel and Alain Trannoy

7 AGAINST POLITICS
On government, anarchy and order
Anthony de Jasay

8 MAX WEBER AND MICHEL FOUCAULT
Parallel life works
Arpad Szakolczai

9 THE POLITICAL ECONOMY OF CIVIL SOCIETY AND HUMAN RIGHTS
G. B. Madison

10 ON DURKHEIM'S *ELEMENTARY FORMS OF RELIGIOUS LIFE*
Edited by W. S. F. Pickering, W. Watts Miller and N. J. Allen

11 CLASSICAL INDIVIDUALISM
The supreme importance of each human being
Tibor R. Machan

12 THE AGE OF REASONS
Quixotism, sentimentalism and political economy in eighteenth-century Britain
Wendy Motooka

13 INDIVIDUALISM IN MODERN THOUGHT
From Adam Smith to Hayek
Lorenzo Infantino

14 PROPERTY AND POWER IN SOCIAL THEORY
A study in intellectual rivalry
Dick Pels

15 WITTGENSTEIN AND THE IDEA OF A CRITICAL SOCIAL THEORY
A critique of Giddens, Habermas and Bhaskar
Nigel Pleasants

16 MARXISM AND HUMAN NATURE
Sean Sayers

17 GOFFMAN AND SOCIAL ORGANIZATION
Studies in a sociological legacy
Edited by Greg Smith

18 SITUATING HAYEK
Phenomenology in the neo-liberal project
Mark J. Smith

19 THE READING OF THEORETICAL TEXTS
Peter Ekegren

20 THE NATURE OF *CAPITAL*
Marx after Foucault
Richard Marsden

21 THE AGE OF CHANCE
Gambling in Western Culture
Gerda Reith

22 REFLEXIVE HISTORICAL SOCIOLOGY
Arpad Szakolczai

23 DURKHEIM AND REPRESENTATIONS
Edited by W. S. F. Pickering

24 THE SOCIAL AND POLITICAL THOUGHT OF NOAM CHOMSKY
Alison Edgley

25 HAYEK'S LIBERALISM AND ITS ORIGINS
C. Petsoulas

26 METAPHOR AND THE DYNAMICS OF KNOWLEDGE
Sabine Maasen and Peter Weingart

27 LIVING WITH MARKETS
Jeremy Shearmur

28 DURKHEIM'S *SUICIDE*
A century of research and debate
Edited by W. S. F. Pickering and Geoffrey Walford

DURKHEIM'S *SUICIDE*

A century of research and debate

Edited by W. S. F. Pickering and Geoffrey Walford

Published in conjunction with the
British Centre for Durkheimian Studies

London and New York

First published 2000
by Routledge
2 Park Square, Milton Park, Abingdon, Oxfordshire OX14 4RN

Simultaneously published in the USA and Canada
by Routledge
711 Third Avenue, New York, NY 10017

First issued in paperback 2014

Routledge is an imprint of the Taylor and Francis Group, an informa company

Transferred to Digital Printing 2006

Typeset in Garamond by
The Running Head Limited, www.therunninghead.com

British Library Cataloguing in Publication Data
A catalogue record for this book is available
from the British Library

Library of Congress Cataloging in Publication Data
Durkheim's Suicide : a century of research and debate / edited by
W. S. F. Pickering and Geoffrey Walford
p. cm.
Includes bibliographical references and index.
1. Durkheim, Emile, 1858–1917. Suicide. 2. Suicide.
I. Pickering, W. S. F. II. Walford, Geoffrey.

HV6545.D833 2000
394′.8—dc21
99–059080

ISBN-13 978-0-415-20582-5 (hbk)
ISBN-13 978-1-138-00730-7 (pbk)

Publisher's Note
The publisher has gone to great lengths to ensure the quality of this reprint but points out that some imperfections in the original may be apparent

CONTENTS

NOTES ON CONTRIBUTORS

Philippe Besnard is Research Director at the Centre National de la Recherche Scientifique (CNRS) and teaches sociology at the Paris Institut d'Etudes Politiques. He heads the Observatoire Sociologique du Changement, a research centre of the Foundation Nationale des Sciences Politiques, and is director of the *Revue française de sociologie*. He founded the Groupe d'Etudes Durkheimiennes, an international network of specialists in the history of French sociology, and he has edited several special issues of the *Revue française de sociologie* in this area. His research has also focused on social rhythms and the sociology of taste. Publications include: *Division du travail et lien social: la thèse de Durkheim un siècle après* (Presses Universitaires de France, 1993, editor), *La Cote des prénoms* (Balland, 1998) and *Emile Durkheim: Lettres à Marcel Mauss* (Presses Universitaires de France, 1998, joint editor).

Kevin D. Breault is an associate professor of sociology at Middle Tennessee State University. He has published mainly in the area of deviance and crime. Recent works have appeared in *American Sociological Review*, *British Journal of Sociology*, *Journal of Interpersonal Violence*, *Journal of Quantitative Criminology*, *Social Forces* and *Social Science Research*. With Augustine Kposowa, he is currently working on a book on crime.

Christie Davies, who holds an MA and PhD from the University of Cambridge, is Professor of Sociology at the University of Reading. He has been a visiting lecturer in India, the United States and Poland, and has done empirical research in Canada, Switzerland and the United States. He is the author of several books including *Jokes and Their Relation to Society* (Mouton de Gruyer, 1998) and many articles in leading academic journals (*American Journal of Sociology*, *British Journal of Sociology*, *International Journal of the Sociology of Language*, *Policy Review*, *Humor: The International Journal of Humor Research*, *Journal of Strategic Studies*). He has lectured on Durkheim's *Suicide* for over thirty years and has taught a seven-week module, specifically devoted to *Suicide*, for over a decade.

Mike Gane is Reader in Sociology in the Department of Social Sciences at Loughborough University where he has been teaching since 1972. Born in 1943, he studied sociology at Leicester University (1965–8) and undertook doctoral studies at the LSE (1968–71). His main interests are in the development of social theory particularly in France, Germany, Britain and the United States. He has published widely on Durkheimian sociology: his books include *On Durkheim's* Rules of Sociological Method (Routledge, 1988), and he has edited the collection *The Radical Sociology of Durkheim and Mauss* (Routledge, 1992). He has also written *Baudrillard: Critical and Fatal Theory* (Routledge, 1991), *Baudrillard's Bestiary: Baudrillard and Culture* (Routledge, 1991) and edited *Baudrillard Live: Selected Interviews* (Routledge, 1993). He has edited two collections on Foucault, *Towards a Critique of Foucault* (Routledge, 1986) and (with T. J. Johnson) *Foucault's New Domains* (Routledge, 1993). He has also published a study of the emergence of masculinity as a theoretical issue in *Harmless Lovers? Gender, Theory and Personal Relationships* (Routledge, 1993). His recent writings have concerned Baudrillard, Canguilhem, Comte, Derrida, Durkheim, Lyotard, Marx, Mauss and Virilio. He is a member of the editorial board of *Economy and Society*, and *Durkheimian Studies*.

Alexander Gofman has a doctorate in sociology and is Professor at the Higher School of Economics in Moscow and Senior Researcher at the Institute of Sociology, Russian Academy of Sciences. He is the author of works on the history of sociology, sociological theory, the sociology of industrial design and fashion, including: *Fashion and People: A New Theory of Fashion and Fashion Behaviour* (in Russian, Moscow, 1994) and *Seven Lectures on the History of Sociology* (in Russian, Moscow, 1995, 1997). He has translated several of Durkheim's works into Russian including: *The Division of Labour in Society*, *The Rules of Sociological Method* and a collection of articles.

Robert Alun Jones is Professor of Religious Studies, History and Sociology at the University of Illinois in Urbana-Champaign. Besides Durkheim, his major research interests include the methodology of the history of ideas and the scholarly use of electronic documents and networked information systems. He is the editor of *Emile Durkheim: An Introduction to Four Major Works* (Sage, 1986), *The Development of Durkheim's Social Realism* (Cambridge, 1999), several edited volumes, and numerous journal articles on Durkheim. He has been the editor of *Etudes Durkheimiennes*, and is also responsible for the Durkheim site on the internet. He is currently working on Robertson Smith and the later Durkheim.

Augustine J. Kposowa is an associate professor of sociology at the University of California, Riverside. His interests include the identification of risk factors for violent victimization and the effects of immigration on the

US market. Recent publications have appeared in *British Journal of Sociology*, *Ethnic and Racial Studies*, *Journal of Interpersonal Violence*, *Journal of Quantitative Criminology* and *Social Forces*. He is also the author of *The Impact of Immigration on the United States Economy*.

Mark Neal is Lecturer in Organizational Studies at Aston University. He has a PhD in International Management and teaches business and sociology courses in Aston Business School. He is the author of two books, the most recent of which is *The Culture Factor: Cross-National Management and the Foreign Venture* (Macmillan, 1998), as well as articles in academic journals. His current research interests include the work of Emile Durkheim and comparative business values and management.

W. S. F. Pickering was for many years a lecturer in sociology in the Department of Social Studies, University of Newcastle upon Tyne. His books include *Durkheim on Religion* (Routledge and Kegan Paul, 1975, introduction and translations with J. Redding), *Durkheim: Essays on Morals and Education* (Routledge and Kegan Paul, 1979, edited with introductions), *Durkheim's Sociology of Religion: Themes and Theories* (Routledge and Kegan Paul, 1984), *Anglo-Catholicism: A Study of Religious Ambiguity* (Routledge and Kegan Paul, 1989), *Debating Durkheim* (Routledge, 1995, edited with H. Martins) and *On Durkheim's* Elementary Forms of Religious Life (Routledge, 1988, edited with N. J. Allen and W. Watts Miller). He is currently General Secretary of the British Centre for Durkheimian Studies at the University of Oxford.

William Ramp is Assistant Professor of Sociology at the University of Lethbridge, Alberta, Canada, where he teaches courses in sociological theory and the cultural history of modern selfhood. He is the author of 'Effervescence, Differentiation and Representation, in *The Elementary Forms*' in N. J. Allen, W. S. F. Pickering and W. Watts Miller (eds) *On Durkheim's* Elementary Forms of Religious Life (Routledge, 1998), and 'Durkheim and Foucault on the Genesis of the Disciplinary Society', in Mark Cladis (ed.) *Durkheim and Foucault: Punishment and the School* (The Durkheim Press, 1999). His interests include sociological theories of identity and subjectivity, especially as applied to the cultural history of modern concepts of citizenship, personal and collective identity, and embodiment.

Luigi Tomasi received his PhD in philosophy from the Catholic University of Milan and in sociology from the University of Trento (Italy), where he now works. He is currently Visiting Professor of Sociology at the Royal University of Phnom Penh (Cambodia). He has also been closely associated with the Committee on Social Thought at the University of Chicago, and studied under Edward A. Shils. The editor and author of numerous articles and several well-known monographs on the history of American sociological thought, his most recent publication on the subject is *The Tradition of the Chicago School of Sociology* (Ashgate, 1998). He is a member of the Executive Council of the Research Committee on The History of Sociology, International Sociological Association.

John Varty is currently completing his doctorate on Adam Ferguson's ideas of civil society in the Social and Political Thought Graduate Programme at the University of Sussex. He has taught at the University of Sussex and Anglia Polytechnic University.

Geoffrey Walford is Reader in Education Policy and a Fellow of Green College at the University of Oxford. He was previously Senior Lecturer in Sociology and Education Policy at Aston Business School, Aston University, Birmingham. He has published widely and his recent books include *Choice and Equity in Education* (Cassell, 1994), *Researching the Powerful in Education* (UCL Press, 1994, editor), *Doing Research about Education* (Falmer, 1998, editor), *Durkheim and Modern Education* (Routledge, 1998, edited with W. S. F. Pickering), and *Policy and Politics in Education* (Ashgate, 2000). He is joint editor of the *British Journal of Educational Studies*, series editor of *Studies in Educational Ethnography*, and is currently director of a three-year Spencer Foundation funded project on 'Faith Based Schools in England and The Netherlands'.

PREFACE

The chapters of this book, at least most of them, began as papers given at an international conference organized by the British Centre for Durkheimian Studies. The Centre is based in the Institute of Social and Cultural Anthropology at the University of Oxford. The three-day conference was held in December 1997 in conjunction with the Maison Française, Oxford. It commemorated the publication of Durkheim's book on suicide, which appeared a hundred years earlier. The wide range of papers dealing with this classical and still much used text in sociology, covered such issues as methodology, the use of statistics, explanations of suicide, anomie, religion, the morality of suicide and so on. One of the aims of the British Centre for Durkheimian Studies has been in holding a number of conferences on Durkheim and the band of scholars who surrounded him, and who after his death in 1917 continued to work on his ideas. Several of the conferences were funded by an award from the British Economic and Social Research Council; this was the last of such conferences.

When the time came to publish a book, such was the variety of papers given that it was impossible to include them all in such a volume. There had to be a selection which displayed a certain unity of style and development. The editors much appreciated those who were willing to let their papers be published and, in some cases, emended. But they are just as grateful to those who delivered papers but then found that their efforts could not be rewarded by having a chapter in the book. In order to give the book greater coherence and make it more comprehensive, one or two scholars who were writing in the field, but who could not attend the conference, were asked to submit contributions.

We are also grateful to those who helped with the organization of the conference and the preparation of the book. Once again our thanks extend to M. Jean-Claude Vatin, Director of the Maison Française, and his staff, and to those at Routledge who have helped with bringing the book to fruition.

Finally, it is necessary to forewarn readers of a particular technical point in the references in this book. Steven Lukes' dating–enumeration system for Durkheim's work has been followed throughout. In this system each original published work has its own specific identification. Unless otherwise specified, references to Durkheim thus give the date of the French original (followed by an identifying letter), then, where applicable, the date of the English translation used (again followed by an identifying letter). This system allows a precise identification of any quotations.

W.S.F.P.
G.W.

1

INTRODUCTION

W. S. F. Pickering and Geoffrey Walford

Many undergraduate students in the past, certainly in Britain and the United States, have been introduced to Durkheim's thought by reading his book on suicide (see chapter 12 here). Talk to them about Durkheim and immediately they refer to it. Of its kind, it is generally recognized as a classic, and if teachers want the students to encounter Durkheim's sociology, probably no other book written by him will create such a spark of enthusiasm.

Of course it has its own intrinsic fascination. The subject of suicide – unlike, for example that of the division of labour – frequently arouses the emotions. The feelings of would-be readers may be stimulated by the fact that they have known friends who have committed suicide or tried to do so. The violence of self-destruction prompts the enquiring mind to search for a cause. Durkheim probably had a similar experience, based on evidence to be found in his long obituary of a close friend, Victor Hommay, who at an early age apparently committed suicide (Lukes 1973:49–51). The starkness of the English title, *Suicide*, tempts one to take the book down from the shelf and browse through it.

But another reason for focusing on the book is that it employs, at least at first sight, the validity of an empirical methodology, attractive at least to some minds which like to start with 'facts' – if possible, statistical facts – from which a cause or causes for the 'abnormal' social phenomenon can be postulated. It has its appeal for those who are convinced that sociology should avoid grand theories or philosophical speculation. Whether Durkheim was successful in establishing causes by this method is something which remains open to debate, as will be shown here (see chapter 2).

In France, judged by the number of copies sold over the years, *Le Suicide* has not been the most popular of Durkheim's books (see Besnard 1993 for details about the number of books sold). That honour goes to *The Rules of Sociological Method*. *Le Suicide* comes roughly an equal second with *De la Division du travail social*. Why *Les Règles* has turned out to be the most widely purchased of all Durkheim's books is perhaps due to the alleged fact that the French academic mind prefers a more theoretical or philosophical book than *Le Suicide*. A more sceptical reason might be that it is a smaller and cheaper book than that on suicide!

The first edition of *Le Suicide* appeared in June 1897. According to the recently published *Lettres à Mauss*, Durkheim said he had finished the manuscript in February 1897, although he was still making finishing touches to it until the last moment (Durkheim 1998a:51). He appears to have handed it over to the Paris publishers, Alcan, who accepted all the books he wrote, early in March, perhaps 14 March. Remarkable is the fact that compared with our own age, with all its sophisticated electronic machinery, the book only took three months to produce. Durkheim was correcting the proofs on 4 April (1998a:63). In 1930 a new edition was brought out with a preface by Marcel Mauss. The page numbers of the two editions have remained the same.

The book was translated into English relatively late, in 1951, by the Americans J. A. Spaulding and G. Simpson, and turned out to be one of the most satisfactorily executed of all the early translations of Durkheim's works, although some would question the translation of the psychiatric terms used at the time (Berrios and Mohanna 1990:1). It was the last of the four great books to be translated. *The Elementary Forms of the Religious Life* was the first and appeared in 1915, only three years after the French publication. *The Division of Labour* came out in English in 1933 and *The Rules* in 1939. All the translations appeared first in America but were frequently published by an English press shortly afterwards. Thus *Suicide* officially appeared in England in 1952, published by Routledge and Kegan Paul, via the American publishers, Free Press of Glencoe.

Students in their undergraduate days may associate Durkheim's study of suicide with Max Weber's classical text, *The Protestant Ethic and the Rise of Capitalism*, which appeared shortly after Durkheim's book, around 1904. Indeed, there are striking, but some would want to say superficial, parallels. Protestantism, be it in the seventeenth, eighteenth or nineteenth centuries, is according to Max Weber the key factor in the rise and development of bourgeois capitalism. For Durkheim, however, Protestantism in the nineteenth century was associated with a relatively high level of suicide in Europe.

But the analysis has further parallels in so far as both Durkheim's and Weber's contentions fail at the same point. Given the sociological correlation that Protestantism is related to both the rise of capitalism and high levels of suicide, the problem is to know precisely what in Protestantism brings about these consequences. One comes face to face with endless possibilities, none of which by itself seems satisfactory. For example, why is it that capitalists of a Protestant disposition were so successful? Was it on account of their disposition to hard work, to honesty, to dealing with persecution, for being open to change, and so on? All these can be said to be characteristics of various Protestant churches. Each characteristic rationally offers a possible answer. To posit multiple 'causes' in a random fashion is not convincing. And in the matter of suicide, what is the factor operating in Protestantism which could be said to give rise to a relatively high level of suicide? That Protestants were of an individualistic disposition? That the control of ministers over their flocks was not as authoritarian as that in Catholic parishes? That Protestant churches did not have that level of social cohesion or solidarity present in Catholic churches? And if one factor is singled out, should it not apply to other religious groups in accounting for varying levels of suicide?

But to return to the production of the book and Durkheim's attitude towards it. He was certainly proud of what he had written. After he had delivered it to the publisher he wrote: 'Pauvre bouquin, cela me fait de la peine de m'en séparer' (Poor old book, it is painful to be separated from it) (Durkheim 1998a:65). Does this also imply that he was a long time writing it, as Gaston Richard, a former colleague of Durkheim, seemed to indicate? But he was also keen to know how it would be received by the academic world. An early reaction on his part was that it was all a wasted effort (un coup de l'épée dans l'eau) (Durkheim 1998a:78), for early reviews were far from encouraging (for a more detailed account of the reception of the book, see chapter 10 here). He became somewhat depressed at this time, not least because of the pressure of producing what he thought was a significant book but also of having to prepare the first volume of the journal, *L'Année sociologique*, which was intended to further the cause of sociology. Further, emotional tension was heightened over the possibility of his receiving a chair at the Collège de France, which in the end eluded his grasp (for Durkheim's mental troubles see Mucchielli 1998).

Despite the final popularity of *Le Suicide* to which we have referred, it is remarkable that in later years Durkheim made little or no reference to it. Why was this so? Three answers are possible. First, he was completely satisfied with what he had written and there was no need for further statistical research which would modify his theories. Second, he lost all interest in the subject as other issues, such as religion and morality, became more important to him. And third, that he did not refer to suicide much in later years might have been due to what he saw as a theoretical or methodological flaw which he later realized but did not wish to speak about. He was sometimes sceptical about the use of statistics, and his next book – his *magnum opus*, *The Elementary Forms* (1912a) – used as its data, not statistics about contemporary religion, but ethnographic material from preliterate societies in central Australia. Did a sense of failure cause him to seek empirical data of a totally different kind? We can only speculate as to possible reasons. Of course, it could be argued that he always sought to work on primal or primitive forms of social institutions as a key to understanding later and more complex ones, and that statistics would be out of place.

With the expansion (in the western world) of universities after World War II and the accompanying rapid growth of social sciences in university curricula, *Le Suicide* tended to be portrayed as a worthwhile text for students (see chapter 12 here). Such approval gradually gave way to more serious criticisms as sociology became increasingly sophisticated and as methodology became more and more a subject of debate and even acrimony. With the advance of statistical analysis it was evident that Durkheim's use of statistics was inadequate. Its naïveté gave rise to facile conclusions as was evident in both early and late criticisms of the book. The result in some circles was to degrade it so that in the hands of some teachers it became popular only on the grounds that it showed the way how not to do sociology!

Durkheim's contribution to the study of suicide has often been said to be his theoretical approach. He made his nephew Marcel Mauss work extremely hard on the book in compiling statistical tables. Mauss said he classified 26,000 suicides, all arranged on cards (1979). But, of course, they were available from statistics from government and other sources throughout Europe, which had been collected by various bodies and commented on by scholars, not least Morselli. Durkheim's specific contribution to the study of suicide was not so much in producing more statistics but in his carefully argued rejection of psychological, geographical, sexual and similar approaches to an understanding of suicide. Instead he placed an overriding emphasis on social characteristics, for suicide is seen as a social act, not an essentially individual one. Perhaps less convincing in some people's eyes is the fact that he felt it necessary to subdivide the phenomenon of suicide into types or classes, in which each is related to corresponding social factors.

The various criticisms that have been levelled against the book are dealt with in the pages ahead. Nevertheless these criticisms only partially detract from the book's continued popularity as a text with which sociology students have to grapple. It is highly fitting that a book should be devoted to the reassessment of Durkheim's classic work over one hundred years after its publication.

Following this introduction, the chapter by Luigi Tomasi gives a broad overview of Durkheim's contribution to the sociological explanation of suicide. He argues that the sociological explanation of suicide is both awkward and also slightly disturbing because, according to sociologists, people do not kill themselves. Instead, those who commit suicide are always, at least partly, killed by the social conditions in which they live. The suicide phenomenon is sociological in so far as it is considered from the point of view of a way of reasoning which is typical of sociology. This chapter highlights how the work of Emile Durkheim on suicide represents a significant stage in our knowledge of the phenomenon. Tomasi focuses on how Durkheim was able to present voluntary death – traditionally seen as an individual event or act – as a sociological fact, in order to demonstrate that an event as definite as suicide can be explained on the basis of variations in suicide rates. In making evaluations and judgements on suicide as a 'social factor', special attention is given to type, the result of a differentiated analysis, which is to be considered Durkheim's most long-lasting contribution. Furthermore, the chapter tackles the problem of the recontextualization of suicide in today's society and, at the same time, discusses the 'rather inaccurate' interpretations made by Durkheim himself. Finally, Tomasi argues that the strength of *Suicide* lies in its being a work produced in a precise social context, using pioneering methodology typical of earlier sociology and based on a theory whose validity is primarily provided by the discussion which arises from it one hundred years on.

The next three chapters focus on methodological and theoretical issues. The third chapter, by Mike Gane, considers the many critical issues that are raised by Durkheim's statement that in *Suicide* he reversed the method advocated in *The Rules of Sociological Method*. This chapter outlines what this reversal meant in practice, and discusses whether the alteration was a minor adjustment once the epistemological space of sociology was established or, on the contrary, raises fundamental questions as to the relation between the theoretical framework, sociological analysis and methodological procedures. Gane argues that Durkheim improvises a quite different solution from the one expected of him, and that by so doing, initiated an auto-deconstruction of key methodological propositions.

In the fourth chapter Christie Davies and Mark Neal discuss the neglect by subsequent sociologists of Durkheim's concepts and discussion of altruistic and fatalistic suicide. This is contrary to the symmetrical quality of Durkheim's work in which those forms of suicide are balanced by egoistic and anomic suicide. Durkheim's critics have tended to argue that he did not give enough modern examples of altruistic and fatalistic suicide and that his only substantive example of altruistic suicide is that of the military. However, such suicide is in itself important enough to justify the use of the idea of altruistic suicide, and Durkheim in fact provides a complex and subtle set of comparisons between military rank and unity to support his thesis.

Durkheim's critics are sadly Eurocentric. A study of Asian suicide rates and notably of the very high suicide rates among young (15- to 24-year-old) women in rural China indicates that altruistic and fatalistic suicide are major phenomena in those societies. Durkheim was right in seeing a curvilinear relationship between egoistic and anomic suicide on the one hand, and altruistic and fatalistic on the other, with a notional 'low point' somewhere in between.

However, there remains a serious problem: the fall in the suicide rate of the military (both army *and* navy) in wartime, which ought not to happen according to Durkheim as increased integration and regulation are being imposed on an already excessively integrated and regulated institution. What this phenomenon and a consideration of the unstable suicide rate of religious orders and sects reveal is that the suicide rate under conditions of extreme altruism and fatalism is indeterminate; it depends on the content of the rules and the nature of the ethos of the institution concerned in a way that is not true of egoistic or fatalistic suicide. The curvilinear Durkheimian model thus fails and in this chapter is replaced with a new and more sophisticated model which coincides with the Durkheimian model at high levels of egoism and anomie but is deliberately indeterminate at the altruistic and fatalistic end of the spectrum.

In the fifth chapter John Varty assesses Douglas' analysis of Durkheim's use of statistics in *Suicide*. Some time ago Jack Douglas raised the most comprehensive critique of the reliability of the official suicide statistics that Durkheim used. Douglas' analysis broadens out to a wider questioning of how one should study suicide sociologically. Should the focus be upon suicide rates or individual acts of suicide? Should it be upon the external, social causes of suicide rates or the shared and personal meanings that cause individual acts of suicide?

In order to provide a critical account of the Durkheim–Douglas debate Varty focuses on Durkheim's use of suicide statistics and his discussion of their accuracy and meaning; he discusses the problems arising out of Durkheim's definition of suicide, and outlines and assesses Douglas' critique of Durkheim.

Producing a verdict of suicide is a complex process involving a coroner's investigation into possible motivations that lie behind someone's death. Durkheim was aware of this problem and the difficulties it raised for his study. He observed that the official statistics of motives 'are in fact the statistics of the opinions about motives held by officials'. Durkheim doubted the reliability of the statistics on suicide motives yet he did not extend this uncertainty towards statistics of the number of suicides. Douglas argues that Durkheim should have taken a further step in questioning not just the validity of the official judgements of motives but also of the suicide statistics themselves.

The following pair of chapters focus on the moral aspect of *Suicide*. In chapter 6 W. S. F. Pickering asks readers to give more attention than they have before to the conclusion of *Suicide*, and to understand Durkheim's view of morality and religion presented there. *Suicide* is concerned with social phenomena other than suicide. As Durkheim admitted, his book raises questions which are associated with serious practical problems of the day. It is in the last chapters in the conclusion that several such issues are raised. Particularly important are those which relate to aspects of morality and religion, some of which are not considered elsewhere in the book and in his other writings. Durkheim presented a brief history of the moral attitudes of rulers, philosophers and theologians towards suicide. In some instances he misunderstood the writings of Christian theologians. The criticisms of Bayet, who was inspired to write his long book on morality and suicide as a result of reading Durkheim on the subject, are briefly stated, as are the problems of humanists with regard to the morality of suicide. What is not often stressed is that Durkheim committed himself to a strong position in considering suicide as absolutely immoral. In *Suicide* religion is portrayed very much in terms of its function of social control and the influence it can have on those given to suicide. Finally, secularization and the origin of religion, mentioned in these final chapters, are critically analysed.

This is followed by William Ramp's chapter which explores the moral discourse of Durkheim's *Suicide*. The status of *Suicide* as a methodological classic is reinforced by Durkheim's own description of it as a 'concrete and specific' example of sociological method. But his characterization begs a question about the topic: why suicide? The chapter seeks answers both in the context in which the work was written and in Durkheim's own justification of his topical choice, suggesting that suicide was more than a convenient occasion to demonstrate a sociological perspective and method. Durkheim attempted an ambitious moral theory of society organized around one of the most symbolically troubling features of modern life.

Suicide was part of, and addressed, a prolific nineteenth-century literature on 'problems of modern life' (excessive individualism, isolation, neurasthenia, a decline in traditional moral regulation): even its method was anticipated by moral statisticians. It exemplified the growth of professions, disciplines and policies concerned with the productivity, health and order of national populations as objects of study and intervention (Foucault's 'governmentality'). In this context, suicide was a resonant issue: an ultimate act of self-sovereignty in a culture of individualism, it was also a symbolic challenge to the moral integrity, productivity and welfare of national societies.

Durkheim himself claimed to have chosen the topic because few subjects were 'so accurately defined' (or had generated so much statistical data), and because suicide was instructive concerning the 'cause of the general maladjustment being undergone by European societies and concerning remedies which may relieve it'. A third reason appears in the course of the study: suicide not only mirrors the social malaise of the time, it can pose a threat to the moral order itself. Ramp argues that *Suicide* not only reflects but transcends its context. It may be seen as a unique moral statement, proposing a relentless *sociological* morality, as attuned to the consequences and social meanings of self-destruction as to its causes.

Chapter 8, by Philippe Besnard, considers the reception, acceptance and eventual place in the academic world of Durkheim's *Suicide*, based on the evidence of reviews at the time of the book's publication. Reference is also made to contemporary correspondence between Durkheim and other academics – in particular his letters to Marcel Mauss. The reception of the book was a disappointment to Durkheim. It was largely neglected by his followers between the wars, along with other studies on suicide. This was despite Halbwachs' book, which attempted to extend Durkheim's work although he disagreed with Durkheim theoretically. *Suicide* was also seldom mentioned in studies on social disorganization in the United States, certainly in comparison with allusions to other books that Durkheim wrote. This was the position until about 1950, but from then on and in the decade that followed, the book was increasingly referred to. Other issues raised in the chapter are the book's influence on the sociology of suicide and whether the theory is still valid.

In a somewhat similar way the next chapter, by Alexander Gofman, contains a description and an analysis of the Russian reception of Durkheim's *Suicide* until the 1930s. Although Durkheim did not consider Russian suicide statistics, his study provoked a great interest, and Russia was the first place where Durkheim's classical essay was published outside France. There were many reviews and extensive analysis of this classic text. In general, in spite of rare criticism, the reception of *Suicide* was favourable, certainly more favourable than, for example, the reception of Durkheim's *Division of Labour* or *Rules of Sociological Method*. This attitude can be explained by the growth in the number of suicides in Russia at the turn of the century, as well as by the character and the scale of the sociological object of study. As the subject was relatively narrow and did not obviously consider the global and fundamental problems of the nature of society and sociology, Durkheim's *Suicide* did not affect the profound 'theoretical emotions' that had existed in Russian society. Thus, rather than provoking lively conceptual discussions and debates, it was warmly received.

The following two chapters present research that deals with suicides in the present day. Chapter 10, again by Philippe Besnard, is concerned with the relationships between marriage and the frequency of suicide. This chapter was originally published in French in the *Revue française de sociologie* and it is here translated into English. Following an analysis of Durkheim's theory and a review of the relevant literature, Besnard seeks to determine whether the theory of marital regulation can still shed light on variations in suicide rates by marital status – and developments of these variations – in France. First, Besnard compares the suicide rates of 1889–91 and 1981–91. There is a remarkable stability in the rates for women, but significant changes for men. Next, the chapter examines an area hardly discussed by Durkheim: the possible effect of a change in marital status. The effect of widowhood as an event rather than a state is examined in detail.

At the heart of the chapter is a very detailed discussion of the effects of recent changes within the institution of marriage, where time series correlations are presented between various marital indicators and suicide rates. This analysis gives fragmentary but convergent results that tend to confirm the central thesis of Durkheim's theory of marital regulation: marriage as an institution protects men from the risk of suicide more than women. Correlations between time series for the years 1968–93 suggest that the deinstitutionalization of marriage has essentially affected suicide rates among young married men, whereas it has not affected rates for married women. This is consistent with Durkheim's theory.

Data on individuals reveal that widowhood and divorce, whether as events or conditions, increase the risk of suicide more for men than women. Familial integration – the presence of children – can play a role in this difference, because many more divorced women than men live with children. But this factor cannot suffice to account for the differential effect of widowhood by gender. It is true that widows live more often than widowers with their own or other children, but this difference is not at all proportional to the enormous difference between the sexes in the effect of widowhood on suicide. The loss of one's spouse (event) or the spouse's absence (state) fragilizes men much more than women. If we add that this difference has strongly increased over the century, we can find support here for the Durkheimian thesis that the interests of the respective sexes within the marriage institution are antagonistic to each other.

Chapter 11 by K. D. Breault and Augustine J. Kposowa presents an analysis of 30,157 suicides recorded in the United States. It uses individual level statistics drawn from the *Mortality Detail File* produced by the US National Center for Health Statistics. It is thus the largest study ever completed, covering males, females, white, African American, Hispanics, Asian Americans and Native Americans for the single year 1992. In some contrast to the previous chapter, these results indicate little support for Durkheim's social integration thesis concerning marital status. None of the ten sex and race/ethnic groups followed the general marital status pattern predicted by Durkheim, and in no group is marriage of greater benefit (in terms of protection from the risk of suicide) than the other three categories. Of 30 comparisons between marriage and other marital statuses, Durkheim's predictions are supported in only eight, six of which concern divorce/separation. The most important result of the study is that single status is of greater benefit than marriage for white, black and Hispanic males. Widow status is similarly beneficial to white and Hispanic women. Unemployment is positively significant only for white females. Foreign-born status is a significant suicide risk for black males and females, Hispanic males and females, and Asian American females. The discussion focuses on methodological approaches to suicide and to theoretical alternatives to social integration.

Finally, in chapter 12 six academics discuss teaching Durkheim's *Suicide*, one of the few classic studies in sociology that is still studied by undergraduates and postgraduates. It is still frequently a key recommended text in many British and American undergraduate sociology courses. It is studied not only for its contribution to the understanding of suicide and to methodology, but also for its development of theory. In essence, it presented an example of sociological study that Durkheim wished others to follow. Although Durkheim was writing about a century ago, the uncertain and rapidly changing situation that France faced at the time has many similarities with the present day. Durkheim's focus on the moral base of society and his insistence of the importance of the social and society have important implications for today.

This chapter brings together a range of contributions from a sample of university lecturers in sociology and other linked disciplines who focus on *Suicide* within their teaching. For some contributors, *Suicide* is the central reference within a course lasting most of a first undergraduate year. For others it is the topic of just one or two lectures. In all cases the authors believe that the text should be studied not just because of its historical contribution to the development of sociology, but for what it still has to add to sociological enquiry. Each contribution discusses the task of teaching *Suicide* in a different way, with some being more theoretical and others more practical in orientation, but each in its own way seeks to answer such questions as:

Why still study *Suicide*?
What are the ways in which *Suicide* is used within teaching?
How do students react to *Suicide*?
What do students gain from the study of *Suicide*?

As such, this last chapter provides a suitable finale to the book.

Bibliography

Berrios, G. and Mohanna, M. (1990) 'Durkheim and French Psychiatric Views on Suicide during the 19th Century: A Conceptual View', *British Journal of Psychiatry* 156:1–9.

Besnard, P. (1993) 'La diffusion de l'édition française', in P. Besnard, M. Borlandi and P. Vogt (eds) *Division du travail et lien social. La thèsis de Durkheim un siècle après*, Paris: Presses Universitaires de France.

Durkheim, E. (1897a) *Le Suicide: étude de sociologie*, Paris: Alcan.

(1912a) *Les Formes élémentaires de la vie religieuse. Le système totèmique*, Paris: Alcan.

(1998a) *Durkheim. Lettres à Marcel Mauss*, Paris: Presses Universitaires de France.

Lukes, S. (1973) *Emile Durkheim*, London: Penguin Books.

Mauss, M. (1979) 'L'Oeuvre de Mauss par lui-mème', *Revue Française de Sociologie* 20:209–20.

Mucchielli, L. (1998) 'Autour de la "révélation" d'Emile Durkheim', in J. Carroy and N. Richard (eds) *La Découverte et ses récits en sciences humaines*, Paris: L'Harmattan.

Richard, G. (1923) 'L'Athéisme dogmatique en sociologie religieuse', *Revue d'Histoire et de Philosophie Religieuses* 1923:125–37, 229–61, translated (1975) by J. Redding and W. S. F. Pickering, in W. S. F. Pickering (ed.) *Durkheim on Religion*, London and Boston: Routledge and Kegan Paul.

2

EMILE DURKHEIM'S CONTRIBUTION TO THE SOCIOLOGICAL EXPLANATION OF SUICIDE

Luigi Tomasi

Emile Durkheim's thought needs to be interpreted in relation to the historical background of French culture. At the time the French nation was refinding its identity as it sought to assert itself in Europe and in the pursuit of colonial ambitions through conquests in Africa and Asia. France's ambitions were those of a bourgeoisie compelled to find moral justification both for the economic system that it was then engaged in constructing and for the institutional framework in which that system was located.

In his treatment of ethical problems Durkheim followed closely the thought of Immanuel Kant and his school, while his sociology was influenced by Auguste Comte and a detailed knowledge of eighteenth-century French culture. His intellectual formation was such that, once he had begun his scientific career, he was never again completely able to separate the sociological from the ethical-philosophical dimensions, although he always harmoniously blended the two aspects.

At the more strictly sociological level, as was just mentioned, Auguste Comte and also Herbert Spencer were the authors to whom Durkheim often referred, although in developing his theories he also drew on the most disparate of sources, from classical authors to historians. Behind these authors, however, and behind the construction of Durkheim's thought itself, lay an endeavour to give a moral foundation to the political and social system: an implicit endeavour which explains not only the logic of Durkheim's thought but also the emphasis that he placed on some issues rather than others.

For Durkheim the moral rules that govern society are grounded in the belief systems from which they ensue, in religious systems, in the legal institutions, in languages, and in customs. All these must be studied by the sociologist, whose task it is to specify the value-premises on which rest social morality and the collective conscience. Accordingly Durkheim sought to clarify the function of moral values embraced by society as a whole in individual action.

Judged solely by its title, Durkheim's work *Le Suicide* (1897a) seems to have little relevance to the problem of social order, whereas it is exactly this question that the book addresses. Durkheim, in fact, considered suicide above all to be a signal of crisis in a society riven by constant and excessively rapid change, a phenomenon which threatened the existence not only of society but also of the individual. His choice of theme was determined both by a desire to give social relevance to science and to challenge and defeat the utilitarians on their own ground, explaining in social terms a phenomenon, namely suicide, which was generally believed to stem from individual motivations.

Over one hundred years have passed since the publication of *Le Suicide* in 1897, a work which is a milestone in the history of sociology. In the intervening period the book has proved to be one of the most influential studies published in the social sciences. For the understanding of suicide – or at least in so far as it is a valid starting point for analysis of the phenomenon – *Le Suicide* has been considered a work of major importance. It is also one of the most outstanding examples in the history of sociology of research based on statistics: using innovative methods it sought to verify hypotheses deduced from sociological theory. Today, the sociocultural explanation of suicide has changed, and because of its heuristic and hermeneutic implications research and sociology are obliged to take this changed interpretation into account, but this in no way diminishes the value of the work as a serious attempt to adopt an analytic approach. Sociological interest in suicide grew out of the increased quantity and accessibility of literary and scientific documentation, first as regards the relationship of ethics with nature and the social order, and later in the sectors of psychiatry, psychology, medicine and Romantic literature. In the second half of the nineteenth century, the cultural factors adduced in the explanation of suicide were joined by progress in statistics. Thus the collection of data on suicide and their organization into statistical surveys became the real source of the social explanation of the phenomenon, with particular emphasis placed on their role as resources for interpretation and knowledge.

The writing of *Le Suicide* was stimulated and made possible by the publications containing suicide statistics then making their appearance in several countries, and also by the academic studies from which Durkheim drew data and with which he polemicized – most notably *Il Suicidio* by Enrico Morselli, which had acquired a certain reputation (Morselli 1879). Although the explanation of suicide as a sociocultural phenomenon was not created by the science of statistics, the latter highlighted its quantitative dimensions through measurement and theory-based estimation. Sociology replaced the quantification of individual units and the dimensions of morphological facts performed by statistical etiology with analysis of qualities and measures in terms of social differentiation (Tomasi 1989).

Of its kind, *Le Suicide* was Durkheim's first and only empirically based sociological study. The data used in writing it were in part first-hand, but to a much larger extent they were drawn from second- or even third-hand sources. Moreover, Durkheim expected his data to yield more information than they were capable of delivering, and he did not possess statistical tools adequate to the task. Suffice it to point out that his constant use of the method of concomitant variation was not backed by the coefficient of correlation, and that he sometimes employed the method in a logically inexact manner.

How, in the circumstances of his time, did Durkheim perceive the relationship between society and the individual? Put briefly, he simply posited voluntary death (traditionally considered by philosophy, ethics and psychiatry to be an individual act or event) as a 'social fact', and he did so in order to prove that a fact defined as suicide could be explained by variations in the suicide rate.

Durkheim used the method of concomitant variation in an attempt to demolish the purported relationships between psychopathological states and suicide, between alcoholism and suicide, and between genetic factors and suicide. In doing so, he probably went too far in his destructive endeavour, and especially with regard to the first of the three relations.

He also committed a number of errors in his rebuttals. Despite these reservations, however, one must admit that his *pars destruens* managed to prove that suicide is, at least in part, caused by general social conditions. Moreover, one must acknowledge that in his uncompromising critique of the alleged non-social causes of suicide – the physical environment and heredity in particular – he abided by the rule that social facts like the suicide rate should only be explained in terms of other social facts.

Durkheim showed that if ever there was a phenomenon linked more than any other to the variability of the relations between society and the individual, it was suicide. Evidence was to be deduced from social statistics, notwithstanding the private reticence and public visibility which for many decades made statistics on suicide so unreliable and difficult to interpret. It was unclear how much weight should be attributed to social factors that worked in favour of or against the exercise of free will.

The data on suicide and its variable rates made a substantial impression on early sociological research. It became increasingly possible to determine suicide rates in a direct, concomitant or participatory fashion as suicide and the processes that induced it grew apace, with social transformations such as greater mobility of individuals and families, migration, industrialization, urbanization, and so on.

Despite the causalism of the variables assumed by Durkheim's typology, and despite the criticisms that have been made of this typology, the sociological viewpoint on suicide initiated by Durkheim – whose merit it was to render the phenomenon observable from the societal exterior – can be stated as follows: voluntary death is neither conventional nor inspired by sociologism; rather, it is an act against solidarity, a rejection of society itself, related above all to the state of integration of the individuals and groups who live in that society.

Social statistics in the second half of the nineteenth century recorded an increase in suicide rates in concomitance with enormous social changes; at which point it became far too easy to correlate the malaise provoked by social change with practices, attitudes, fads and even trends inducing suicide, whether successful or only attempted.

Correlations among variables – and therefore differences in suicide rates by age, marital status, sex, profession, urban or rural residence, religion, season of the year, climate, political crisis, economic instability, the methods and means used to commit suicide, and the ratios between statistics on suicide and homicides – raised the problem of how certain statistical dimensions and quantities could have moral qualities and social significance.

Attempts were made to find a benchmark for these qualities, given that statistical measurements of social facts like suicide, as well as technical aspects (such as, for example, correlation coefficients, which were unfortunately unknown to Durkheim), were deliberately designed to demonstrate the irrelevance of free will and thereby invalidate it as a metaphysical presupposition.

In reality, and also with regard to the difficulty of interpreting data and suicide rates, social statistics encountered the problem of moralization, where the principal issues were on the one hand deciding whether social statistics gave rise to moral data, and on the other, whether with their conceptual and technical tools, social statistics could in fact give a cultural interpretation to material data.

It is interesting to enquire if and how the problem of the 'moralization' of statistics in the mid-nineteenth century anticipated or interwove with methodological debate on the social sciences and their growing hermeneutic needs as historical-cultural – or comprehensive – sciences.

Sociology assumed the task of 'moralizing' the presence of morphological factors, measurements and statistical estimates by adopting the viewpoint of social differentiation. And Durkheim made a decisive contribution to this shift from a science of synthesis to the scientific analysis of society.

The distinction drawn between the normal and the pathological undoubtedly had a significant effect on Durkheim's conception of suicide, for it implied that in a normal society the suicide rate should fall, and the rate of fatal self-aggression could reasonably be attributed to individual free will. By contrast in a pathological society, or in one with a low level of integration, the percentage of socially induced fatal aggressiveness should increase.

However, Durkheim considered the two types of aggression to be heterogeneous in their causes and effects. His distinction between egoistic and altruistic types of suicide, as well as anomic suicide, demonstrates the extent to which they were tied to the influence of the dichotomy between the normal and the pathological. This had important effects, most notably the 'demoralization' of the phenomenon of suicide from the point of view of its contextual identification.

'Egoistic' suicide is so called because it is an act in which the individual self overwhelms the social self. This can obviously only happen in a society characterized by organic (or excessively individualistic) solidarity, so that the collective conscience loses that grip which Durkheim believed so necessary for the health of individuals. However, he did not elucidate this relationship, or at any rate he did not do so initially. He developed it implicitly by examining the relationship between suicide rates and the degree of social integration in the three most important forms of society: religious, familial and political. He sought to show, again using the method of concomitant variation, that suicide rates were higher among Protestants than among Catholics or Jews. Concentrating his analysis on the two Christian groups, he sought to explain the difference between them in terms of the different natures of their religious systems.

The crucial factor, he argued, was the free examination of conscience permitted to Protestants but denied to Catholics, and which among Protestants was accompanied by the absence of an ecclesiastical hierarchy and a multiplicity of sects, whereas Catholics were subject to an ecclesiastical hierarchy and to the monolithic unity of the Church. Protestants were less integrated within their community than Catholics, and more liable to be pushed into suicide by egoism. Durkheim argued that only the group could furnish the individual with valid reasons for his or her existence.

It should be pointed out that Durkheim's celebrated assertion of the relationship between suicide and religion is open to some criticism. He did not thoroughly investigate the historical context of his data on religious membership. And yet it had been known for some time that the Protestant areas of the world were those most closely associated with the economic-social growth of capitalism. Even within the German regions of mixed religion, the Protestant population was mainly concentrated in the cities, where it engaged in more modern economic activities; the Catholic population, by contrast, lived mainly in rural areas and devoted itself to agriculture. Owing to his unfortunate habit of using data aggregated by region, Durkheim committed an error which somewhat undermines the validity of his results. It is probable, in fact, that the label 'Protestant' frequently conceals a process of de-Christianization in the most advanced capitalist countries and regions. This, however, Durkheim did not accept, declaring instead that Protestantism was the result of the breakdown of traditional beliefs which proved impossible to replace with others.

Durkheim then passed to consideration of familial society. In *Le Suicide* he sought to show that the family, when it is properly developed and defended, is a safeguard against suicide and therefore a factor in social and personal order. Using the method of concomitant variation, he demonstrated that married individuals with numerous children were less likely to commit suicide. However, he did not put forward alternative hypotheses, for example that the personalities of individuals who marry and have children are not prone to suicidal tendencies.

Durkheim drew the general conclusion that the suicide rate varied in inverse ratio to the integration of a community and then attempted to explain egoistic suicide. His theory started with the fact that man is in part a child of nature and in part a child of society, but it is to society that humans owe their higher activities such as morality. Consequently, an excess of individualism removes all value from the latter. In particular, suffering becomes bereft of every moral value, and the individual prefers to take his or her life; which amounts to the assertion that life is generally unbearable for those who do not have ends that transcend it.

Society has self-consciousness: it is aware of the fact that it is disintegrating, and it thus realizes that the individuals whom it has shaped and who posit it as their end, are losing every reason to exist. Consequently society grows melancholic. Given the intimate relationship between individuals and society, currents of depression and disenchantment traverse every aspect of existence. Life-denying ideologies arise, followed by new moral codes which recommend suicide, or at least covertly urge it. Caught in the cross-fire, so to speak, assailed from within and without, individuals take their lives and the suicide rate rises.

The most significant type of suicide is anomic suicide, which Durkheim viewed as resulting from rapid and uncontrolled change, and therefore as the form of suicide typical of a society in crisis. Initially, Durkheim concentrated on economic crises with their correlated increases in the suicide rate. He believed that every change, for better or worse, made individuals more vulnerable to suicidal tendencies. The essential fact, he claimed, was that the material needs of individuals are limited, but their moral needs are boundless and can never be fully satisfied. Social order and personal equilibrium are closely interconnected, and they can only be achieved if external restraints are imposed on desires by a higher power; a power obeyed not only out of fear but also out of respect. Here Durkheim anticipates the position that he later developed in *L'Education morale* (Durkheim 1925a) and which brought him only a step away from discovery of the internalization of norms as the basis of the social order.

Why do rapid and unexpected changes increase the suicide rate? Why do they interfere with the regulatory action of society? Because crises compel those affected by them to learn a new way of life. But before society is able to repair their moral education, many of them commit suicide. By contrast, economic growth and enrichment increase desires and consolidate the relationships among the classes, which find themselves in an absolute and, more importantly, relative position better or worse than before. Durkheim points to the close connection between anomic suicide and contemporary society, where chronic anomie in industry and commerce has come to pervade the whole of society.

Durkheim believed that he had proved that the suicide rate depended not on changeable human motives but on suicide-inducing processes. These collective forces operated independently of individuals, acting constrictively on them according to the logic of egoism, altruism and anomie. They were objective, measurable and comparable: social facts which allowed the growth of sociology as a science, as he declared in *Rules of Sociological Method* (1895a).

Society is reality *sui generis*, and social states arise from the substrate of the collective conscience. The suicide rate is the result of suicide-inducing forces which arise from an excess of one of three elements – egoism, altruism or anomie – present in all societies. Durkheim sought remedies to the ills he diagnosed. He ruled out the possibility that the state could do very much against suicide, because it was too distant from individuals, and recommended that, as a measure to curb suicide, marriage should be made indissoluble.

Through analysis of suicidal practices, he was able to show persuasively and enduringly that every action – even a person's most individual action – does not take place in a vacuum of sociostructural reflexes or effects; in other words, it is always socially determined and it is always socially explained. He was firmly opposed to two types of explanation – those based on merely statistical units or measurements, and those based merely on psychological data – and he was especially critical of the medico-psychiatric and psycho-collective theories propounded respectively by Etienne Esquirol and Gabriel Tarde.

Assessments of Durkheim's contribution to the study of suicide as a 'social fact' tend to dwell on his typology, neglecting that this is the result of a different analysis, which should be perceived as his more lasting achievement, namely his shift from morphological to structural factors in the determination of social differentiation. In other words, the tripartition of suicide – egoistic, altruistic and anomic – distinguishes among modes of being and objective states of society before it distinguishes among types of suicide (Tomasi 1993).

The causal explanation *à la Durkheim* naturally has its shortcomings. These shortcomings, however, do not lie in the contextualization of suicide in states of society's 'moral density', or in the normal–pathological dichotomy, or in the consequent attribution of suicide to social pathology and to the relative over-exposure of the suicide victim to anomie and deviance.

Today, suicide requires recontextualization. There is no doubt that for many years analysis of suicide has been strongly characterized by theoretical presuppositions of causal type, and therefore by their relative methods. But the problem of suicide, as a voluntary act and a form of action, cannot be understood using an approach that overlooks its social and cultural coordinates. The growing suicide rate among young people, for example, can be significantly correlated with experiences of a social 'void' and, at times, with imitative trends whose social geography is not given by material data, primitive measurements or theoretical, late-positivist analyses.

It is the changes in the sociocultural explanation of suicide which, in the final analysis, direct current interest. In the context of the society of the first and second industrial revolutions, suicide and suicide-inducing factors appeared to be linked with, and therefore explained by, structural processes. Although the sociocultural explanation of suicide has changed since Durkheim's time, this does not detract from the sociological importance of the phenomenon in terms of causal and structural analysis, even if the problem of the relationship between the analysis of differentiation and the analysis of identification arises once again.

Numerous studies have been based on Durkheim's work in the course of these hundred years since publication, from a reappraisal of the role of religion as one of the aspects most closely studied (Bainbridge and Stark 1981; Breault and Barkey 1982) to the debate on the 'women–suicide–work' relationship, the interpretation of which certainly differs today from that provided by Durkheim. Indeed, the theory of economic anomie itself requires reformulation.

Many studies, therefore, and also many 'inexact' interpretations have appeared, the most significant of which has seen *Le Suicide* as a model for modern positivist sociology (Wacquant 1993). While there are certainly positivist elements in Durkheim's work, the theoretical position set out in *Le Suicide* differs from that of positivism. Durkheim explained the stable correlation between suicide rates and the various forms of 'external' association in terms of 'suicide-inducing currents' which stem from the moral forces generated by collective life which give rise to suicidal impulses.

The ascription of positivism to *Le Suicide* is therefore incorrect, because neither the facts–values dichotomy, nor the distinction between theoretical and real categories distinctive of positivism, are to be found in the work. Durkheim's contention was that sociology had to produce explanations and objective data concerning the relationship between collective life and the actions of the individual. In *Le Suicide* he showed that societies are more than the sum of their parts, and that they have generated a collective conscience or some sort of shared group thought.

I feel it necessary, however, to recall the work of this eminent French sociologist not so much by considering the criticisms brought against *Le Suicide* over the years, as by emphasizing that analyses of the book have often omitted to mention the 'originality' of his insights. In this regard it should be pointed out that suicide is sociological in that it is considered from the point of view of the laws which regulate social phenomena, and of the inferences that can be drawn by reasoning and exploration typical of the science of sociology. It is evident that, for example, an anthropological conception of suicide can never coincide with the sociological view developed by Emile Durkheim.

The end of the nineteenth century saw the establishment of a society which had emerged from a communitarian and agrarian society to a more individualistic one, from a rural population to an urban labour force. The transition to the modern age involved the broad 'realignment' of traditional forms of societal organization with the forces now emerging. Objective appraisal of Durkheim's work necessarily involves reflections on urbanization, industrialization and secularization: three concepts fundamental to his theory, and three factors fundamental to suicide. As Travis (1990) points out, Durkheim equated social change with the erosion of social control. In this respect, a decisive role in the process of secularization was played by religion, which increased egoism and the risk of suicide. In other words, religious individualism was engendered by Protestantism. Shared beliefs were weakened, so that life grew less meaningful and the risk of suicide increases.

Also part of this process was the spread of education in Europe. The desire for greater knowledge inevitably undermined obedience to cultural and historical traditions and fostered a 'scientific culture', thereby changing the family structure and kinship ties. In addition, there was the increased *laissez faire* that ran parallel to a lack of rules governing the economic sector. The burgeoning global economic system, with its quest for unlimited profits, seemingly encouraged anomie.

Durkheim wrote *Le Suicide* in his own times – times he saw as constituted by a 'collective sadness' that was undermining the old social order based on the general sublimation of the individual in collective life. He did not conduct longitudinal studies on suicide. To sustain his theory he merely asserted that over the previous fifty years, in countries for which data were available, the suicide rate had tripled. He may have underestimated the ability of city-dwellers to adapt to urban life and their capacity to maintain kinship ties, to develop relational networks in the suburbs, to create a village out of the city (Gans 1961). And he very probably underestimated the extent to which, with industrialization accomplished, affective bonds would develop in cities as well, and the risk of suicide would decrease.

Le Suicide is strongly influenced by the profound macro-social evolution then transforming society's institutions. The slowdown in this evolution during the twentieth century entails re-examination of many of Durkheim's basic axioms, and emphasizes the need to consider various 'extra-social factors' relevant to suicide which he was unable to assess.

Various issues have been raised with regard to the importance and relevance of Durkheim's original theory to the analysis of current aspects of suicide. It is clear that these issues cannot be resolved, first because one hundred years have passed since Durkheim wrote *Le Suicide*, and second because these one hundred years have been marked by profound social changes and substantial sociological development. The contradictions to be found in Durkheim's work were the contradictions of almost the whole of nineteenth-century sociological thought. Sociology was left in mid-air, so to speak, as a science still searching for foundations and rationale in the society within which it developed.

Durkheim was the son of his times, for good or ill. Born into a nascent industrial society, he based his analyses on the novel features emerging in that society. He had an ability theoretically to isolate, explain and utilize one of these new features, perhaps the most important of them, thrown up by the economic and social dynamics of the nineteenth century. His weakness lay, first, in his tendency to give value and significance to a factor which, although new, was neither the only nor the decisive element in an interpretation of the problems of society and social change. Second, he attempted to present as scientific an approach which, in its method, logic and ends, was tied more to a philosophical past than to the future of the social sciences.

Despite Durkheim's contribution to empirical inquiry, his was not an experimental method. Rather, it was a comparative historical method, an analysis of institutions, and overall a medley of heterogeneous tools and data. The logic of his proofs was very distant from that of exact causes, and he drew on other human sciences which in their turn were methodologically unsound. In short, his merits belonged just as much to his time as did his flaws. For this reason, one may look with interest at Durkheim's theories while at the same time distancing oneself from them; one may appreciate his often original and stimulating insights while bearing in mind that they are only intuitions. And one must do so for two reasons: first, because Durkheim lacked the methodological tools of the human sciences; second, because the human sciences now constructing a unitary model of mankind's needs, and of the social framework in which these needs are expressed, were either flawed or non-existent in Durkheim's time.

One may reasonably suggest that, although later theoretical and statistical studies have helped to extend the range of Durkheim's analysis, and to clarify the more obscure aspects of its interpretation of suicide, they have not diminished the validity of the work itself, both because the hypothesis of social integration has been invariably corroborated, and because these sociological studies have proved too fragmentary and unable to offer valid alternatives to Durkheim's explanation.

Bibliography

Bainbridge, W. S. and Stark, S. (1981) 'Suicide, Homicide and Religion', *Annual Review of the Social Sciences of Religion* 5:33–56.

Baudelot, C. and Establet, R. (eds) (1986) *Durkheim et le Suicide*, Paris: Presses Universitaires de France.

Besnard, P. (1987) *L'Anomie*, Paris: Presses Universitaires de France.
Breault, K. D. and Barkey, K. (1982) 'A Comparative Analysis of Durkheim's Theory of Egoistic Suicide', *Sociological Quarterly* 23:629–32.
Cuin, C. H. (1997) *Durkheim d'un siècle à l'autre. Lectures actuelles de* Règles de la méthode sociologique, Paris: Presses Universitaires de France.
Durkheim, E. (1895a) *Les Règles de la méthode sociologique*, Paris: Alcan.
(1897a) *Le Suicide: étude de sociologie*, Paris: Alcan.
(1925a) *L'Education morale*, Paris: Alcan.
Gans, H. (1961) *The Urban Villagers*, New York: Free Press.
Giddens, A. (1971) *The Sociology of Suicide*, London: Frank Cass.
Lester, D. (ed.) (1989) *Suicide from a Sociological Perspective*, Springfield, OH: Charles C. Thomas.
(1994) *Emile Durkheim:* Le Suicide *100 Years Later*, Philadelphia: The Charles Press.
Minois, G. (1995) *Histoire du suicide. La sociétè occidentale face à la mort volontaires*, Paris: Fayard.
Lukes, S. (1972) *Emile Durkheim: His Life and Work*, New York: Harper and Row.
Morselli, E. (1879) *Il suicidio. Saggio di statistica morale comparata*, Milano: Dumolard.
Orrù, M. (1987) *Anomie: History and Meanings*, Boston, MA: Allen and Unwin.
Pope, W. (1976) *Durkheim's* Suicide*: A Classic Analyzed*, Chicago: The University of Chicago Press.
Prades, J. A. (1990) *Durkheim*, Paris: Presses Universitaires de France.
Taylor, S. (1982) *Durkheim and the Study of Suicide*, New York: St Martin's Press.
Tomasi, L. (1989) *Suicidio e società. Il fenomeno della morte volontaria nei sistemi sociali contemporanei*, Milan: Angeli.
(1993) 'Social Differentiation and the Current Significance of Emile Durkheim's Anomie', *Social Compass* 3:363–74.
Tragott, M. (ed.) (1978) *Emile Durkheim on Institutional Analysis*, Chicago: The University of Chicago Press.
Travis, R. (1990) 'Halbwachs and Durkheim', *British Journal of Sociology* 41:225–43.
Wacquant, L. (1993) 'Positivism', in W. Outhwaite and T. Bottomore (eds) *Twentieth Century Social Thought*, Oxford: Blackwell.

3

THE DECONSTRUCTION OF SOCIAL ACTION

The 'reversal' of Durkheimian methodology from *The Rules* to *Suicide*

Mike Gane

> Nous pouvons arriver à notre but par une autre voie. Il suffira de renverser l'ordre de nos recherches.
>
> (Durkheim 1897a:141)

As Steven Lukes has pointed out, Durkheim claims that in studying suicide he made a contribution to sociological methodology (Lukes 1973:192). In fact Durkheim says that the 'chief methodological problems elsewhere stated and examined' (i.e. in *The Rules* 1895a) arise again in a new context (1897a/t.1951a:37). In the Preface to *Suicide* he emphasizes that these methodological problems are above all those relating to the definition of the 'social fact' – a phenomenon conceived by Durkheim as being external to individuals: 'any way of acting, whether fixed or not, capable of exerting over the individual an external constraint' (1895a/t.1982a:59). This definition in its simplicity does not prepare us for the complexity we encounter in the study of suicide.

Even if Lukes did not notice it, there can be little doubt that there is a more dramatic issue raised in *Suicide*: the fact that in this work Durkheim claimed to have applied the order of analysis prescribed in *The Rules* in reverse. If this has been noted by commentators it has rarely if ever been the subject of serious and critical reflection. But since it was noted briefly in my study of Durkheim's method (Gane 1988) a discussion has emerged on the significance of this reversal. On the one hand there are those who see in it nothing of any great significance, following Durkheim's own comments in *Suicide* itself (see Schmaus 1994:8, 150–84; Berthelot 1995). On the other hand other writers have begun to read the reversal as a significant event in Durkheim's development (see Steiner 1994:40). As yet, however, the real significance of the issue remains ill-defined. In this chapter I hope to clarify what is at stake in this debate. My argument is that in trying to work with suicide statistics Durkheim was forced to override the principles he laid out so brilliantly in 1895; and, as I have argued elsewhere (Gane 1994), this very fact reveals a great deal about Durkheim's conception of the inventive, flexible, undogmatic role of methodology. But it also led him to face more radically the possibility that his position in *The Rules* had been, in part, misconceived – a possibility which would have important and wide ramifications for his sociology.

In this chapter I want to examine and discuss the following problems: first, the method prescribed in *The Rules*; second, just how it should, if Durkheim had been consistent, have been applied to suicide; third, what Durkheim actually did in *Suicide*; fourth, to what 'discovery' his 'reversal' of methodological practice corresponds; and to discuss an alternative way of looking at the significance of this issue, particularly the relation of method to the substantive content of Durkheim's sociology.

The method of *The Rules*

Although Durkheim tried to crystallize his method in *The Rules of Sociological Method*, his writings on method are not limited to the formulations in this work. Indeed it is possible to argue that even this work exists in two, three, even four different versions (see Gane 1994). Many writers have argued that Durkheim changed his methods, and some have argued that his real method was different from his stated or 'official' method (e.g. Lukes 1973). It seems clear that he redrafted his manuscript on key points between 1894 and 1895 (Berthelot's 1988 edition gives only some of the changes) following a decision to study not consolidated social facts, but ones which were identifiable as independent from their individual manifestations (Durkheim 1895a/t.1988a:138). *The Rules* is clearly very ambitious, seeking not only to define procedures, but also strategic priorities.

The steps prescribed in Durkheim's work are as follows. First, the book demands that sociologists first define the kind of social facts which form the object of investigation. These facts are to be treated 'as things' – that is, are external to individuals, having the force of a collective phenomenon. Second, they are to be defined by characteristics observed to belong to the order of facts themselves, not by commonly held presuppositions or previously conceived judgements. The sociologist must follow rules for treating the reliability of data. Third, the sociologist must follow rules for distinguishing between normal and pathological forms. This is done by determining the character of normal features of the social species. Social types are, fourth, to be classified: morphologically at this stage. The social facts under study are to be interpreted through an understanding of the inner social milieux of societies (moral volume and density) in order to discover social causes. These suggest possible invariant relations. The proofs, finally, concerning these relations are to be administered by comparative analysis through a sufficient number and quality of comparative series, and aim to establish laws of co-variation.

This brief outline of Durkheim's procedure shows just how systematic and comprehensive the sociological method is. It is certainly not restricted to techniques of investigation and gathering of evidence. The general character of the method is to present elements of rationalism, objectivism and experimental reason (Berthelot 1995:140). A key feature is the application of the division between normal and pathological facts which Durkheim uses to link his method with practical intervention (see Gane 1995:185–205). Essential to the method is the specific requirement, in Comtean fashion, that observation take precedence over imagination. Durkheim insists on this point throughout *The Rules*: scientific sociology is only possible if the order of analysis begins with the work of objective observation and rational classification of objects. Durkheim argues that there are a number of facts in society which are observed to have the character of being necessary, determined and determining, independent of the subjective or objective will of individuals. It is to this body of phenomena that sociologists must attend, and without prejudgement. However, he does make room for a second order of analysis which might be applied as a 'verification' of the first. An example of this is his set of famous rules for determining the division between normal and pathological facts. The preferred method is one which identifies 'some immediately perceptible outward sign, but an objective one, to enable us to distinguish these two orders' (1895a/t.1982a:91). In cases where this is difficult, or in periods of transition, a second method is required to verify the first (p. 94). The rule for determining the normal in the second method is as follows: the results of the first method 'can be verified by demonstrating that the general character of the phenomenon is related to the general conditions of collective life in the social type under consideration' (1895a/t.1982a:97). He says of this second and more theoretical procedure, however, that it 'should in no case be substituted for the previous one, nor even be the first one employed' (p. 96). This is reiterated time and time again: analysis must begin with observation, never in a way which 'presupposes that either causes or functions' are already known (p. 96).

How should the study have been conducted?

Suicide was not studied according to the set of rules just mentioned. How should it have been studied if it had followed these rules? Here there are some remarks in *Suicide* that are of some help. Durkheim says that the preferred method would be to group together suicides by specific characteristics that they are discovered to have in common; to subdivide them by these resemblances and differences, for there are 'as many suicidal currents as distinct types'. The sociologist should 'then seek to determine their causes and respective importance' (1897a/t.1951a:145–6). He says at this point, 'we have pursued some such method in our brief study of insanity' ('C'est a peu près la méthode que nous avons suivie dans notre examen sommaire au suicide vésanique' 1897a:140). Let us turn to this study in Chapter 1 of Part Three of *Suicide*.

Here Durkheim reports a remarkable attempt to classify suicides of the mentally ill by their morphological characteristics. Four different types are found from the detailed investigation (manical, melancholy, obsessive, automatic). What Durkheim does is to examine the evidence with a view to establishing social causation. He subjects the evidence to comparative analysis with respect to sex, religion, age, more general social suicide rates, and to time sequences. He notes a rule *en passant*: 'To estimate the possible effect of psychopathic states one must eliminate cases where they vary in proportion to the social condition. They must be considered only where they are in inverse proportion to one another; only when a sort of conflict exists can one learn which is decisive' (1897a/t.1951a:70). His conclusion is that 'the social suicide rate . . . bears no definite relation to the tendency to insanity' (p. 76). He says these particular psychopathological types lie outside the influence of social forces, and outside the field of sociology. His method is instructive: suicides are classified morphologically in the first instance as 'insane suicide', and these groups are then analysed with reference to other known social phenomena in order to discover patterns of agreements or differences.

Thus what Durkheim should have done, if he had been following his rules throughout his study, is the following. The analysis would commence with the obligatory definition of suicide. In fact this is done of course in the Introduction:

> the term suicide is applied to all cases of death resulting directly or indirectly from a positive or negative act of the victim himself, which he knows will produce this result.
>
> (1897a/t.1951a:44)

Interestingly Durkheim notes that in the case of the mentally ill the suicides are 'either devoid of any motive or determined by purely imaginary causes' (1897a/t.1951a:66). These suicides are included as a definite category since the question of motive is not part of Durkheim's definition. But the crucial point here is that, if Durkheim had followed this method throughout his study, suicide statistics would then be classified by the whole character of the act itself; that is, as a voluntary 'passive or active' act based on a real understanding of its consequences. We could say this would involve an idea of the context and resolve, and the way the suicide was committed but not its motive. Durkheim's methodological imperative is based on the thesis that the rational definition of suicide, identification of the objective character of the act, is the specific, empirical and only route to a scientific analysis of the facts themselves: this is because the unknown causes are expressed in these objective manifestations. Grouped by these characteristics (positive, negative, etc.) such facts would be subject to comparative analysis to discover the causes of the different types of suicide expressed in them. In Durkheim's own words the order of research is the following: 'one would admit as many suicide currents as there were distinct types, then seek to determine their causes' (1897a/t.1951a:145). But, as noted, given the possibility of a second kind of analysis which seeks to explain these facts by relating the phenomena to 'the general conditions of collective life in the social type under consideration' (1895a/t.1982a:97), Durkheim might also be expected to follow through his analysis by relating suicide rates to the conditions of collective life. He would then present his proofs by testing the evidence in search of 'inverse' co-variation.

How was the study conducted?

Durkheim is disarmingly open, at the beginning of Book Two of *Suicide*, about the fact that the study was based on the quite different principle: '*we shall be able to determine the social types of suicide not directly by their previously described characteristics but by the causes which produce them*' (1897a/t.1951a:147, my emphasis). He is quite prepared to identify the presumed costs of such a move: it assumes there are different types without being able to identify them at the start; it may indeed prove the existence of types but not their characteristic forms. Durkheim is very insistent at this point that *because the cause is expressed in the effect* it is possible to 'deduce' these morphological characteristics from the causes identified. The method 'in reverse' also depends on the unbroken link between cause and effect (1897a/t.1951a:147).

At the moment he discusses motives, Durkheim offers an important clarificatory comment. He says that on inspection, the similarity of suicide motives given in statistics across very different occupational groups (rural and urban) suggests that motives are only 'apparent causes' – an effect of 'moral casuistry' (1897a/t.1951a:151). He announces at this point that because of this immediately evident problem, 'we shall try to determine the productive causes of suicide directly, without concerning ourselves with the forms they can assume in particular individuals' (1897a/t.1951a:151). The famous chapters which follow examine three types of suicide: egoistic, altruistic and anomic. After determining and analysing these types the final chapter of Book Two returns to examine 'Individual Forms of the Different Types of Suicide'. Now it is precisely this order of inquiry which is at issue. The key methodological problem here is why should this order of investigation stand? How did Durkheim come to establish his aetiological classification?

If we examine Durkheim's analysis of egoistic, altruistic and anomic types of suicide, we can see that it certainly does not proceed from the characteristics of each type of suicide considered as an act. His analysis of *egoistic* suicides proceeds via an analysis of suicide rates relative to religion, sex, education, etc. Crucially it does not work *directly* with comparisons of sex, age, region, etc. (see Pope 1976:142ff.; Baudelot and Establet 1984:101). It concludes that this particular type is revealed to vary inversely with the degree of social integration of these milieux (the famous formulation is given on p. 208). He explains this law at two levels: first, individualism simply produces insufficient social cohesion (p. 210) but, more profoundly, there is an essential requirement, absent here, for transcendent objects, since man is essentially *homo duplex*: Durkheim's proof – society expresses its own disintegration at certain periods in waves of sadness and despair (pp. 213–14). The discussion of *altruism* is again different in structure. It begins more theoretically and works by comparison to and contrast with the established egoistic form (p. 221). Durkheim notes that this type is chronic in the military milieux; where there is a coefficient of aggravation of suicide, identified with the intensity of the spirit of abnegation (p. 237). He adds: 'the facts prove that the causes of military suicide are not only different from, but are in inverse proportion to most determining causes of civilian suicide' (p. 236). His discussion of the third type of suicide, the *anomic*, begins with an analysis of economic crises (p. 241). He notes that this concerns patterns of deregulation, and declassification, and works towards a definition (p. 258). With the decline of religion and in the absence of strong moral codes, and the absence of secondary institutions, a certain anomie has become chronic in modern civilized cultures. There is also a type of anomic suicide which appears in the family, a conjugal anomie which is associated with the strength of the marriage bond and the conjugal relation. Durkheim has presented in these central chapters a mixture of statistical analysis and theoretical investigation. His discussion is organized around the identification of three quite different suicide types which he concludes are produced by three distinct social causes, and three suicide currents. He sums up as follows: 'Egoist suicide results from man's no longer finding a basis for existence in life; altruistic suicide, because this basis for existence appears to man situated beyond life itself. The third sort of suicide . . . results from man's activity's lacking regulation and his consequent sufferings' (p. 258). His method is circular in the sense that because he has grouped his material by the category of each suicide he comes to discover a proof that there are indeed such groups – a circularity his method was supposed to avoid.

In the final chapter of Book Two he therefore returns to the question of individual forms or morphology. He notes, in its first section, that this 'morphological classification, which was hardly possible at the commencement of this study, may be undertaken now that an aetiological classification forms its basis' (p. 277). He again emphasizes that what is required is 'to see the characteristics of special suicides grouped in distinct classes corresponding to the types just distinguished' (p. 277). The explanation for this, it is made clear, is to follow the work of expressive causation in reverse, to follow the way that these causes go 'from their social origins to their individual manifestations' (p. 277), for each type has a 'special mark' carried from its cause to its effect. The analysis here proceeds 'deductively' (p. 278). Durkheim gives a warning at this point, that this procedure involves making purely 'logical' implications and these 'may not be able to receive experimental confirmation' (p. 278). This procedure is always open to question, for it may seem that what is achieved is merely a presentation of illustrative material to give a 'concrete character' for results attained by other means. The following brief account concerns clear examples of egoistic suicide (Lamartine's Raphael) as a 'lofty' form, the Epicurean as a contrasting form (pp. 278–83); altruistic suicide contrasting violent and emotional with calm and dutiful forms (pp. 283–4), and the anomic form, associated with disappointment (pp. 284–5). He then presents a sketch of combined types 'ego-anomic' (p. 288), 'anomic-altruistic' (p. 288) and 'egoistic-altruistic', the stoic type (p. 289).

This brief analysis provides us with a good idea of what Durkheim meant by 'individual manifestations' or key 'special marks' of the way suicides were committed, but the second section of this chapter, however, introduces a complete bombshell. It is at this moment that Durkheim chooses to explain the real reasons for his very drastic change of mind on methodology. It is worth quoting the passage in full:

> One might think a priori that some relation existed between the nature of suicide and the kind of death chosen by the one who commits it. It seems quite natural that the means he uses to carry out his resolve should depend on the feelings urging him on and thus express these feelings. We might therefore be tempted to use the data concerning this matter supplied us by statistics to describe the various sorts of suicides more closely, by their external form. But our researches into this matter have given only negative results. (p. 290)

This is in some respects a devastating statement with important implications and ramifications on all of Durkheim's methodological pronouncements. To repeat, the study discovers that the expected continuity of social causation into the 'external form' of the act has not been confirmed. As the whole procedure outlined in *The Rules* is based on this 'a priori' assumption, *this discovery, even if a negative one, ranks as a central finding of the study*. It has long been overlooked, one suspects, because it is negative on the one hand, and because it intervenes at the level not of empirical finding but of methodology itself. Methodology is revealed here in a way not fully exposed before to be closely bound up with substantive sociological assumptions and presuppositions. One might say that Durkheim discovered one of his own crucial ideological prejudgements had not been removed.

Durkheim immediately announces a curious aspect of the new finding: 'social causes certainly determine the choice of these means; for the relative frequency of the various ways of committing suicide is invariable for long periods in a given society' (p. 290). Durkheim presents his statistics for the *different* ways suicides are committed in four different countries in the 1870s. It is clear that his investigation into the 'external form' of the suicide was not prevented for lack of evidence. What the figures reveal, says Durkheim, is that '[t]he social causes on which suicides in general depend . . . differ from those which determine the way they are committed; *for no relation can be discovered between the types of suicides which we have distinguished and the most common methods of performance*' (p. 291, my emphasis). Curiously, the modes of committing suicide are more stable than suicide rates (p. 291).

Durkheim provides a consolation. A set of hypotheses is presented about the ways certain of his types might have been expected to affect the mode of performance and which therefore would have confirmed his methodological assumption. Altruism might show a link through death by firearms, but this is not confirmed. Egoism might have its 'natural expression' through hanging, but this is not confirmed. Durkheim interprets these figures to show that the motives for suicide are quite different from motives for choice of means. The latter is influenced by available technology ('under trains'), and by the very prestige of certain means. He concludes with the unexpected but typically extreme formulation: 'the form of death chosen is therefore *something entirely foreign to the very nature of suicide*' (p. 293, my emphasis). And consequently 'the first has nothing to teach us about the second; it was discovered by a wholly different study' (p. 291).

The final section, Book Three, of *Suicide* deals with suicide as a 'social problem'. But its first chapter is again highly theoretical, concerning in the main a long critique of Quételet's conception of the average (pp. 300–6). Durkheim uses this topic as a vehicle to develop a detailed exposition of his conception of the difference between his idea of social facts as collective causes and any kind of averaging from individual forms. When he discusses methodology it is to stress that his findings confirm the proposition that social facts are objective (p. 310) and external to individuals (p. 313) and this confirms the principles set out in *The Rules* (p. 310). What is striking about this recapitulation of themes from *The Rules* is that it reiterates many of the formulae which contain the thesis of expressive causality relating internal and external characteristics. For example, 'we start from the exterior because it alone is immediately given, but only to reach the interior. Doubtless the procedure is complicated; but there is no other unless one would risk having his research apply to his personal feeling concerning the order of facts . . . instead of to this factual order itself' (1897a/t.1951a:315). This return to *The Rules* and its emphasis on the objectivity and externality of social facts effectively closes off an appreciation of what Durkheim has actually just discovered. But he wants to end the chapter with an investigation into a theory of social life as a process of equilibration of the three currents, egoistic, altruistic and anomic, and in particular the idea that 'no moral idea exists which does not combine in proportions varying with the society involved, egoism, altruism, and a certain anomie' (p. 321). In this discussion it is striking that Durkheim again resorts to a notion of expressive causation. The causes of the tendency to egoism and anomie also affect the mental constitution of individuals at a deep level, for 'they are expressive of the same cause: this makes them combine and become mutually adapted' (p. 323). But then Durkheim recoils. He concludes with the more subtle observation that '[t]he productive cause of the phenomenon naturally escapes the observer of individuals only; for it lies outside individuals' (p. 324). Thus the effect on the mental constitution is not a cause of suicide but of certain effects which might lead to predispositions to suicide in certain groups depending on the intensity and direction of suicide currents (p. 324).

In the final two chapters Durkheim attempts to complete other tasks demanded by his method: a wide comparative analysis over historical time (that is, across different social species) a diachronic analysis from antiquity to the present (pp. 326–38); a synchronic analysis, varying suicide with other social criminal and moral facts in contemporary society (pp. 358–60); and finally he comes to examine the question of normal and pathological suicide rates and what might be done practically about the rise in the reported rates of suicide (pp. 361–92). The first and second problems deal, according to Durkheim, with the question whether suicide should be considered an immoral or criminal act; the third problem concerns the question of the state of modern society itself. Durkheim reaches complex conclusions: first, the tendency towards thinking suicide might become entirely a matter of individual volition is an error; second, there is no simple connection between suicide and other criminal forms, so no formula can be used to determine the solution to forms of sanction against them. Finally, Durkheim works systematically to a conclusion that the current rates of suicide in France and modern Europe are rising in an abnormally rapid way. His remedy, as is well known, is the reintroduction of secondary occupational groups between the state and the individual: institutional socialism. In Durkheim's words 'we may believe that his aggravation springs not from the intrinsic nature of progress but from the special conditions under which it occurs in our day' (p. 368). This modern crisis is not part of a 'regular evolution' since completely abnormal causes are at work (p. 370). Durkheim's solution is spelt out: it involves a complete restructuring of the state – even its forms of democratic representation (p. 390). Durkheim's analysis is really only intelligible in the context of this theoretical envelope established elsewhere.

How important is the reversal of method? Could the study simply have been presented differently?

I now want to examine the question of the importance of Durkheim's decision to change his method. What difference does it make in the analysis? Is it fundamental and does it arise from a discovery concerning the nature of suicide itself?

Let me begin by suggesting that there are enough elements presented in the book *Suicide* to piece together what might have been the outcome had he placed these pieces in a different order. What is at issue in this examination is what has been called the problem of the 'order of exposition' and the 'order of explanation'. Durkheim's work has these elements:

1 a definition and theory of social causation of suicide as a social fact: an idea that there are currents and countercurrents;
2 a large array of suicide statistics, and a project to determine if the suicides are at a normal or abnormal level;
3 an examination of the kinds of suicides as they change with different social species, and as they vary with different milieux;
4 an attempt to determine if suicides are immoral acts or are destined to become a freely chosen type of act;
5 an attempt to produce a scientific explanation of suicide rates not simply to reproduce the statistics in a more rational manner.

One can go on to ask: what alternatives did he have? How could Durkheim have proceeded otherwise?

The definition of suicide could have been broader. It could correspond to Durkheim's wish to make a rational definition of suicide an act, and to eliminate motives. The fact that the theory of the nature of the act of suicide is complex and is the result of the interaction of two quite different forces (the suicidal current, and the current determining the nature of the act itself) could have been presented early in the study. Durkheim could have presented his theory of abnormal social equilibrium and then attempted to provide proof – the study could then have looked at the evidence and have presented the material in a more empirically led mode. The substance could have been analysed differently: co-variational analysis – sex, age, occupation, urban distribution, etc., which Durkheim could have taken as social facts (but did not); co-variations – homicide, criminal statistics; genealogical evidence on suicide rates and types of sanctions; evidence on normal and pathological rates of suicide could have been given a more direct presentation, even have framed the analysis and determined the order of the work.

This study would have been largely a presentation of statistics but not a purely empirical study. It might have resembled Comte's own prescription of a positive method, one devoted to establishing laws of concommittance and co-variation with the addition of causal analysis (recently discussed by Schmaus 1994 and Cherkaoui 1997:153ff.). If this is one alternative to the present form, it is also important to note that *Suicide* is clearly not the empiricist study it is sometimes mistaken to be.

What Durkheim achieves in his study, however, is quite different. Ironically the empirical 'discovery' that the mode of the suicidal act is quite external to the cause of suicide is the basis on which Durkheim very suddenly and dramatically renounces the logic of 'expressive causality'. He was thus provoked into the theory of complex social mal-integration in a way which he could not handle with any degree of assurance. It seems that the theory presented through a method of 'deduction' (see Gane 1988:49–51) remains radically incomplete, for it does not provide us with a good statement of what Durkheim actually did in *Suicide* from a methodological point of view. It does not on the other hand genuinely reflect the sociological discovery of the complexity of certain kinds of human 'acts' like suicide, and the domain of sociology is made up of such acts, religious, political, cultural and so forth.

Quite unlike the route which Parsons, Douglas and Lukes and others have identified – that is, towards an interpretative understanding of human action which they argue Durkheim secretly followed – Durkheim's analysis led in quite the opposite direction, to an unexpected but specific kind of *deconstruction* of action. He analyses suicides as the meeting of at least two heterogeneous currents: the suicidogenic current giving rise to the resolve itself, and the different current which furnishes the means. Both are outside the immediate rationalization of action by the agent and the immediate triggers of such phenomena. Such 'ways of acting' (if we return to the definition of a social fact) are complex, made up of elements which come together but do not mutually express or cause each other, for they are 'foreign' to each other. The implication for methodology is that sociology should not assume that by following the natural logic of action it is following a privileged linear causal chain. Importantly, the presupposition that sociology can work from the external features of a given social fact directly to its internal cause is thrown into doubt.

One could say, however, that the delayed explanation of the full complexity of the suicide act – the devastating thesis that the mode of committing the act is foreign to the nature of suicide itself – leads to the greatest surprise of all, the greatest ruse of *Suicide*, *that he did not use his method in reverse*. Because the causal chain is broken, Durkheim could not work back from the causally determined types to the 'external manifestations' as effects in any completely continuous analytic sequence (the method of deduction).

If the reverse method is impossible what was his method?

What he did in the famous Book Two was the following: first, he grouped the facts relating to egoistic suicide in such a way that he was able to discover the condition of egoism (a completely circular manoeuvre). He then found contrasting forms of altruism and anomie (and fatalism). He followed, in effect, the method he called in *The Rules* an analysis of the relation of the phenomenon 'to the general conditions of collective life'. The rule he broke was the injunction that 'this method should in no case be substituted for the previous one, nor even be the first one employed' (1895a/t.1982a:96). From these aetiologically determined types he suggested the phenomenological moods that expressed them in illustrations which might resemble the proposed 'manifestations' and their 'rationalizations'.

But this means that there is, in *Suicide*, no analysis of any suicide act, no analysis of any suicidal process. Indeed, as Pope has noted, 'nowhere is evidence presented to demonstrate that some or all of the suicides of a particular sociological type actually experience the subjective states attributed to them. Although Durkheim characterised the egoistic suicide as apathetic and anomic as angry, there is no evidence for rejecting the reverse possibility. Durkheim offered virtually no empirical evidence to link his etiological classification with his morphological one' (Pope 1976:198). There is no attempt at all to analyse the complex interaction or meeting of the suicidal causal chain and that which determines the means to achieve it. Durkheim is content to provide, first, a theory of differential forms of social integration and social regulation; second, to present evidence on inverse co-variation of social integration and suicide rates; and third, to provide a brief imaginative evocation of what might be expected of the subjective mood under which the act is committed and its associated 'co-enaesthetic' forms. He can engage in this elaborate fiction-theory only as a ruse that the general deconstruction of the act of suicide has not been effective.

Conclusion

In conclusion therefore we might say that in *Suicide* we find:

1. a specific kind of methodological disobedience, and complex forms of displacement of practice;
2. a work producing different kinds of rhetorical effects related to a simultaneous acceptance and rejection of expressive causal linearity;
3. a work of imaginative reconstruction of suicidal moods hypothetically linked as 'currents' to suicide causes identified in sociological theory;
4. the discovery of a fundamental finding about the nature of suicide as a social act, a finding both presented and denied at the same time.

It is the first of these which perhaps most of all reveals Durkheim's ability to overrule his own rules with superb assurance and therefore to have created something of an intellectual puzzle which we are still trying to solve a hundred years after it was constructed. Getting through to the important problems for Durkheim overrides any methodological dogmas, but when the findings are truly revolutionary and profoundly disturb, even to the basic frame of sociology, the official methodological formulae may come to play an entirely different function.

Bibliography

Anderson, O. (1987) *Suicide in Victorian and Edwardian England*, Oxford: Clarendon Press.

Atkinson, J. M. (1978) *Discovering Suicide: Studies in the Organisation of Sudden Death*, London: Macmillan.

Baudelot, C. and Establet, R. (eds) (1984) *Durkheim et le suicide*, Paris: Presses Universitaires de France.

Berthelot, J.-M. (1995) *Durkheim: l'avènement de la sociologie scientifique*, Toulouse: Presses Universitaires de Mirail.

Borlandi, M. and Mucchielli, L. (1995) *La Sociologie et sa méthode.* Les Règles *de Durkheim un siècle après*, Paris; L'Harmattan.

Cherkaoui, M. (1997) in C.-H. Cuin, *Durkheim d'un siècle a l'autre*, Paris: Presses Universitaires de France.

Cuin, C.-H. (1997) *Durkheim d'un siècle a l'autre*, Paris: Presses Universitaires de France.

Douglas, J. (1967) *The Social Meanings of Suicide*, Princeton, NJ: Princeton University Press.

Durkheim, E. (1897a) *Le Suicide: étude de sociologie*, Paris: Alcan.

—(t.1951a) by J. A. Spaulding and G. Simpson, *Suicide: A Study in Sociology*, edited with an introduction by G. Simpson, Glencoe, IL: Free Press (London, Routledge and Kegan Paul, 1952).

(1895a) *Les Règles de la méthode sociologique*, Paris: Alcan.

(1988a) *Les Règles de la méthode sociologique*, edited by J.-M. Berthelot, Paris: Flammarion.

—(t.1982a) by W. D. Halls, *The Rules of Sociological Method*, edited with an introduction by S. Lukes, London: Macmillan.

Gane, M. (1988) *On Durkheim's* Rules of Sociological Method, London: Routledge.

(1994) 'A Fresh Look at Durkheim's Sociological Method', in W. S. F. Pickering and H. Martins (eds) *Debating Durkheim*, London: Routledge.

(1995) in C. Baudelot and R. Establet (eds) (1984) *Durkheim et le suicide*, Paris: Presses Universitaires de France.

Giddens, A. (1978) *Durkheim*, London: Fontana.

Hamilton, P. (ed.) (1990) *Emile Durkheim: Critical Assessments, vol. 3*, London: Routledge.

Huff, T. (1975) 'Discovery and Explanation in Sociology: Durkheim on Suicide', *Philosophy of the Social Sciences* 5:241–57.

Jones, R. A. (1986) *Emile Durkheim*, London: Sage.

Lacroix, B. (1981) *Durkheim et le politique*, Paris: Presses de la Fondation Nationale des Sciences Politique.
Lehmann, J. (1993) *Deconstructing Durkheim*, London: Routledge.
Lukes, S. (1973) *Emile Durkheim*, London: Penguin Books.
Parsons, T. (1937) *The Structure of Social Action*, New York: Free Press of Glencoe.
Pickering, W. S. F. and Martins, H. (eds) (1994) *Debating Durkheim*, London: Routledge.
Pope, W. (1976) *Durkheim's* Suicide*: A Classic Analyzed*, Chicago: University of Chicago Press.
Schmaus, W. (1994) *Durkheim's Philosophy of Science and the Sociology of Knowledge*, Chicago: University of Chicago Press.
Steiner, P. (1994) *La Sociologie de Durkheim*, Paris: La Découverte.
Taylor, S. (1982) *Durkheim and the Study of Suicide*, London: Macmillan.
(1988) *Suicide*, London: Longman.
(1983) 'Durkheim as a Methodologist', *Philosophy of the Social Sciences* 13:425–50 and 14:51–71.
Watts Miller, W. (1996) *Durkheim, Morals and Modernity*, London: UCL Press.

4

DURKHEIM'S ALTRUISTIC AND FATALISTIC SUICIDE

Christie Davies and Mark Neal

Durkheim's categories of altruistic and fatalistic suicide have been much neglected by later sociologists in comparison with the attention bestowed on anomic and egoistic suicide. Indeed, one sociologist has spoken of Durkheim's 'one cause of suicide' (Johnson 1965). Such radicals wish to eliminate, or at least to forget about, altruistic and fatalistic suicide altogether (Johnson 1965; see also on fatalistic suicide Marra and Orrú 1991:284), and some also wish to fuse egoism and anomie into one single concept conveying an absence of both integration and regulation. From this crude point of view there is one simple explanation of suicide rates: the lower the levels of integration and regulation, the higher the suicide rate (Johnson 1965).

This will not do. Whether or not we treat egoism and anomie as separate variables or as different aspects of the same thing is largely a matter of convenience depending on the phenomenon under examination. Although they are closely related, they are also, as Durkheim (1897a/t.1951a:258) himself emphasizes, analytically separable. More to the point for our present purposes, it is worth noting that there are many important examples of both altruistic and fatalistic suicide that cannot be dismissed or swept aside. The concepts of altruistic and fatalistic suicide are both essential to the comparative study of suicide rates and to an understanding of Durkheim's sociology, rooted as it is in an Aristotelian perception of the 'golden mean' (La Capra 1972:158; Aristotle 1976, Book 2:1104 and 1107a28 to 1108b9). For Durkheim, suicide rates are high at the extremes, both where there is very strong integration or very strong regulation, and also in the cases of weak integration and weak regulation that constitute egoism and anomie respectively (Alpert 1961:100–1). For such a model to be coherent and falsifiable it must of course be clearly postulated that there is an intermediate area of moderate integration and moderate regulation where suicide rates are low, as shown in Figures 4.1 and 4.2.

The diagrams are of course purely schematic; they could equally well have been drawn in a curvilinear way (Pope 1975:429; cf. Pope 1976:106). They

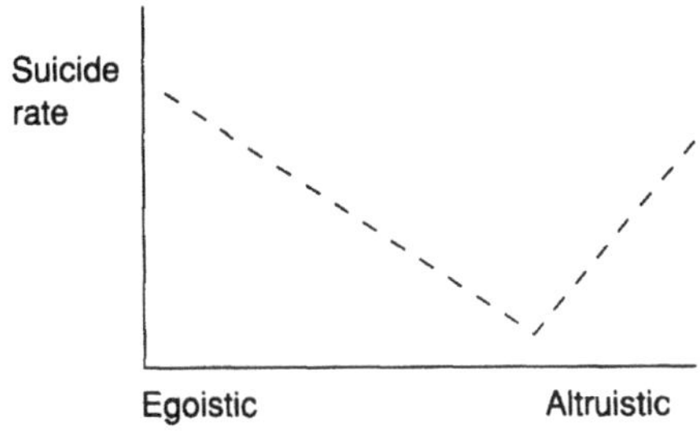

Figure 4.1

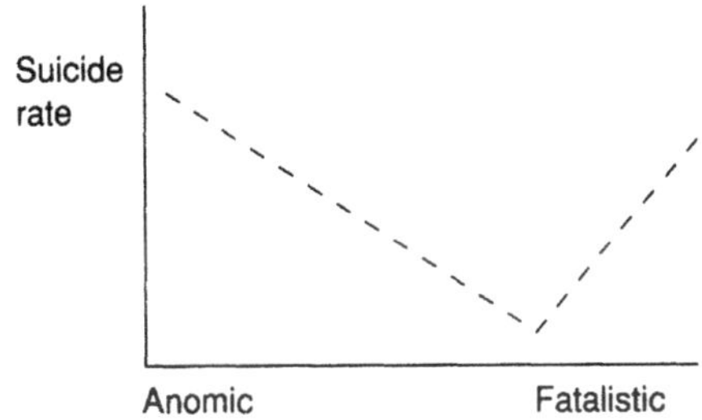

Figure 4.2

are both asymmetrical such that the low point comes nearer to the altruistic or fatalistic rather than the egoistic or anomic end of the spectrum. This pattern is quite arbitrary, though. It reflects the fact that nearly all of Durkheim's data and a large part of our modern information about suicide rates refer to the highly individualistic and anti-traditionalist countries of Europe. The most altruistic and fatalistic societies in Europe have the lowest suicide rates, and in no European country does any significant group of *civilians* have an elevated suicide rate because of 'excessive' integration and regulation. As a consequence any kind of notional median point for egoism–altruism or anomie–fatalism for Europe will lie well to the egoistic and anomic side of the minimum suicide-rate point. So far as Europe is concerned, only the military consistently display high levels of altruistic suicide (Durkheim 1897a/t.1951a:228).

It is for this reason that in the last half of the twentieth century some sociologists have sought to do away with Durkheim's categories of altruistic and fatalistic suicide. Altruistic suicide, it is argued, can be ignored because it is restricted to the military (Johnson 1965), and fatalistic suicide is, even in Durkheim's treatise, a mere footnote, a ragbag of very young husbands, older childless married women and slaves (Durkheim 1897a/t.1951a:276).

This view does less than justice to Durkheim's detailed and subtle analysis of altruistic suicide. It ignores the care with which Durkheim has dissected the military statistics to show how the suicide rate is higher among elite troops than among ordinary soldiers, higher among NCOs than among officers, who in turn have a higher suicide rate than privates, and higher in combat units than among those performing support functions. In each case it is the category whose members have most clearly subordinated and sacrificed their individuality to the group and most strongly submitted to its dictates, who have the highest suicide rate (Durkheim 1897a/t.1951a:233–4, 237). Thus in his analysis of the military Durkheim has provided not one but several examples of altruistic suicide. They cannot be dismissed.

Durkheim has skilfully linked the frequent but in no sense prescribed or expected suicides of individual soldiers in European armies with the obligatory or at least socially recognized and approved suicides to be found in other civilizations. Clear examples are *seppuku* (suicide by ritual disembowelling) in Japan and suttee (suicide by a widow burning herself to death on her husband's funeral pyre) in India. It is noticeable that both in Japan and in India there are several special names for different kinds of altruistic suicide, indicating that they are a recognized part of social behaviour and the social order. There are no such terms in English. As Durkheim (1897a/t.1951a:217–40) shrewdly noted, European military suicide and Asian customary suicide are closely related phenomena, even though European military suicide is an aggregate of voluntary acts, and the Asian examples are obligatory suicides, or at least governed by social convention as to their context and the method used. Both are the product of hierarchical collectivist societies or institutions in which the individual's fate is unimportant and the group alone is what matters (Durkheim 1897a/t.1951a:83; Bellah 1973:xviii). The connection is indeed even closer than Durkheim suggests. Suttee was often voluntary (Thompson 1928:119, 123, 125, 138–9), though in some cases the women concerned came under intense social pressure to die by fire (Thompson 1928:138–9). Even in the most suttee-prone areas and periods, only a very small proportion of Hindu widows ever committed suicide (Baechler 1979:362). It was most common among the warrior castes and was imitated by the Sikhs whose *khalsa* was a brotherhood of pious warriors (Thompson 1928:52–3, 90–100, 117). Suttee was rare among the Hindu lower castes; it was primarily the privilege of the widows of warriors, who were seen as exhibiting the same bravery and self-sacrifice by their fiery suicide as their husbands were expected to show on the battlefield. After such a woman's death a *sati* stone might be erected in her honour; it had much the same significance as a war memorial (Thompson 1928:30–4; O'Malley 1935:183; Baechler 1979:362). Greater love hath no woman than to lay down her life for her dead husband, whether on his funeral pyre or by self-immolation by fire on learning of his death in battle.

Likewise *seppuku* is the Samurai custom of those professing bushido (the way of the knight) (Nitobe 1905) and one which in the twentieth century has been mainly practised in the Japanese armed forces. It was, like many other forms of suicide in the Japanese military, an expression of the subordination of the individual to the group, to an institution and to the Emperor, and of the individual's consequent lack of significance (Nitobe 1905:116–22; Stokes 1975:96; Morris 1980:299). In the past it could be obligatory but more usually it was chosen by the individual in the same sense that a Japanese naval officer might *volunteer* to be a *kamikaze* pilot or to ride a human torpedo (Hoyt 1985:165, 174–5, 235). The latter cases are *not* suicides, whatever Durkheim (1897a/t.1951a:44) may have argued, but Durkheim was right to see the close connection between the habit of passive submission leading to a willingness to die in battle for one's country and altruistic suicide (1897a/t.1951a:234, 237; see also Thompson 1928:138–9). It is but a short step from *dulce et decorum est pro patria mori* to honourable suicide by falling on one's sword. Today when a terrorist from a culture that is neither Christian nor individualist dies by driving a truckload of explosives into the midst of his enemies and blowing himself up, Westerners are apt to call it suicide. Such a phenomenon is not suicide but it does underline the close connections between a willingness to die in battle and altruistic suicide in the military that was emphasized by Durkheim.

Also there is a form of 'obligatory' altruistic suicide in the West and one that also has a military connection: the custom of the captain remaining on board and going down with his ship after everyone else has left. He is so strongly identified with his vessel, a self-contained social institution that is embodied in a physical object, that he sacrifices himself when it sinks. The custom is of course not always followed but it is so strongly ingrained among naval captains that during World War I several members of the French Chamber of Deputies demanded a law forbidding naval officers from doing so (Baechler 1979:359–60), as it meant that the unfortunate loss of a warship was accompanied by the unnecessary loss of an expensively trained, highly skilled and experienced, difficult to replace, senior officer. From a utilitarian point of view this practice hampered the war effort, but altruistic suicide is not a matter of calculation. Indeed, that is what makes it suicide. Altruistic suicide is an end in itself, unlike the death of the *kamikaze* pilot which is the unfortunate by-product of some other purpose; the efforts by the Japanese navy to design ejector seats for their human torpedoes are proof of that (Morris 1980:300). The same point may be made in relation to the (potential) British kamikaze pilots of World War I defending London against Zeppelin raids. Charles Hobhouse wrote of them: 'Churchill has sent 100 aeroplanes to Dunkirk. In the last resort the officers in charge of aeroplanes will charge the Zeppelins but in view of the certain death have arranged to draw lots for the task' (David 1977:187). The drawing of lots demonstrates that their sacrifice is *not* suicide, but it also shows how close to suicide it is. Durkheim was wrong to blur the distinction between altruistic suicide and military sacrifice by adopting a peculiar definition of suicide, but he was right to stress the connection between a willingness to sacrifice one's life in the service of an institution and a proneness to commit suicide; both of these phenomena are most commonly found in the military but that does not in any way diminish their sociological importance. Altruistic suicide does exist and it is the opposite of the egoistic version.

Fatalistic suicide, as described by Durkheim, appears to be more problematic, mainly because Durkheim says so little about it. Also his examples are not convincing. The high suicide rates of very young husbands and of older childless married women that he observed are perhaps better explained in terms of the rival theory of a lack of status integration (Gibbs and Martin 1958, 1964) than seen as fatalistic suicide. Even in Durkheimian terms it might be better to see these as an anomic phenomenon. The marital constraints on the very young husband are no different from those that impinge on husbands in general and which slightly 'preserve' them from suicide, according to Durkheim (1897a/t.1951a:186, 274). For Durkheim to suggest that very young husbands have stronger 'passions violently choked by oppressive discipline', which in turn leads to enhanced suicide rates is to invoke the kind of biological variable that he himself tried to exclude by his doctrine of the supremacy of social facts (1897a/t.1951a:276). The problem very young husbands face is that most boys of their age are not married and that they have two incompatible statuses with associated regulations and expectations, those of their age group and those of husbands. Because very young husbands were rare in Europe, even in Durkheim's day (Durkheim 1897a/t.1951a:178), their expectations would therefore have been uncertain and confused – a classic case of anomie. The same point may be made in relation to the high suicide rate among the older married women of Durkheim's day who found themselves childless when their contemporaries were all engaged in bringing up families and who lived in a society where no alternative roles were available for married women. Again it was an anomic situation.

The case of the high suicide rate of slaves, mentioned by Durkheim (or, come to that, the high suicide rate among prisoners in our own time, which shows that the issue is one of contemporary and not just as Durkheim thought of 'historical interest'), is a better example of fatalistic suicide 'deriving from excessive regulation, that of persons with futures pitilessly blocked and passions violently choked by oppressive discipline' (Durkheim 1897a/t.1951a:276). However, the high suicide rate of slaves and prisoners cannot be compared with the high suicide rate of army NCOs or elite troops. The latter are committed to their institution and to its rules which are, therefore, not perceived as oppressive. Slaves and prisoners do not internalize the harsh rules of their masters and jailers but see them as alien and external and *in contradiction* to the very different rules that had controlled their lives before their enslavement or those which govern their interactions among themselves. Perhaps this situation too should be seen as a case of anomie. If it is, it creates a problem for Durkheim's (1897a/t.1951a:271–3)

Table 4.1 Suicide rates per 100,000 people in 1988

	Male (all ages)	*Female (all ages)*
Ireland	11.0	4.0
Greece	5.9	2.3
UK	13.0	4.6
Austria	36.6	13.3
Denmark	33.3	19.0
USA	20.1	5.0
France	30.2	11.7
Singapore	16.4	11.2
Hong Kong	10.9	9.5
Germany	25.0	10.8
Japan	23.8	13.7

perception of rules as being social facts in and of themselves, regardless of whether those who are governed by the rules accept them. From such a viewpoint countries with strict divorce laws cannot be regarded as less anomic than countries with lax divorce laws, if a large part of the population of that country has ceased to believe in the validity of the laws. This was, for example, the case in Italy or Ireland immediately prior to the referendums that allowed divorce.

However, the reality of fatalistic suicide and the widespread existence of altruistic suicide in the modern world can easily be demonstrated if we abandon the Eurocentric point of view taken by Durkheim and many of his successors. In particular, the extremely high suicide rate among young women in the rural areas of the People's Republic of China is a striking example of both fatalistic and altruistic suicide. The rural areas of China alone have a population of several hundred million people, which is comparable with that of the whole of Europe. The exceptionally high suicide rates of young women in rural China can be demonstrated by comparing the age–sex suicide profile for rural China with that of Hong Kong and of urban industrial and increasingly capitalist China. Here, the age–sex pattern of the suicide rates is much more comparable with those of the West (Pritchard 1993:10–12). In all Western and industrialized East Asian countries female suicide rates are much lower than male rates, as can be seen from Table 4.1 (compiled from Pritchard 1993:10–11). At least in the European countries and the United States, this one-way sex disparity is true for *all* age groups.

It should also be noted from Table 4.1 that the male suicide rates are not only higher than the female rates in all the European countries but *much* higher, a phenomenon that was also true in Durkheim's day. This is the case in both Europe's very high suicide rate countries such as Austria, Denmark and France and the low suicide rate countries such as Ireland, Greece and the

Table 4.2 Suicide in China by age and sex per 100,000 people in 1988

Age	*Male suicide rate*	*Female suicide rate*	*Female:male ratio* as %
General	15.0	19.5	130
15–24	15.8	30.4	192
25–34	13.8	17.7	128
35–44	15.4	18.4	119
45–54	16.0	18.6	116
55–64	27.7	26.5	96
65–74	49.9	44.3	89
75+	90.1	71.0	79

UK. Males are also more likely to commit suicide than females in Asian countries – such as Hong Kong (later annexed by China), Japan, Republic of Korea, Singapore and Sri Lanka (Iga and Tatai 1975:256; Pritchard 1996:365) and indeed throughout most of the world (Diekstra 1989:3–4). The reason lies in the far more egoistic and anomic existence led by males relative to females. Males are more likely to become loners and isolates, to become cut off completely from kinship and other ties, to abandon religion altogether and to exhibit behaviour such as crime or drug and alcohol addiction associated by Merton (1957:185–248) with anomie. In consequence they are far more likely to commit suicide for the egoistic and anomic reasons advanced by Durkheim. Women by contrast only make suicide *attempts*, whose purpose is to achieve an improved level of integration. We do not need to consider seriously Durkheim's (1893b/t.1933b:57–8) other type of explanation, that women in advanced societies such as late nineteenth-century Paris are more primitive and have smaller brains. One hundred years on this seems a little eccentric and rooted in the prejudices of *fin de siècle* Paris, the sexist capital of Europe where women could not vote until after World War II and where investigation into the paternity of illegitimate children was forbidden, regardless of the mother's need and desire for maintenance.

When we look at the figures for China a marked contrast emerges, as can be seen from Table 4.2 (Pritchard 1993:12). It is very striking that the female suicide rate in China is higher than the male rate in general and for all age bands except the three oldest; only among *very* old people is the female rate substantially lower than the male. The excess of female over male suicide is especially high in the age group 15–24 where nearly twice as many women as men kill themselves, a situation that is the exact opposite of what is found in Europe or those other parts of East Asia for which suicide statistics are available. If a differentiation is made between rural China with its very strong kinship ties and (in 1988) a collectivist socialist economy, coupled with a minimum of domestic and economic anomie, and urban China, which has recently enjoyed a capitalist revolu-

Table 4.3 Suicide rates in the People's Republic of China in 1988 by age, sex and urban and rural areas

		All age groups	*Age group 15–24*
China in general	Male rate	15.0	15.8
	Female rate	19.5	30.4
	Ratio female:male	130%	192%
Urban China	Male rate	8.0	7.3
	Female rate	10.0	12.9
	Ratio	125%	177%
Rural China	Male rate	23.1	25.0
	Female rate	30.3	47.8
	Ratio	131%	191%

tion, the figures become even more striking. This can be seen in Table 4.3 (Pritchard 1993:12).

It is worth noting (a) that the rates of suicide in general are *much* higher in rural than in urban China for both sexes, which is *in marked contrast* to what Durkheim found in Europe, (b) that although the female suicide rate is much higher than the male throughout China, the *disparity is greater* in rural China.

The rate of successfully completed suicides among young females in Europe, the USA and modern Japan is very low; and in *all* of these countries the suicide rate of young women is lower (in 1988) and usually *much* lower than that of women in general (Tatai 1983:21–5; Pritchard 1993:11). Occasionally at other times and in other places the suicide rates of young and older women have been roughly equal and, indeed, the suicide rate of young women has exceeded that of women in general in Sri Lanka (Pritchard 1996:365) and in Mexico and Venezuela (Diekstra 1989:7). What is striking is that the suicide rate of young females in rural China is *very high indeed*, both when compared with the male suicide rate for the same age group in rural China, and in comparison with the far lower suicide rates of females aged 15 to 24 in Hong Kong, Japan, the Republic of Korea and Singapore. In Sri Lanka the suicide rate among young women is even higher than for young Chinese women but it is much lower than for young male Sri Lankans of the same (15–24) age group (Pritchard 1996:365). Only in China do young females stand out as having a much higher suicide rate than both their male contemporaries, and women in general. China is unique in having a high female suicide rate relative to most other countries, a higher female than male suicide rate, especially in rural areas, a higher rural than urban suicide rate and a higher suicide rate among young women than among women of all ages taken together, again especially in the rural areas. Any one of these phenomena may be found elsewhere, again particularly in Asia (Chia and Mehta 1983:118; Headley 1983:350–3; Diekstra 1989:3–4, 7; Travis 1990:242) but the combination of them is peculiar to China and is a clear indication of a Chinese pattern of altruistic–fatalistic suicide in marked contrast to the dominant Western pattern of egoistic–anomic suicide.

The higher male relative to female suicide rates in Europe reflect Durkheim's notions of egoism and anomie. By contrast the higher female and exceptionally high young female suicide rates in rural China are best explained in terms of Durkheim's categories of fatalistic and altruistic suicide. The suicide of young Chinese women is indeed 'suicide deriving from excessive regulation, that of persons with futures pitilessly blocked and passions violently choked by oppressive discipline' (Durkheim 1897a/t.1951a:276), i.e. it is fatalistic suicide. A woman in the age group 15–24 in rural China is and always has been expected to marry a husband chosen for her by her family; she has had very little choice (Butterfield 1982:167). She can neither refuse to marry this person, nor refuse to marry at all, nor marry someone else. The family has been all and all-powerful. On her marriage she has traditionally entered her husband's household and lived under the tyranny of her mother-in-law (Mosher 1984:196). There are many bitter Chinese proverbs and jokes about the unhappy fate of the daughter-in-law (Levy 1974). Her situation is, however, not that of a slave for she is part of a system in which everyone accepts the legitimacy of these harsh rules and expectations. Indeed, she in turn may become a harsh mother-in-law and bully her own daughters-in-law. Traditionally such a woman may even in some areas have deliberately sought to find a subservient daughter-in-law by adopting a young girl to be brought up as a sister to her son and who is later expected to marry him. The marriages are unhappy because the young couple's relationship is quasi-incestuous, but that consideration is subordinate to the mother-in-law's desire for total compliance (Fox 1980:45–6). In modern rural China, though, it is the wife's total material and moral subordination to an often brutal husband (Mosher 1984:208–23) that is the main problem, and it is not surprising that many women of the marrying age group commit suicide to escape this pitiless future. When young women commit suicide in China it is clearly a case of fatalistic suicide.

The domestic fate for these young women is made worse by their economic situation. In urban China the existence of a thriving capitalist economy enables some women to escape from the now attenuated tyranny of their families by achieving a measure of economic independence. It is at least possible to get a job or start up a business of one's own. By contrast, in peasant China young women are trapped in the harsh idiocy of socialist rural life (Mosher 1984:199) where the men of the village control its economy and rural women are a trapped, unskilled, underpaid, overworked, proletariat for whom there is little room for manoeuvre (Butterfield 1982:165–6; Mosher 1984:204–23). Stable poverty is no protection against suicide in such a fatalistic society. There is no escape other than suicide, and many women take it. Durkheim (1897a/t.1951a:254–8) associated commercial life and capitalism with increasing suicide rates because of the greater egoism and anomie of an individualistic and unregulated modern capitalist economic system. This is so when contrasted with the economic way of life of traditional rural Europe. However, it was only the case because traditional rural European societies were not very collectivistic by Chinese standards; they lay close to Durkheim's nominal suicide low point rather than being at the fatalistic and altruistic end of the spectrum. By contrast, rural socialist China with its traditional and restricted sex roles for women lies close to the fatalistic–altruistic end of the spectrum and thus any shift in a capitalist direction should produce a fall in the suicide rate. This is in fact what seems to have happened in urban China with its lower suicide rates. Something similar happened in Japan in the 1960s when the suicide rate *fell* after the old altruistic–fatalistic, militarist society of Imperial Japan had been securely replaced by a more individualistic, less regulated and less integrated, democratic capitalism. Believers in a one-cause egoistic–anomic model of suicide and society were surprised that when the immediate post-war upheavals had been overcome, the suicide rate in Japan fell considerably. It was much lower in 1970 than in highly integrated and regulated pre-war Imperial Japan between 1920 and 1935 (Iga and Tatai 1975:276; Tatai 1983:20; Retterstol 1993:12). These changes once again confirm that the relationship between suicide and society is of a curvilinear kind. The idea that Durkheim's thesis can be reduced to a 'one-cause' theory has thus been demonstrated to be utterly false, and his Aristotelian-ethic model of the low suicide society as a form of moderation between two extremes has, thus far at least, been vindicated.

The Chinese data strongly support Durkheim's model of the four cases of suicide and of the curvilinear relationship between them. However, there remain problems. These problems stem from anomalies *within* Durkheim's own model. It is not necessary to take an un-Durkheimian or anti-Durkheimian perspective in order to make the criticisms that follow. The inconsistencies lie within Durkheim's work but are nonetheless best analysed from a Durkheimian perspective.

Durkheim noted that suicide rates fall in wartime because of a fall in egoistic suicide as societies become more strongly integrated. In peacetime people do not have enough social integration to 'protect' them from suicide. The suicide rate is higher than the minimal level possible on the egoistic–altruistic dimension (see Figure 4.2) owing to egoistic suicide. Soldiers, however, whether volunteers or conscripts, commit altruistic suicide because, according to Durkheim (1897a/t.1951a:234), they have excessively committed themselves to the group at the expense of their own individuality. On this argument the suicide rate of soldiers and sailors in wartime ought to rise as they move from a position of excessive integration to one of

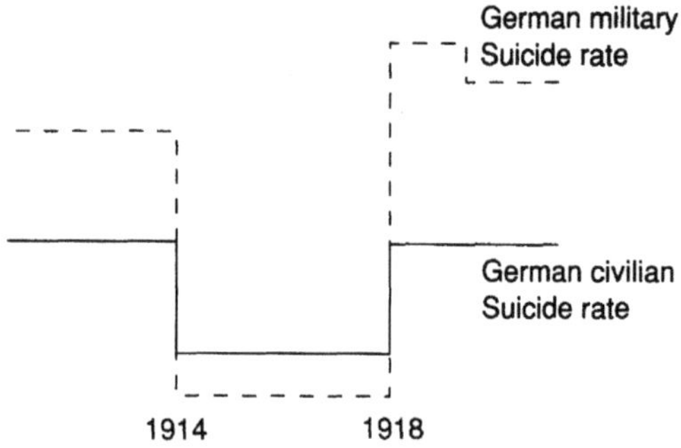

Figure 4.3

Table 4.4 Comparative suicide rates in war and peace per 100,000 Germans for selected years

Year	*Army*	*Navy*	*Total population*
1890	55	–	27
1913	43	46	23
1914–18	15	17	18
1921	110	141	21
1934	38	39	29

super-excessive integration following the outbreak of war. This will intensify the solidarity of those in the military even more than in the case of civilians. However, it does not happen, as can be illustrated from the suicide rates of soldiers and sailors in the German armed forces in World War I, as shown schematically in Figure 4.3, which is based on the statistics in Table 4.4 (Brickenstein 1965).

During World War I the suicide rate among the German military dropped dramatically until it was even lower than the (also diminished) civilian rate of suicide. That it should fall below the civilian rate at all is proof that the drop in military suicides was not due to the influx of conscripts into the army in wartime diluting its military ethos. Besides, most of the new arrivals in the army would have already served a period of prior military service before the war, since Germany had peacetime conscription. Many of them, too, would have served in the reserve; indeed, a reserve officer's commission was the height of status for members of a large middle class aping the aristocratic and gentry-based military caste of their society (Shirer 1960:96; Craig 1964:238; Balfour 1975:431). It was common for such individuals to fight duels with pistols at point-blank range so that one or both of them was likely to get killed. They had a code of 'honour' in which one's standing depended on a willingness to risk sudden and violent death over some trivial dispute (McAleer 1994). In England at the time the one survivor out of two duellists would have been hanged for murder, but in Germany he was a hero and, if an army officer, would be protected by his superiors from any serious consequences. In other words, Germany was a thoroughly militarized society, a society in which, as Prince Bernhard von Bülow (1914:181) noted with pride, even the Social Democratic Party marched in an orderly way with banners, thus displaying the virtues of a unit under military discipline. Civilians of this type who were conscripted into the army would not have seriously diluted its ethos or led to a loss of solidarity within its ranks.

We should also note that the suicide rate in wartime dropped as much among naval personnel as among those in the army. This is important since it is sometimes alleged that there is no *real* fall in suicide in wartime but that it simply ceases to be measured (O'Malley 1975:349, 353–5). In particular a soldier who wishes to kill himself has the option of dying in battle through deliberate recklessness. Such men may even be posthumously perceived as heroes sacrificing themselves for their country and not as suicides at all. However, this again illustrates the strength of Durkheim's insight that the two phenomena are closely connected. The connection, though, does not make sense from a utilitarian point of view, and a wise officer will refuse to accept a potentially suicidal man who volunteers for a raiding party, lest he endanger all the others by his heedless search for death.

It is for this reason that it is important to note that the naval suicide rate fell by the same order of magnitude as that of the army. Naval personnel do not have the same opportunities for individual recklessness that soldiers do. Their fate is tied to that of their ship or U-boat and they cannot commit disguised suicide. Only the commander of the fleet could really decide to commit suicide in this way. It was the fear that a senior commander might seek death with honour in this fashion that led to the German sailors' mutiny in Kiel in 1918 (Pitt 1962:265), when they turned against their officers and helped to bring about the collapse of the entire system. Also, most of the German *surface* fleet remained in port throughout the entire 1914–18 war except for a few forays into the North Sea (Halpern 1994:287, 387–80, 417–21), such as one that led to the Battle of Jutland (Halpern 1994:310–29). There were no opportunities for suicide disguised as fighting; a sailor, hanging himself in a secluded corner of a naval barracks or in a Kiel brothel, would have been meticulously recorded as suicide by the German equivalent of a coroner. Thus the drop in military suicides in wartime is a real phenomenon and not a mere artefact of measurement.

This fall in the suicide rate in wartime among the military is a phenomenon which, from a Durkheimian point of view, should not have happened. Durkheim's theory leads us to a hypothesis that predicts that the military suicide rate would have *risen* in wartime, and the massive fall in suicide that in fact occurred falsifies Durkheim's prediction, hypothesis and theory. The very idea of altruistic suicide has collapsed under the weight of its own inner contradictions.

However, this should not unduly surprise us. The problem that Durkheim never faced is that most other European institutions at the altruistic end of the spectrum do not have high suicide rates, even though their level of integration is as great as that of the military. Members of religious orders, for instance, have a low suicide rate despite their total commitment to what Coser (1974) has termed a greedy institution, i.e. one demanding the total submersion of the individual into the collectivity. They are as close to the altruistic end of the spectrum as those enrolled in the military but they have a far lower suicide rate. At the same time their situation can be unstable, as can be seen from the 'waves of suicides in monasteries in medieval times' noted by Durkheim (1897a/t.1951a:228). In the more distant past there were also fears that Christians would commit suicide through martyrdom, as persons who wished to die chose to do so by insulting the heathens and defiling their idols and graven images, or by cursing their god or gods while the heathen were at prayer. The occurrence of hysterical religious suicides once caused 'Augustine to abandon his customary delicacy and to ask during a sermon at Cyprian's grave why those who were obsessed with the desire for a martyr's death never employed the rope which offered a much more comfortable way of taking one's life' (van der Meer 1961:84).

In our own era it is the suicidal behaviour of sectarians that best fits this pattern. In normal times members of small, tightly bound religious sects such as the Amish have a low suicide rate, partly because of an absence of egoism and anomie (that is, because of strong integration and regulation), and partly because of the distinctive content of their religious beliefs (Kraybill, Hostetler and Shaw 1986). Yet every so often there will be an outbreak of suicide in the midst of a tightly knit sect, sometimes sponsored by the leadership, as in the case of the Jonestown massacre, the Solar Temple and Heavensgate in California (Weightman 1983; Saraswati 1997).

What we can see from this is that altruistic suicide and, indeed, fatalistic suicide are indeterminate. At the egoistic–anomic end of the spectrum suicide rates are always high but at the altruistic–fatalistic end they can be *either very high or very low* depending on circumstances that lie outside Durkheim's model. The pattern is shown in Figure 4.4.

At the altruistic–fatalistic end of the spectrum almost anything is possible. The suicide rate could be very high as in Case A or very low as in Case B, and anything in between. This is a completely different pattern from that of Figure 4.2 which we derived from Durkheim's model; indeed, the new model completely supersedes that of Durkheim.

On further consideration it can also be seen that the new model flows logically from the difference between the nature of egoistic–anomic and

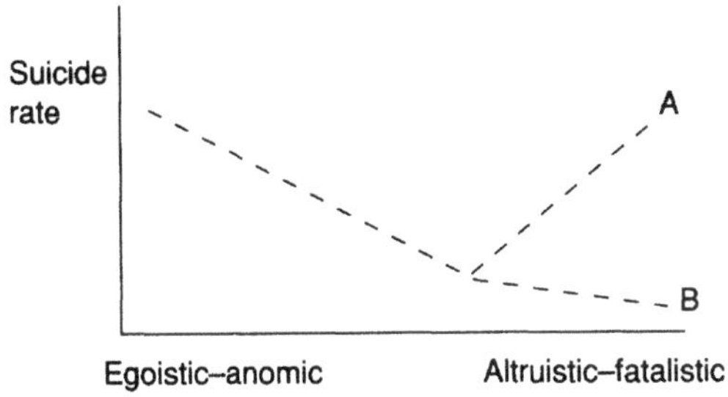

Figure 4.4

altruistic–fatalistic suicide. In an egoistic–anomic society individuals are weakly attached to groups but are feebly regulated. Therefore the nature of the group and the content of the regulations *does not matter*. All egoistic and all anomic societies are the same, since all weak forces are *weak in the same way*. By contrast, if individuals are strongly integrated and strongly regulated, then their behaviour, including the committing of or restraining oneself from suicide, must depend on the nature of the group and the content of the rules. This is why NCOs commit suicide and parish priests do not. The nature of strong groups and strong rules will differ markedly from one case to another and produce different consequences for suicide, as when soldiers who readily commit suicide in peacetime refrain from doing so when war breaks out. It is not simply a question of whether or not the group strongly forbids, is indifferent to, encourages or enforces suicide, though (contrary to what Durkheim says) this will be important at the altruistic and fatalistic end of the spectrum. Rather it is the entire ethos of the group, its values, lifestyle and patterns of internal interaction that are involved. Once this is recognized, it becomes clear that Durkheim's concepts of altruistic and fatalistic suicide are badly flawed. We can still go on using them – indeed they can illuminate cases such as that of the age–sex pattern of suicide in China in a way that no other theory can – but we must recognize that they are problematic in a way that egoistic and anomic suicide are not. There is no symmetrical relationship between the egoistic–anomic and the altruistic–fatalistic cases, and no Aristotelian golden mean of maximum 'protection' from suicide. The low point of suicide will indeed lie somewhere towards the altruistic–fatalistic end of the spectrum but we have no way of knowing where. There may be a golden mean or there may be an altruistic–fatalistic golden extreme: it will differ from one group to another depending on sociological characteristics and contexts that lie outside Durkheim's model. Equally, a society at the extreme altruistic–fatalistic end of the spectrum may be characterized by a very high, a very low or a moderate level of suicide, and Durkheim's model is of no help in telling us which it will be.

Bibliography

Alpert, H. (1961) *Emile Durkheim and His Sociology*, New York: Russell and Russell.

Aristotle (1976) *Ethics (The Nicomachean Ethics)*, translated by J. Thomson and H. Tredennick, Harmondsworth: Penguin.

Baechler, J. (1979) *Suicides*, Oxford: Basil Blackwell.

Balfour, M. (1975) *The Kaiser and His Times*, Harmondsworth: Penguin.

Bellah, R. N. (1973) 'Introduction' to E. Durkheim (t.1973a) *Emile Durkheim on Morality and Society, Selected Readings*, translated by M. Traugott, edited with an introduction by Robert N. Bellah, Chicago: University of Chicago Press, pp. vii–lv.

Brickenstein, R. (1965) 'Faktoren für das Zustandekommen von Selbsttotungen bei Soldaten der Bundeswehr', *Der Nervenarzt* 36(10):437–41.

Bülow, Prince Bernhard von (1914) *Imperial Germany*, London: Cassell.

Butterfield, F. (1982) *China. Alive in the Bitter Sea*, London: Hodder and Stoughton.

Chia, H. B. and Mehta, K. K. (1983) 'Singapore', in L. A. Headley (ed.) *Suicide in Asia and the Near East*, Berkeley: University of California Press, pp. 101–41.

Coser, L. A. (1974) *Greedy Institutions: Patterns of Undivided Commitment*. New York: Free Press.

Craig, G. A. (1964) *The Politics of the Prussian Army*, New York: Oxford University Press.

David, E. (ed.) (1977) *Inside Asquith's Cabinet: From the Diaries of Charles Hobhouse*, London: John Murray.

Diekstra, R. F. W. (1989) 'An International Perspective on Suicide and Its Prevention', in S. D. Platt and N. Kreitman (eds) *Current Research on Suicide and Parasuicide*, Edinburgh: Edinburgh University Press, pp. 2–21.

Dissanyake, S. A. W. and de Silva, P. (1983) 'Sri Lanka', in L. A. Headley (ed.) *Suicide in Asia and the Near East*, Berkeley: University of California Press.

Durkheim, E. (1893b) *De la Division du travail social: étude sur l'organisation des sociétés supérieures*, Paris: Alcan.

— (t.1933b) by G. Simpson, *The Division of Labor in Society*, New York: Macmillan.

(1897a) *Le Suicide: étude de sociologie*, Paris: Alcan.

— (t.1951a) by J. A. Spaulding and G. Simpson, *Suicide: A Study in Sociology*, edited with an introduction by G. Simpson, Glencoe, IL: Free Press (London: Routledge and Kegan Paul, 1952).

— (t.1973a) by M. Traugott, *Emile Durkheim on Morality and Society: Selected Readings*, edited with an introduction by Robert N. Bellah, Chicago: University of Chicago Press.

Farberow, N. L. (ed.) (1975) *Suicide in Different Cultures*, Baltimore, MD: University Park Press.

Fox, R. (1980) *The Red Lamp of Incest*, London: Hutchinson.

Gibbs, J. P. and Martin, W. T. (1958) 'A Theory of Status Integration and Its Relationship to Suicide', *American Sociological Review* 23:140–7.

Gibbs, J. P. and Martin, W. T. (1964) *Status Integration and Suicide: A Sociological Study*. Eugene, OR: University of Oregon Press.

Halpern, P. G. (1994) *A Naval History of World War I*, London: UCL Press.

Headley, L. A. (ed.) (1983) *Suicide in Asia and the Near East*, Berkeley: University of California Press.

Headley, L. A. (1983) 'Conclusion', in L. A. Headley (ed.) *Suicide in Asia and the Near East*, Berkeley: University of California Press, pp. 350–66.

Hoyt, E. P. (1985) *The Kamikazes*, London: Panther.

Iga, M. and Tatai, K. (1975) 'Characteristics of Suicide and Attitudes towards Suicide in Japan', in N. L. Farberow (ed.) *Suicide in Different Cultures*, Baltimore, MD: University Park Press, pp. 255–80.

Johnson, B. D. (1965) 'Durkheim's One Cause of Suicide', *American Sociological Review* 30:875–86.

Kraybill, D. B., Hostetler, J. A. and Shaw, D. G. (1986) 'Suicide Patterns in a Religious Subculture. The Old Order Amish', *International Journal of Moral and Social Studies* 1(3):249–63.

La Capra, D. (1972) *Emile Durkheim: Sociologist and Philosopher*, Ithaca, NY: Cornell University Press.

Levy, H. (1974) *Chinese Sex Jokes in Traditional Times* (Asian Folklore and Social Life Monograph 583), Taipei.

Marra, R. and Orrú, M. (1991) 'Social Images of Suicide', *British Journal of Sociology* 42(2):273–88.

McAleer, K. (1994) *Duelling: The Cult of Honor in Fin-de-Siècle Germany*, Princeton, NJ: Princeton University Press.

Merton, R. K. (1957) *Social Theory and Social Structure*, New York: Free Press.

Morris, I. (1980) *The Nobility of Failure: Tragic Heroes in the History of Japan*, Harmondsworth: Penguin.

Mosher, S. W. (1984) *Broken Earth: The Rural Chinese*, London: Robert Hale.

Nitobe, I. (1903) *Bushido: The Soul of Japan*, New York: Putnam.

O'Malley, L. S. S. (1935) *Popular Hinduism: The Religion of the Masses*, Cambridge: Cambridge University Press.

O'Malley, P. (1975) 'Suicide and War: A Case Study and Theoretical Appraisal', *British Journal of Criminology* 15(4):348–59.

Pitt, B. (1962) *1918: The Last Act*, London: Cassell.

Pope, W. (1975) 'Conception and Explanatory Structure in Durkheim's Theory of Suicide', *British Journal of Sociology* 26(4):417–34.

(1976) *Durkheim's* Suicide*: A Classic Analysed*, Chicago: University of Chicago Press.

Pritchard, C. (1993) 'A Comparison of Youth Suicide in Hong Kong, the Developed World and the Republic of China, 1973–1988: Grounds for Optimism or Concern?', *Hong Kong Journal of Mental Health* 22:6–16.

(1995) *Suicide – the Ultimate Rejection: A Psycho-Social Study*, Buckingham: Open University Press.

(1996) 'Suicide in the People's Republic of China Categorised by Age and Gender: Evidence of the Influence of Culture on Suicide', *Acta Psychiatrica Scandinavia* 93:362–7.

Retterstol, N. (1993) *Suicide: A European Perspective*, Cambridge: Cambridge University Press.

Saraswati, S. B. (1997) 'This Suicide Got No One to Heaven', *Hinduism Today* July, p. 9.

Shirer, W. L. (1960) *The Rise and Fall of the Third Reich*, London: Secker and Warburg.

Stokes, H. S. (1975) *The Life and Death of Yukio Mishima*, Tokyo: Charles E. Tuttle.

Tatai, K. (1983) 'Japan', in L. A. Headley (ed.) *Suicide in Asia and the Near East*, Berkeley: University of California Press, pp. 12–58.

Thompson, E. (1928) *Suttee: A Historical and Philosophical Enquiry into the Hindu Rite of Widow Burning*, London: George Allen and Unwin.

Travis, R. (1990) 'Suicide in Cross-Cultural Perspective', *International Journal of Comparative Sociology* 31(3–4):237–48.

van der Meer, F. (1961) *Augustine the Bishop: The Life and Work of a Father of the Church*, London: Sheed and Ward.

Weightman, J. M. (1983) *Making Sense of the Jonestown Suicides: A Sociological History of Peoples Temple*, New York: Edwin Mellen.

5

SUICIDE, STATISTICS AND SOCIOLOGY

Assessing Douglas' critique of Durkheim

John Varty

Jack Douglas has presented the most comprehensive critique of the official suicide statistics that Durkheim used in *Suicide*. At the same time Douglas put forward an alternative sociological approach to the study of suicide. This chapter addresses the problems that arise from Durkheim's use of official statistics on suicide and compares the two different approaches to studying suicide. In what follows I focus first on the points in *Suicide* where Durkheim discusses the accuracy and meaning of suicide statistics; I then discuss the problems arising out of Durkheim's definition of suicide; I outline and assess Douglas' critique of Durkheim; and finally I compare Durkheim's study of suicide rates with Douglas' analysis of the collective and individual meanings involved in the suicidal process.

First, I wish to do two things to put the debate in its appropriate context: clarify exactly what it is that Durkheim is being accused of, and then make some observations about various assumptions that seem to be doing a lot of work in the arguments for and against the use of statistics in both Durkheim's time and ours. Taking the latter issue first, making explicit these assumptions may help to explain why Durkheim did not feel much need to defend a move – using official suicide statistics – that his critics now consider to require greater justification, if indeed it can be justified at all. While some of the assumptions may not be explicitly raised in the debates, the role they play – in both the authors' arguments and readers' responses to them – suggests that one needs to be aware of them in order to understand what is going on.

With his study of suicide, Durkheim entered into an ongoing, Europe-wide debate. Much of the data that he used had already been collected and analysed by others. The publication of government statistics on a range of 'social problems' including suicide was one of the reasons the debate about suicide arose when it did and took the form that it did. Participants within the debate were less concerned with suicide as a philosophical issue – is it right or wrong? – than with what they perceived to be abnormally high rates of suicide. The new statistical material was considered to be of ideal value to those interested in a scientific approach to studying society and the 'moral problems' that advanced industrial societies seemed to generate.

The inadequacies of the official statistics on suicide had already been discussed before Durkheim published his book. In his study of suicide, Morselli noted that the official statistics began to be collected in the early nineteenth century. He acknowledged that there were problems in gathering exact data: there were difficulties in distinguishing between suicide, homicide or accidental death, and there were obstacles generated by public prejudices, habits, indifference or bad faith. Despite this, Morselli suggested, as Durkheim would later, that while statistics could not provide useful information on individual motives they were becoming more accurate records of real suicide rates (Giddens 1971:6–8). We can explain the absence of detailed discussion of the possible problems involved in the use of official statistics in *Suicide* once we recognize that Durkheim accepted the orthodoxies of his day and thus saw little need to reproduce the details of a debate that he thought was concluded and that had vindicated his position. Indeed, Douglas suggests that Durkheim must have assumed that Morselli had dealt with such problems and that the issue was 'quiet enough' when Durkheim wrote *Suicide* for him to be able to 'pass over it lightly' and to count on the reader to 'make the appropriate tacit assumptions' (Douglas 1967:178). Such general 'enthusiasm' about official statistics has now been replaced by a general scepticism towards them; this has arisen in part from the deliberate misuse of official statistics by government, e.g. in British government statistics on unemployment the numerous changes of the criteria for what counts as being out of work. While such scepticism will not lead one to give automatic assent to Douglas' critique of Durkheim's use of official statistics, it may lead one to think that Durkheim was somewhat naïve in his use of statistics and insufficiently sensitive to those factors that could lead to their distortion. While Durkheim might have passed over such problems too quickly there is a danger of arriving at – possibly equally erroneous – snap judgements. Expectations that Durkheim could not possibly be aware of such issues seem to be driven by the currently fashionable denigration of 'positivism' in all of its forms. Today 'positivist' is for many little more than a term of abuse (Giddens 1995:136). As Durkheim was some kind of positivist, the current reckoning appears to be that he was theoretically unequipped to recognize, let alone deal with, such issues. Without wishing to go into great detail, it is worth remarking that *Suicide* cannot be easily classified as a positivist work. Durkheim was a naturalist: sociology should be a natural science of society. However, Durkheim's theory of suicide was 'realist': studying the suicide statistics and the different rates dependent on marital status, family structure, religious affiliation, etc. allows one to gain knowledge of real forces – suicidogenic currents – that explain the suicide rate but are otherwise unobservable. This reference to suicidogenic currents has troubled subsequent sociologists within the positivist tradition, who have quietly tended to drop this aspect of Durkheim's theory. Interestingly, Douglas argues against 'positivist' interpretations of *Suicide*. He even suggests that his thesis – that shared meanings are the fundamental causes of suicide – can be found within *Suicide* in embryonic form (Douglas 1967:42).

In a nutshell Durkheim stands accused of the *uncritical* use of official statistics, specifically in the sense of uncritically assuming their validity and reliability. Whether or not this charge is fair, I would first like to make it clear that Durkheim cannot be reproached for slipshod use of statistical material. Indeed, *Suicide* is generally seen to be a pioneering and innovative study. Assuming, for the moment, that the official statistics are both valid and reliable, Durkheim was careful to avoid errors in his study arising from their misuse. For example, when commencing his discussion of why there were different rates of suicide for those of Catholic or Protestant faith, he insisted that it was necessary to compare the two religions in the 'heart of a single society' in order to avoid error (Durkheim 1897a/t.1951a:153). Durkheim avoided a comparison between different countries in order to narrow, as much as possible, the range of variables. Durkheim was critical of what he saw as others' misinterpretations of the statistical data. This would seem to belie Douglas' criticism that Durkheim 'believed that the data spoke for themselves' (Douglas 1967:68). If this were so why would he take issue with others' use of the data? Durkheim was aware that the data needed to be interpreted and that this could give rise to errors. For example, he noted that looking at the absolute figures gave the wrong impression that unmarried persons commit suicide less often than married ones and that Morselli, due to some faulty analysis, over-estimated the tendency of widows to commit suicide. He also found fault with the official statistics when he thought that they had been compiled in such a way that categories that should have been recorded separately were erroneously combined – for example combining widowed persons with unmarried persons (Durkheim 1897a/t.1951a:171, 191 and 176ff.). Having dealt with these preliminaries I will now turn to Durkheim's discussion of official suicide statistics and their place in his study.

Verdicts and motives

The process of producing a verdict of suicide is a complex one involving a coroner investigating the possible motivations that lie behind someone's death. In many cases the evidence might be less than clear. So how certain can one be that the verdict of a coroner will be right? As numbers of suicide per year in any country are low, there will be a tendency to magnify the problem of the reliability of statistics based on such verdicts. Perhaps this element of unreliability of verdicts is enough to make the statistics meaningless and thus any conclusions about tendencies drawn from them arbitrary.

Durkheim was aware of this problem and the difficulties it raised for his study. In a different context, he observed that the official statistics of motive 'are actually statistics of the opinions concerning such motives of officials, often of lower officials' (Durkheim 1897a/t.1951a:148). This quotation is preceded by the comment 'as Wagner long ago remarked', which suggests that Durkheim was simply going along with what had become an orthodox position within an already extensive debate on the matter. We may conclude that Durkheim was simply over-exaggerating when he went on to suggest that 'official establishments of fact are known to be often defective even when applied to obvious material facts comprehensible to any conscientious observer and leaving no room for evaluation' (Durkheim 1897a/t.1951a:148). Durkheim doubted the reliability of statistics on suicide motives, yet he did not extend this uncertainty towards statistics of the number of suicides[1] – which suggests that he was exaggerating in the previous comment. He saw no reason to doubt the ability of officials to record the 'simple fact' of suicide. Such statistics are reliable, the assumption is, because it is easy to look at a body and recognize a suicide. He was confident as to the accuracy of suicide statistics because any errors in suicide verdicts are random and thus do not distort the statistics in any significant way.

Despite his doubts as to the reliability of statistics on motives, Durkheim had confidence in the ability of statisticians to make certain judgements as to the reliability of the information they provided. To back up his argument about the worthlessness of statistics on motives he was pleased to note that in England and Austria official statisticians were abandoning the task of collecting data on 'such supposed causes of suicide' (Durkheim 1897a/t.1951a:151). In order to defend his argument that suicide rates fall in times of national crisis, Durkheim was willing to show his confidence in the official statistics. He directly confronted the objection that such a drop could be explained away in terms of records being inaccurate due to the 'paralysis of administrative authority'. He was adamant that this could not explain the matter. First, the 'widespread occurrence of the phenomenon' told against such a position. Drops in suicide rates are found 'among conquerors as well as vanquished, invaders and invaded alike'. The effects persist a long time after the event. 'Suicides increase slowly; some years pass before their return to their point of departure; this is true even in countries where in normal times they increase with annual regularity.' Though partial omissions are likely in times of trouble, 'the drop revealed by the statistics is too steady to be attributed to a brief inadvertence of administration'. Durkheim closed with what he saw as the knock-down argument against putting such a drop in the figures down to a mistake in accounting: 'Not all political or national crises have this influence. Only those do which excite the passions' (Durkheim

1897a/t.1951a:206). Whether or not one judges this to be a satisfactory counter-argument, it undoubtedly reflects Durkheim's confidence in government statistics, or at least his confidence that, if they are flawed, they are scarcely more so than normal. Any errors that exist are not a result of administrative breakdown.

Durkheim's critics argue that he should have taken a further step in questioning not just the validity of official judgements of motive but of the suicide statistics themselves. Douglas argues that Durkheim never considered the frequency of mistakes in recording motives and what they might imply for his use of official statistics. Furthermore, while he generally took the stability of the statistics to be a sign of their reliability, he assumed that the statistics on motives were unreliable *despite* their stability (Douglas 1967:176–7). Durkheim may be right in both cases but he is wrong simply to assume so. Furthermore, Durkheim overdid the contrast when he suggested that recording motives requires interpreting and explaining complex facts, while recording a suicide involves only making a simple observation of 'obvious material facts . . . leaving no room for evaluation'. Douglas notes that, even in the latter case, one is '*relying upon human judgement for the data, not simply upon sensory experience . . . but actually upon the complex faculties of human judgements in interaction with each other*' (Douglas 1967:170, emphasis in original). And finally, Durkheim did not have to take a huge step, in terms of his own logic, to conclude that the suicide statistics were useless. It is argued that official decisions about motives or their ascribed explanations are not simply 'tagged on' as separate, or supplementary data (Taylor 1982:58–9).[2] One cannot make such a neat distinction between the process of ascertaining motives and verdicts. Ideas about motives are part of the process of coming to a verdict. They acquire a special importance when a coroner is trying to determine between a verdict of suicide or of accidental death. In the absence of other information, if no motive for suicide can be found, a coroner is more likely to come to a verdict of accidental death. Both these points suggest that recording a verdict of suicide is not simply a matter of registering facts, it also involves judgement and interpretation.

On the other hand, in defence of Durkheim's position, while it is correct to point out that ascertaining motives is part of the process by which a coroner comes to his verdict, we could still hold on to the fact that it is only a *part* of that process. A coroner could get the motive wrong and still come to the right verdict, or have little or no information about possible motives yet be certain that a death is a suicide due to the specific nature and circumstances of the death. Certain types of death – hanging, barbiturate poisoning, shooting and drowning – are, once foul play has been excluded, suggestive of suicide. In this sense perhaps it is legitimate to play down the question of motives and, furthermore, to suggest that coroners will not always be able to discern motives for suicide, while still being able to classify suicides correctly. However, it seems that such a defence does not hold water. Evidence from the circumstances of death is rarely sufficient to establish a suicide verdict. Officials also examine the background of the deceased in order to uncover indications of suicidal intent. Taylor refers to a particular case where a man was found dead in his garage sat in his car having suffocated from inhaling petrol fumes. The man died after leaving the car engine running while the garage door was closed. The circumstances strongly suggest suicide but the coroner did not come to such a verdict. As none of the usual problems associated with suicide could be found, a verdict of misadventure was given. The assumption was that, having parked his car, the man fell asleep before switching off the car engine. The investigators then turned to provide explanations as to how the door might accidentally have swung shut, however unlikely such a possibility might seem (Taylor 1982:77–84). These 'secondary investigations' carry greater weight in determining a verdict than the examination of the circumstances of the death. This backs up Taylor's suggestion that deaths are only recorded as suicides when they are accompanied by '*facts* (such as drunkenness, domestic troubles, etc.) which provide, at least in the officials' view, an explanation for the suicide. A "normal", happy, adjusted person killing himself makes "no sense". Therefore, if a death *really* is a "suicide", then there must be evidence of "abnormality", unhappiness, disturbance, etc.' (Taylor 1982:59).

Defining suicide

At the start of his study, Durkheim insisted upon the need for a clear definition of suicide. The definition he settled on was that suicide was any death '*resulting directly or indirectly from a positive or negative act of the victim himself, which he knows must produce this result*' (Durkheim 1897a/t.1951a:44, emphasis in original). For Durkheim the death may not even be self-inflicted to count as a suicide. He later refers to the deaths of the early Christian martyrs as examples of altruistic suicides. The Christian martyrs might not have killed themselves but they voluntarily allowed their own slaughter (p. 227). Durkheim, in contrast to official definitions, focused not on intent but knowledge: whether the victim *knows* the normal result of his or her action with certainty. Durkheim defended this aspect of his definition by arguing that intentions are hard to identify: 'How [to] discover the agent's motive and whether he desired death itself when he formed his resolve, or had some other purpose? Intent is too intimate a thing to be more than approximately interpreted by another.' Furthermore, 'an act cannot be defined by the end sought by the actor, for an identical system of behaviour may be adjustable to too many different ends without altering its nature' (Durkheim 1897a/t.1951a:43).

Durkheim suggested that 'it is not impossible to discover whether the individual did or did not know in advance the natural results of his action' (Durkheim 1897a/t.1951a:44). However, if one cannot accurately interpret the actor's intentions, how can one determine whether an individual knew that their actions would lead to their death? It may be that intentions are more difficult to infer than knowledge of consequences, but this is a difference only of degree. What is involved is still information of the same type: 'information about what is "in the head" of the social actor' (Douglas 1967:380).

Steven Lukes has argued that Durkheim's definition of suicide is also philosophically unacceptable (Lukes 1973:200ff.). The Durkheimian definition cuts across conventional distinctions drawn between acts of suicide and acts of bravery involving self-sacrifice. If we take intentions into account, self-sacrifice is defined by an intention to save others where death is a consequence of such actions. Suicide is defined simply by the intention to kill oneself: there is no intention to save others. Durkheim argued that the differences between acts of self-sacrifice and suicide are merely apparent; they are, in fact, fundamentally identical. He observed that 'Whether death is accepted merely as an unfortunate consequence, but inevitable given the purpose, or is actually itself sought and desired, in either case the person renounces existence, and the various methods of doing so can be only varieties of a single class' (Durkheim 1897a/t.1951a:43). Durkheim does provide his reasons as to why he considers acts of self-sacrifice and suicide to be fundamentally the same, but they do not add up to an argument that would convince someone who accepts the conventional understanding that they are two essentially different forms of renouncing existence.

Durkheim has been criticized for not realizing the significance of the difference between his and officials' definitions of suicide. Having decided he was going to use the official statistics should not Durkheim have used the definition upon which they were based? He considered his definition to be in tune with conventional and official understandings. He noted that his definition would have to determine an order of facts 'sufficiently kin to those commonly called suicide' in order to be able to 'retain the same term without breaking with common usage' (Durkheim 1897a/t.1951a:42). However, Durkheim was wrong in his assumption, and his ignorance of the difference between his and officials' definitions of suicide is no defence for dubious scientific practice. As Douglas (1967:169) states, it makes no sense to propose a definition of suicide and then base one's study on statistics drawn from a different definition. For example, the case of a soldier who dies to save his regiment may be suicide for Durkheim but it will not be recorded as such (Durkheim 1897a/t.1951a:43).[3]

Douglas raises a different problem emerging from 'official' definitions of suicide. He notes that no one has studied what the different groups of officials, who categorize deaths, mean by the term 'suicide'. Until this is known, he suggests, it is an open question whether 'the official statistics labelled "suicide" statistics are measures of the same phenomena' (Douglas 1967:180–1). This raises the problem of the validity of the suicide statistics.

The social construction of suicide statistics

Douglas' general point is that official statistics are 'socially constructed', as opposed to being objective, reliable measures of social phenomena – thus the critique has a much wider scope than Durkheim's *Suicide*. According to Douglas, official statistics are based upon the perceptions, intuitions, and subjective judgements of fallible human beings. He notes that the process of producing a verdict of suicide involves 'the physical scene, the sequence of events, the significant others of the deceased, various officials . . ., the public, and the official who must impute the category' (Douglas 1967:190). He is keen to emphasize that this is a *process* and he suggests that, for the sociologist to understand it, he has to consider two particular problems: '(1) the *objective criteria* used to decide how to categorize a death and (2) the *search procedures* used in determining whether these criteria are met' (Douglas 1967:183). He bemoans the fact that Durkheim failed to determine the criteria upon which officials' judgements were based. He did not look at the relationship between the 'measuring instrument' and the 'phenomena'. If so, Durkheim would have discovered that 'the official statistics on "suicide" wax and wane in relation to a number of different dimensions of "things" called "suicide"' (Douglas 1967:170–1). Douglas suggests that the statistics vary only in relation to changes in what is defined as 'suicide'. The statistics are no measure of objective trends in real suicide rates.

As Steve Taylor notes, Douglas puts forward two arguments: a 'weak' argument that there are *systematic biases* to the suicide rates (Douglas 1967:191), and a 'strong' one that denies the reality of suicide as a unitary phenomenon and thus rejects the notion of a 'real' rate. Douglas argues that the meaning of suicide is neither 'unidimensional, universally agreed upon', nor 'unchanging among the various societies of Europe – and certainly not beyond the cultural borders of Europe' (Douglas 1967:178). For Taylor, the two positions contradict and undermine each other (Taylor 1982:51). If there is no such thing as a real suicide rate why the concern with bias? Bias from what? However, if we take Douglas' intentions into account there is no contradiction. Douglas' ultimate aim is to defend his new sociological approach to studying suicide: the 'intensive observation, description, and analysis of individual cases of suicide', focused upon unearthing 'the whole complex of shared and individual *meanings* of the actions involved in the suicidal process' (Douglas 1967:231). To clear away the ground before illustrating the value of his approach, Douglas first criticizes the dominant sociological approach based on the study of official suicide rates. The argument about systematic bias is put forward with this purpose in mind. The 'weak' argument is a 'negative' one: a tactical manoeuvre designed to shake sociologists out of their complacency. The notion of systematic bias seems to presuppose a 'real' rate of which the statistics are a distorted reflection. However, Douglas is here working within the assumptions of his opponents and challenging them on their own terms. It is only later when he feels that he has raised sufficient doubts about the value of the official statistics that he propounds his more radical argument. In this sense Taylor is right to argue that the two arguments are separate, but perhaps he is wrong to suggest that Douglas contradicts himself by raising them both. I will now turn to the 'weaker' argument.

Durkheim assumed that the statistics showing different rates of suicide within various social groups reflected differences in *actual* suicide rates. He explained these differences in terms of the relative levels of integration and regulation within groups. Douglas puts forward an alternative hypothesis that points to one possible source of *systemic* bias.[4] He starts from the assumption that, due to the stigma that surrounds suicide, coroners are liable to come under pressure to find a verdict of accidental death.[5] According to Douglas, the suicide statistics simply inform us as to the relative stigma that suicide carries within groups and the amount of influence family members of the deceased can exert over coroners. If both factors are high a coroner is more likely to come to a verdict of accidental death. Douglas suggests that 'it *seems most reasonable to expect*' that with different groups 'there will be both differential tendencies . . . to have any "suspicious" deaths within their families categorized as something other than "suicide" and differential degrees of success in these attempts' (Douglas 1967:129, my emphasis).

Assessing the critique

Douglas focused on genuine problems. He is right to point out that producing a verdict is a process and that this process needs to be investigated. However, a number of criticisms can and have been raised against Douglas' argument that there are systematic biases in the official suicide statistics.

As things stand Douglas' account is just an alternative hypothesis in need of evidence in its favour. He notes that some of his argument depends upon analysis of what is plausible (Douglas 1967:167). He insists that what must follow is an 'intensive and extensive empirical investigation of the methods, implicit and explicit assumptions, etc., of the officials who are responsible for the statistics on suicide and of the whole process by which deaths in various societies are brought to the attention of various categories of officials for decisions concerning the "cause of death"' (Douglas 1967:229). His argument that suicide statistics are socially constructed seems to suggest more than is necessarily the case. How far does the process go and just what takes place? How much do families try to influence verdicts? How can they put pressure on coroners and how much are coroners influenced? Halbwachs has argued that suicide is difficult to conceal, because it usually comes as a shock to relatives and friends, who hence do not have time effectively to carry through the necessary dissimulations (Halbwachs 1930/t.1978:23). How many suicides can be passed off as accidental deaths? How much *scope* do officials have to allow their beliefs and preferences to influence their decisions (Taylor 1982:216)? How many problematic cases are there?

Douglas' argument need not be completely wrong for his account of why there are different official rates of suicide for different social groups to be mistaken. While people may attempt to conceal suicides it may not be the case that there are any systematic differences in either the attempts of different groups to conceal suicides from officials or in their degree of success. Thus one could end up with an acknowledgement of sources of possible errors in the official suicide rate but a conclusion that there are no *systematic* biases in the statistics.

Douglas is right when he observes that Durkheim only explicitly considers the validity and reliability of the statistics when they contradict his interpretation (Douglas 1967:173). While Durkheim was aware of a number of the problems that Douglas raises, due to the nature of his study, he did not follow through the further implications of these problems. Douglas' argument is lacking proof but it did shift the focus of attention. Defences of the official statistics have been made (e.g. Barraclough 1987:ch.5) but two empirical studies by Atkinson and Taylor, following Douglas' lead, suggested that his suspicion that the statistics were systematically biased was correct. Taylor noted that if Douglas' position is understood to be a hypothesis about a varying rate of *concealment* of suicides, it is virtually impossible to prove (Taylor 1982:101). If a suicide was successfully concealed it is difficult to see how a researcher could reveal the fact. Atkinson also notes that to understand the issue in this way runs against the grain of another aspect of Douglas' argument. The problem of concealment implies that there are deaths, which are unambiguous examples of suicide, which families then attempt to cover up. However, Douglas also stresses that defining a death as a suicide is a fundamentally ambiguous and problematic process which should be the central focus of research (Atkinson 1978:65–6). Taylor conducted a study of the process of producing verdicts for a number of people killed under London tube trains – a form of death suggestive of suicide. He studied what happened in the coroner's court when the verdicts were being determined. What he found supported the hypothesis that there are tendencies to have certain deaths registered as other than suicide. When evidence about the victim's state of mind and their circumstances is given by family members, they are prone to *resist* the imputation of suicidal intent. Suicide verdicts are less likely to be found (Taylor 1982:107). Thus the differential suicide rates for those individuals who are solitary could, in part, be accounted for by the fact that any witnesses – who are not family members – called to provide background evidence tend not to resist a coroner's imputation of suicidal intent. Taylor suggests that background evidence as to whether there was suicidal intent is negotiated between the coroner and witnesses. He concludes that while his study is not conclusive it raises sufficient doubts as to the reliability of the official suicide statistics.

Two approaches to studying suicide

In the end, the reliability of the official statistics on suicide is not Douglas' primary concern. He would still defend his alternative approach to studying suicide even if an effective defence of the official statistics were to be made. He is interested in interpreting the individual act of suicide: the actors' intentions and individual and collective meanings involved in the act. Atkinson has noted that, for those who wish to take up Douglas' alternative approach to the study of suicide, there is no clear idea as to either what Douglas means when he refers to 'social meanings' or how one could go about analysing them. Nor could one know how whether the true meanings involved in a suicide had been captured, instead of simply reading into the situation what one would expect (Atkinson 1978:79). Douglas just states that he is 'concerned with *certain* ideas concerning the general dimensions of suicidal meanings and of the general properties of suicidal properties'. There is no guidance as to what procedures one should follow in such a study, and Douglas is equally vague as to what counts as the data that one must use to study and analyse meanings: the 'statements, cries, and whatever other real-world phenomena one can come up with' (Douglas 1967:242–3). In the few examples that Douglas discusses he draws his data from diaries, letters and suicide notes discussed in other researchers' work.

Durkheim's approach is the converse of Douglas'. It appears that for Durkheim, a sociologist can find nothing of interest in a study of individual cases of suicide. He was interested in the social suicide rate. He commented on Brierre de Boismont's study of over a thousand individual cases that 'the patient's revelations of his condition are usually insufficient, if not suspect. He is only apt to be mistaken concerning himself and the state of his feelings . . . besides being insufficiently objective, these observations cover too many facts to permit definite conclusions' (Durkheim 1897a/t.1951a:146). Durkheim also argued that the particular private troubles the victim was going through were not the real causes of suicide. Durkheim distinguished, some have thought too sharply, between the proximate or apparent and the effective or real causes of suicide. Study of individual acts of suicide could only unearth the proximate causes of suicide when the real causes of suicide lie elsewhere. 'The reasons ascribed for suicide . . . or those to which the suicide himself ascribed his act, are usually only apparent causes. . . . They may be said to indicate the individual's weak points, where the outside current bearing the impulse to self-destruction most easily finds introduction' (Durkheim 1897a/t.1951a:151). 'The incidents of private life . . . are only incident causes. The individual yields to the slightest shock of circumstances because the state of society has made him a ready prey to suicide' (Durkheim 1897a/t.1951a:215). 'The private experiences . . . have only the influence borrowed from the victim's moral predisposition, itself an echo of the moral state of society. . . . This is why there is nothing which cannot serve as an occasion for suicide. It all depends on the intensity with which suicidogenic causes have affected the individual' (Durkheim 1897a/t.1951a:299–300).

Both approaches to studying suicide have their own problems. It appears that the critical comments of both Durkheim and Douglas are valid: that the official statistics are systematically biased, and that information gathered about individual acts of suicide is often far from complete and not necessarily reliable. The use of official statistics has been defended on pragmatic grounds: they are simply there, immediately available for sociological analysis. By contrast, Douglas' approach is considerably more labour intensive. What seems unfortunate though is that there is in Douglas no attempt to study patterns in suicide rates and possible social causes for such rates. But if the official statistics are systematically biased, such a Durkheimian study of social suicide rates is seemingly impossible.

Notes

1 In a footnote, however, when he was trying to explain why the Spanish figures on women's suicides were different to the rest of Europe, Durkheim observed without further comment that 'the accuracy of Spanish statistics is open to doubt' (Durkheim 1897a/t.1951a:166ff.).

2 Taylor suggests that, given his intentions in *Suicide*, Durkheim did not pursue the implications of his embryonic statistical critique.

3 Douglas notes that if Durkheim had realized that intention was part of the official definition of suicide he should then have concluded, having already noted the difficulty of identifying intention, that the official statistics were unreliable (Douglas 1967:186). See chapter 3 here.

4 Douglas also refers to unreliability resulting from: the choice of official statistics to be used in testing sociological theories; the effects of different degrees of social integration on the official statistics keeping; variations in the social imputations of motives; and the more extensive and professionalized collection of statistics among certain populations (Douglas 1967:203).

5 Durkheim recognized such a possibility: he noted that 'the statistics of English suicides are not very exact. Because of the penalties attached to suicide, many cases are reported as accidental death' (Durkheim 1897a/t.1951a:160n.).

Bibliography

Atkinson, J. M. (1978) *Discovering Suicide: Studies in the Social Organization of Sudden Death*, London: Macmillan.

Barraclough, B. (1987) *Suicide: Clinical and Epidemiological Studies*, London: Croom Helm.

Douglas, J. D. (1967) *The Social Meanings of Suicide*, Princeton, NJ: Princeton University Press.

Durkheim, E. (1897a) *Le Suicide: étude de sociologie*, Paris: Alcan.

—(t.1951a) by J. A. Spaulding and G. Simpson, *Suicide: A Study in Sociology*, edited with an introduction by G. Simpson, Glencoe, IL: Free Press (London: Routledge and Kegan Paul, 1952).

Giddens, A. (ed.) (1971) *The Sociology of Suicide: A Selection of Readings*, London: Frank Cass.

(1995) 'Comte, Popper and Positivism', in *Politics, Sociology and Social Theory: Encounter with Classical and Contemporary Social Thought*, Cambridge: Polity Press.

Halbwachs, M. (1930) *Les Causes du suicide*, Paris: Alcan.

— (t.1978) by H. Goldblatt, *The Causes of Suicide*, London: Routledge and Kegan Paul.

LaCapra, D. (1972) *Emile Durkheim: Sociologist and Philosopher*, London: Cornell University Press.

Lukes, S. (1973) *Emile Durkheim: His Life and Work: A Historical and Critical Study*, London: Penguin.

Pope, W. (1976) *Durkheim's* Suicide*: A Classic Analyzed*, Chicago: The University of Chicago Press.

Taylor, S. (1982) *Durkheim and the Study of Suicide*, London: Macmillan.

(1988) *The Sociology of Suicide*, London: Longman.

6

READING THE CONCLUSION

Suicide, morality and religion

W. S. F. Pickering

Introduction

Durkheim's *Le Suicide* is not just about suicide. As he himself admitted, 'the questions it [suicide] raises are closely connected with the most serious practical problems of the present time' (1897a/t.1951a:391). The book covers nearly all Durkheim's ideas, from those relating to methodology to those concerning education. It presents a mirror of his thought as it was at the turn of the nineteenth and twentieth centuries and, although it was to be modified and expanded, his thought did not radically change from then until his death.

Of all the questions the issue of suicide raises at the hands of Durkheim, that of religion in its moral dimension has a prominent place. What comes quickly to the minds of those who know the book is his assertion that religion is a key variable – perhaps *the* key variable – in analysing rates of suicide. As we all are well aware, he holds, for example, that suicide rates are lower in Catholic countries and provinces than in those dominated by Protestants of various kinds. That assertion, stated earlier by Morselli and much worked-over by later commentators, I leave to one side, at least for the moment. But I would refer in passing to Maurice Halbwachs' long commentary on the subject, which is all too frequently overlooked (Halbwachs 1930:ch.9). Here are a few words in his conclusion which I do not think can be faulted:

> That diverse religious persuasions, as such, produce more or fewer suicides is one of the most impressive of the conclusions in Durkheim's study, but it may also be the most questionable.
>
> (Halbwachs 1930:316)

And surely it is now generally agreed that Halbwachs was right in asserting that it is extremely difficult to isolate religion from other variable factors.

This chapter is not so much focused on Durkheim's attempt to account for social facts about suicide and the alleged causes of the phenomenon, as on his concern for remedying what he held was a morbid situation, and on the basic assumptions of his remedy. The truth of the matter is that he was as much concerned with finding scientific causes of suicide as he was of pointing to practical measures to contain suicide. In this respect I draw on ideas prominent in the last two chapters of the book (Chapters 2 and 3 of Book Three) – chapters all too readily glossed over. Commentaries on Durkheim's book usually stop when once the issue of causation has been dealt with. The import of these two chapters presents a number of interesting and important issues, as well as difficulties. Some of these I wish to examine.

So to a brief look at the text itself. The book concludes with a section, 'Du Suicide comme phénomène social' (Book Three). In it Durkheim goes over much of the ground he has already covered, emphasizing in an examination of suicide the priority of the social (Chapter 1 of Book Two) and continues by drawing on generalizations derived from a limited historical account of the morality of suicide, declaring his own moral position; finally he offers a way of limiting suicide through the influence of decentralized occupational groups (Chapters 2 and 3). One might have thought that some of this – the historical/moral sections – should have come at the beginning of the book rather than the end. Perhaps Durkheim might be excused by holding that it was unwise in a scientific book to declare his moral hand at the outset. But it should not be forgotten that as always for him, practical problems or matters of policy are to be based, at least ideally, on scientific analysis and theory – what he calls social reality (1897a/t.1951a:370). Analysis must always come first.

Let us then look at some of the issues raised in these last two chapters in slightly more detail and not in the order in which they appear.

Normal/abnormal levels of suicide

Durkheim published *The Rules of Sociological Method* in 1895, just a little earlier than his book on suicide. In his manifesto for the science of sociology, the distinction he makes between the normal and abnormal brought forth criticism, not least on account of his position that crime should be viewed as a normal social phenomenon. He takes the same line over suicide. It is a universal social phenomenon, although complete anthropological evidence of its existence in all preliterate societies has still to be confirmed (413ff./361ff.). What alarms Durkheim is that in nineteenth-century Europe, suicide, excluding any altruistic forms of suicide, had reached abnormal levels, multiplying by a factor of 3 or 4 or 5 compared with past times (1897a/t.1951a:368). This is nothing more than a reflection of the sorry state of contemporary society, which urgently needs to be redressed.

What gives rise to abnormally high levels of suicide is not the current economic progress or a high level of intellectual or social achievement. To be sure, western societies of his day were witnessing outstanding developments in the arts and sciences, as well as consolidating empires overseas, but the crucial issue is that all this has been accompanied by a morbid effervescence [*effervescence maladive*] . . . 'the grievous repercussions of which each one of us feels' (1897a/t.1951a:368). This pathological state is a very possible, probable source of the rising tide of suicide (1897a/t.1951a:368). Indeed, so grave and rapid have been the changes in society, accompanied by corresponding social currents, that the outcome can be none other than one of morbidity. A society cannot, Durkheim asserts, change its structure so suddenly (1897a/t.1951a:369). Evidence that the pervading pessimism has reached an abnormal intensity is reflected in the writings of such philosophers as Schopenhauer and Hartmann, and also in the existence of anarchists, aesthetes, mystics, socialist revolutionaries, who all 'share a common hatred and disgust for existing order' – 'a single craving to destroy or escape from reality' (1897a/t.1951a:370).

One of the causes of this – shall we call it *le malaise social*? and I steer clear of the contested word anomie – is, Durkheim alleges, a failure to acknowledge boundaries and limitations. 'Competition is of course becoming keener every day' and with it aggression, because 'greater ease in communication sets a constantly increasing number of competitors at loggerheads with one another' (1897a/t.1951a:386).

Such a state of morbidity can uproot institutions of the past and put nothing in their place. The work of centuries cannot be remade in a few years (1897a/t.1951a:369). New social institutions cannot be manufactured overnight. (What better words can be found to describe what has so suddenly happened in Russia over the past ten years, or less radically in Britain covering a slightly longer period?)

The issue of morality

One matter of crucial importance to Durkheim is the moral status of suicide. He argues that suicide, apart from altruistic suicide, is to be seen as an immoral act: 'the individual is forbidden to destroy himself on his own authority' (1897a/t.1951a:332). He points, however, to evolutionary changes in moral attitudes towards suicide. In the western world there have been two phases. The first occurred in a period when societies permitted suicide, provided it was sanctioned by the state or some civic authority. Here Durkheim refers to legislation enacted in Greek civilization, in Athens, Ceos and among colonists in Marseilles, where those wanting to commit suicide and who put forward their reasons for so doing, were allowed and even helped in the act (1897a/t.1951a:330). In Rome the situation was somewhat more complex but finally a similar attitude to that found in Greece emerged

(1897a/t.1951a:331). The point Durkheim wishes to hammer home is that in this stage religion had no say whatever in the moral status of suicide. The second phase of attitudes towards suicide occurs when suicide is condemned as immoral, absolutely and universally (378ff./333ff.). The right to commit suicide is denied to the collectivity as well as to the individual. Suicide is immoral in and for itself. It is in this second phase that Durkheim in his limited historical treatment of the subject offers more detail in turning to religion as the key factor. Christianity is seen as the agent which turned suicide into an absolute sin. Sometimes that sin was seen to be diabolically inspired – certainly near the top of the table of serious sins (1897a/t.1951a:327). And not only was it a sin full stop, but inevitably ostracism, negative rituals and economic penalties were the consequences of committing it. These were not only enacted by the Catholic Church but were taken over without question by Protestants at the time of the Reformation. In England suicide was declared a felony and the property of the suicide reverted to the Crown. That particular law was abolished only as late as 1870 (1897a/t.1951a:328). In France, bodies of those who had committed suicide were drawn through the streets face down and were dumped on rubbish tips. Noblemen posthumously lost their nobility and their castles were demolished. As late as 1749 some of these rituals and penalties were confirmed legally. And it was the Revolution some forty years later which abolished them.

In Russia penalties were even more severe, and Durkheim referred to practices in Spain, the United States and in Islamic countries.

To sum up, most religious groups, churches and denominations have strongly asserted over the length of their history that suicide is a heinous, sinful and criminal act which carries with it undesirable penalties.

I might add that in the decade immediately following World War II in Britain, clergy of most denominations debated among themselves whether a person who had committed suicide should be granted a Christian burial, and if so, what form of Christian burial. Today a suicide appears to raise no problem. Its criminal nature was taken off the statute book as late as 1961. Today, in matters of ritual, little distinction is made between someone who has died 'naturally' and someone who has committed suicide. And that applies as much to the Roman Catholic Church as to other denominations. Burial rituals in general have tended to become occasions of celebration of the dead person, not of mourning or, in the case of suicide, of moral censure.

Given these social facts, the question arises, why did the churches condemn suicide so violently? For Durkheim there is no problem. He held that according to Christian doctrine, man has an immortal soul – a spark of divinity. He wrote: 'We belong completely to no temporal being because we are kin to God' (1897a/t.1951a:334). This he rephrased in a formula he first enunciated here and which he continued to use until the end of his life – 'man has become a god for man' (ibid.). The implication is that what is sacred must not be profaned: that is, irreverently abolished or annihilated. This is precisely what a man or woman does when either commits suicide.

But are the facts and arguments accurate? For Christians, as well as for Muslims (1897a/t.1951a:329), a common standpoint is that suicide is wrong because the giving and taking of life is in God's hands. Taking one's life is usurping the work of God. Thus, it is not so much that man is sacred, as God is sacred. The decision rests entirely with him, not the individual. External influences may decide the time when the end of life on this earth arrives but it is not for the individual to decide. Where a religion provides a strong sense of providence or personal oversight by God, the wish to commit suicide will be weak since it is seen as evil. So it is assumed. Islamic teaching, which stems from both Christianity and Judaism, is even stronger in this respect than Christianity, as indeed Durkheim noted. The will of Allah is a central, all-dominant theological belief. To commit suicide amounts to blasphemy.

The issue of self-destruction has been recently revived and sharpened in the west by debates over euthanasia, which in many instances can be seen as being akin to suicide. Here the individual, or someone speaking for him or her, decides when life will be terminated. On this point there is division in various churches. The church most opposed to euthanasia, not surprisingly, is the Roman Catholic Church. The issues are very similar to those associated with suicide and, with Roman Catholics, to abortion also.

But let us return to the more academic issue of historical facts related to Durkheim's simple evolutionary pattern, so reminiscent of the categories in *De la division du travail social* (1893b) and 'Deux lois de l'évolution pénale' (1901a(i)). What Durkheim asserts is all-too simple. For example, in Judaism, out of which Christianity grew, there is no moral condemnation of suicide. Indeed, an equivalent word for suicide is not found in the Hebrew scriptures, nor does the word appear in the New Testament. In the Hebrew scriptures there are only four cases of suicide or what might be thought of as being suicide, the best known of which is the death of Saul, but none is condemned. And in the New Testament, there is only one recorded suicide, in the account in Matthew's gospel of the death of Judas, the betrayer of Jesus, where it appears to be readily accepted. There is a different account in the Acts of the Apostles. In cases where there is silence about a suicide, the implication is justification.

From all the existing evidence the Jews have always had a low level of suicide, although the interdict against it is not found in scripture. Rabbinic teaching has been that suicide is permissible in order to avoid the three cardinal sins of murder, adultery and idolatry (forced conversion to another religion).[1]

Albert Bayet was inspired to write a book from reading precisely the same chapters of Durkheim's *Le Suicide* on which this chapter is based, and more particularly by Durkheim's assertions about the history of moral attitudes to suicide. Published in 1922 as a doctoral thesis which took ten years to write, Bayet's *Le Suicide et la morale* turned out to be a refutation of some of Durkheim's ideas, and to do it some 800 pages had to be written! It is a remarkable book, as Maurice Halbwachs has observed (Halbwachs 1930/t.1978:13).[2]

Bayet was a pupil of Lucien Lévy-Bruhl and, like Lévy-Bruhl, he stood apart from the Durkheimians before World War I. Bayet, a convinced rationalist, thought Durkheim too conservative. After the war he associated himself with those disciples of Durkheim who survived it and, historian though he was by early training, he became professor of sociology in the Sorbonne. He wrote a great deal on ethics during the 1930s and was involved in underground activities during World War II. He died in 1960 at the age of 80.

There was much in Durkheim's writing he admired. For example, he accepted Durkheim's definition of suicide, and also the principles of the *Rules*. But by way of criticism he sought to show that the social facts about the morality of suicide were not those Durkheim put forward. Durkheim's error was that he relied too much on the historical study of suicide made by Garrisson, which contained many inaccuracies (Durkheim 1897a/t.1951a:326, 327; Bayet 1922:9. Incidentally both misspelt Garrisson).

Not only was Durkheim historically inaccurate in his assertions about the evolution of the morals of suicide, his method was inadequate. Bayet's other criticism was that Durkheim relied too much on written law.[3] A similar criticism might be made of *De la division du travail social*. His thesis in *Le Suicide* drew not only on law, but on jurisprudence, custom (*mœurs*) and literature (Bayet 1922:16).

Bayet divided moral attitudes to self-destruction into two groups: *la morale simple* (straightforward) and *la morale nuancée* (qualified). *La morale simple* has as its criterion doctrines, attitudes, judgements which condemn suicide out of hand. Suicide is always morally wrong irrespective of circumstances or motivation. *La morale nuancée* consists of moral attitudes which hold that suicide is permissible under certain or all circumstances. There can be no absolute judgement on acts of suicide. What has to be taken into consideration is the examination of the circumstances in which the individual finds himself or herself.

In contrast to Durkheim's generalized approach, Bayet holds that the historical situation is always complex – complex because throughout history these two groups of attitudes have struggled for supremacy. It is true that during the Christian period *la morale simple*, firmly undergirded by theologians and ecclesiastical leaders, was dominant, but exceptions were always to be found. Similarly in the 'pagan' period there can be found examples where suicide was held to be absolutely immoral. Today *la morale simple* is waning and *la morale nuancée* is in complete ascendancy. The agents for change (that is, those who have initiated and supported *la morale nuancée*) have mostly been an élite, consisting of aristocrats, academics and literary figures. The future so far as one can see will be a continuation of the present where *la morale nuancée* stands triumphant.

But let us return to Durkheim's arguments.

Suicide and the cult of the individual

Why does Durkheim pursue the false argument that suicide was condemned by the churches on account of the alleged basic doctrine that the individual was held to be sacred? There are two possible answers. One, that in all honesty he got the theology wrong or that he assumed too much theologically and allowed his imagination full play. Or two, that he over-emphasized a strand of Christian theology that suited his own purposes. Those purposes related to extending what he imagined was the theology behind the condemnation of suicide to a similar moral position in the cult of the individual: the religion of contemporary society, as Durkheim held it to be. By so doing he could demonstrate that certain moral aspects of the new religion of man evolved out of traditional Christianity. What is remarkable is this. In his condemnation of suicide as a totally immoral act he strongly supports the moral teaching of the churches on suicide as it had become established down the ages and it was so apparent in the nineteenth century. There are some parallels between his thought and that of an earlier writer on suicide, Louis Eugène Bertrand, a Catholic doctor who, in 1857, condemned suicide as being a sin against God, one's family and one's country (Bertrand 1857). The book was 'scientific', ethical and theological but was not mentioned by Durkheim in his study of suicide.

So suicide for Durkheim is immoral because it is always an act of profanation. The individual, argues Durkheim, shares 'in some degree that quality *sui generis* ascribed by every religion to its gods' (1897a/t.1951a:333). For a person to take his or her own life is an act of sacrilege, because whoever rejects life or cannot accept the suffering that he or she has to endure, denies the very sacredness of life (cf. Halbwachs 1930/t.1978:297). Thus, suicide undermines the cult of the individual on which, Durkheim argues, all modern morality rests. It is better to endure the suffering in the present, which may be seen as a sacrifice, rather than to take the path of self-destruction (1897a/t.1951a:333). But there is also a social reason why Durkheim, as a rational humanist, sees suicide as an immoral act for and in itself (1897a/t.1951a:337). Quite simply it injures society. The bonds between members become weakened if suicide is carried out with impunity. It must therefore be seen as taboo: it cannot be tolerated under any circumstances, since society itself is sacred.

As is well known, Durkheim always contrasted the cult of man with egoistic individualism. This is evident in *Le Suicide* and it is elaborated in his article on individualism and the intellectuals (1897a/t.1951a:336; 1899c).

Personal drives and predispositions must not be given full rein but have to be checked by external forces. Thus suicide which is clearly a case of egoistic individualism is immoral because the individual does not 'subordinate himself to the general interests of human kind' (1897a/t.1951a:337). Durkheim uses the notion of universality – 'what I can morally do should be applicable to everyone'. If suicide were moral and people could commit suicide indiscriminately this would imply the end of society. Here are surely overtones of Kant?

There are, however, difficulties in maintaining that suicide is absolutely immoral on humanistic grounds. One such problem that arises is the fact that the individual has to be subservient to or accept the authority of some higher power. Durkheim wrote:

> Man cannot become attached to higher aims and submit to a rule if he sees nothing above him to which he belongs. To free him from all social pressure is to abandon him to himself and demoralize him.
> (1897a/t.1951a:389)

But what is this power above man? This higher authority? The demands of society – as it was for Durkheim? And, we also know, Durkheim was never able to solve the ambiguous relation between the individual and society. It is surely legitimate to argue on humanistic grounds that the well-being of the individual is supreme and that current morality should undergird this, provided that the well-being of the individual does not vitiate the well-being of others. Euthanasia is acceptable on such humanistic grounds – people in extreme circumstances have the right to terminate their lives.

How far would humanists today support Durkheim? Surely for them suicide is morally acceptable under certain personal and social conditions, leaving to one side the issue of insanity. Who today would condemn those Jews who committed suicide when faced with life under Nazi persecutors outside and inside concentration camps?

The fact remains that although Durkheim implied a condemnation of the ritual, economic and social barbarities that were associated with cases of suicide until recent times, he did not want to change the associated moral doctrine that makes suicide a 'sin'. To the contrary he offered a powerful defence of the doctrine. And here he must have alienated fellow freethinkers, liberals and humanists, who were similarly divided over his concept of the cult of the individual, particularly with its religious implications.

Religion as social control

We have briefly focused on the morality of suicide. Durkheim firmly associates morality with religion. He holds that historically it has always been the case: morality springs from religion. Other scholars of his day such as

Guyau and Belot took an opposite position. But to religion we now turn, for it was religion in connection with suicide that was raised at the very outset of this essay.

Hardly surprisingly Durkheim made no attempt to deal with religion as a whole in *Le Suicide*: he undertook the task only towards the end of his book of 1912, *The Elementary Forms of the Religious Life*. But nothing becomes more obvious in the closing chapters of *Le Suicide* than the fact that religion performs the function of social control, exercised through moral edict. Durkheim was never a grand or uni-functionalist. But the one thing that religion has done in the past has been to curb and check people's 'natural' or 'egoistical' psychological drives. Here is a key characteristic of religion. If a religion does not demand some form of self-denial or sacrifice, it is no religion. But how is this demand communicated? First and foremost at the level of teaching, of ideology, and more specifically here through the moral condemnation of suicide as an immoral act.

Religious beliefs are disseminated by educational processes, for education is the servant of ideology. With religion in mind, Durkheim could write: 'we are only preserved from egoistic suicide in so far as we are socialized' (1897a/t.1951a:376). But the controlling function of traditional religions – and here Durkheim refers specifically to Christianity – is not to be seen just in negative terms. Its controlling mechanisms transpose people's thoughts and actions. 'If religion teaches that our duty is to accept with docility our lot as circumstances order it, this is to attach us exclusively to other purposes, worthier of our efforts; and in general religion recommends moderation in desires for the same reason' (1897a/t.1951a:383). Religion not only teaches man to accept suffering but, having accepted it, he is to turn to other, more positive possibilities. Hence religion is seen as comfort and consolation for the poor and oppressed – a function condemned by Marx.

A consequence of the controlling function of religion in connection with suicide is that where religion is weak, where it does not impinge on people's lives, the level of suicide will be relatively high, as for example in contemporary secular society. Again, the controlling factor becomes more explicit as one examines and compares different religious groups. Various groups use different techniques to enforce moral prohibitions. Thus, Roman Catholic clergy have at their disposal the power of the confessional, and some might argue Protestants, certainly in the past, have driven home immorality by direct teaching – not least from the pulpit – and by social sanctions. And while Durkheim suggests that Protestant churches place emphasis on individual responsibility and exert fewer ritualized controls, he should have been reminded of Calvin's Geneva, in which controls over individuals exercised by church bodies reached levels so rigorous that they were impossible to maintain over any length of time. What were the levels of suicide in that remarkable period, one wonders?

The question arises as to whether these denominational differences really affect potential immoral actions. A law or a doctrine is one thing: its application and efficacity another.

What of the case of suicide and auricular confession? It does seem likely that through confessing sins to a priest the actions and thoughts of a would-be suicide can be modified. If such a suicidal person confessed his or her intentions, the person might be restrained by the reactions of the priest or by his withholding absolution. But owing to the seal of the confessional it is extremely difficult (if not impossible) to gather evidence. All that can be deduced is that the confessional can direct people's minds to the existence of sin and immorality, but little more can be proved.

Durkheim's argument about the controlling function of religion is based on the assumption of prevention. And like all such arguments, notably in penology, effectiveness is everlastingly open to debate. Durkheim is honest enough to admit that certainly in his day, and in generations before, barbaric rituals and other oppressive measures associated with suicide (and one might add murder) did not restrain others from committing suicide (or murder) (1897a/t.1951a:370).

In the last analysis, Durkheim's unit of analysis is society not the individual. Societal influences cannot be reduced to individual psychological factors. The social has priority. Each society has its own proclivity to suicide. This inclination is made up of various kinds of social currents running through society, among which of course morality is one (1897a/t.1951a:299). Nevertheless, if a society is dominated by a Catholic ideology, a Protestant or a secular one, what has to be demonstrated empirically is the effectiveness of moral teaching *vis-à-vis* suicide within those social currents.

Durkheim's unproven premise therefore is that, all things being equal, moral teaching and socialization in which suicide is held to be wrong, lowers rates of suicide. His rationalism is such that he assumes there is a direct relationship between moral teaching and levels of suicide. That seems sensible enough: were it not so, it could be argued that moral teaching is irrelevant to practice. The problem is to go beyond such an obvious assertion.

This form of rationalist argument is surely of limited merit when considering suicide. For example, in the nineteenth century and in previous centuries the teaching against suicide in the Catholic Church was just as strong as that in Protestant churches, as Durkheim indeed noted (156ff./157ff.). Yet levels of suicide among Protestants were higher than among Catholics. Durkheim is thus forced to explain differences in levels of suicide by going beyond doctrinal beliefs, which contain moral interdicts. Bayet makes the same point (1922:808). Durkheim examines social factors which differentiate the religious groups. He points to what might be called levels of integration (156ff./157ff.). Where integration is high, suicide rates will be low. But as is commonly realized, this is difficult to sustain. Exceptions have to be accounted in comparing social factors among Catholics and Protestants and this undermines Durkheim's thesis. Bayet offered an exception, not mentioned by Durkheim, that in the armed forces – where there is assumed to be a high level of camaraderie and where there exists a strong interdict against suicide – the numbers of those committing suicide is relatively high (1922:808; see chapter 4 here). And among Jews, where the teaching against suicide is not so strong but where the notion of community is strong, the level of suicide is lower than that among Catholics (149ff./152ff.). The notion of being integrated in a community remains unconvincing as a key in helping to explain rates of suicide in the past among Catholics, Protestants, Anglicans, Jews and – we might add – freethinkers. In examining the relation between closely-knit communities and suicide, it would be helpful to turn to anthropological studies.

The failure of traditional religions

'While it is no remedy to give appetites free rein, neither is it enough to suppress them in order to control them' (1897a/t.1951a:383). Here Durkheim asserts that the regulation of people's appetites once provided by traditional religions has become of little value in recent times. He goes so far as to add that religion's 'lack of present usefulness . . . causes evil' (1897a/t.1951a:383). Why? Within its circle of influence traditional religion modifies the inclination to suicide 'only to the extent it prevents men from thinking freely' (1897a/t.1951a:375). Traditional religions cannot be accepted at the present time because they contradict the general law that 'the history of the human mind is the very history of the progress of free thought' (1897a/t.1951a:375).

While traditional religions fade away and will continue to do so, because they do not allow for freedom of thought, new ones, Durkheim suggests, will emerge allowing the right of criticism and individual initiative (1897a/t.1951a:375). They will be more radical than Protestant sects or the religious modernism then becoming apparent in Protestantism and Catholicism. But it is doubtful if the new forms emerging out of the old religions will have the power to curb suicide as did previous religions. The reason? 'When religion is merely a symbolic idealism, a traditional philosophy subject to discussion and more or less a stranger to our daily occupations, it can hardly have much influence upon us' (1897a/t.1951a:376). But would not the same criticism apply to the cult of the individual, which he so much supported? Clearly this new secular (*laïque*) religion, which he sees as the theoretical foundation for contemporary morality and which has been mentioned before, will not perform the same functions as traditional religions. It means not least that the function of social control exerted by religion may well disappear. How can the cult of the individual control egoistic tendencies? And in the matter of suicide, how is one to proclaim suicide as a thoroughly immoral act, for not all humanists would see suicide as immoral, almost profane? Little wonder then that Durkheim, the humanist, stands somewhat alone.

La vie sérieuse

One characteristic or role of religions, which Durkheim strongly approves, is that they bring before mankind the serious side of life. He wrote, doubtless casting an eye on what was happening in France at the time: 'Life is often harsh, treacherous or empty' (1897a/t.1951a:366) and this is reflected in the fact that 'the great religions of the most civilized peoples are more deeply fraught with sadness than the simpler beliefs of earlier societies' (1897a/t.1951a:366). Anthropological data would probably force us to challenge the comparison Durkheim makes, but the fact is that most religions – if not all – take suffering seriously, and one might add none more so than Christianity with a cross at the centre of its belief-system, and Judaism, which has been sustained by a group who by dispersion have suffered so much, and most certainly in recent times.[4] Durkheim would contrast this characteristic of religion with facile moral systems, especially contemporary ones. 'Too cheerful a morality is a loose morality: it is appropriate only to decadent peoples and is found only among them' (1897a/t.1951a:366). Here is the undaunted puritanical sociologist!

The origin of religion

Durkheim's awareness of the suffering of individuals and societies might lead one to suppose that in *Le Suicide* he saw it as the key to the origin of religion. We all know that in his last book, *Les Formes élémentaires* (1912a), he rejects the then current arguments about the origin of religion as put forward by Tylor and Müller. Indeed, all such arguments appear to be contrary to his thinking. However, quite apart from the general notion that religion is related to the social, in *Le Suicide* he puts forward a view which really is an argument for the origin of religion, or at least the basis of religion. His starting-point is the concept of transcendence: of the existence of something greater than ourselves which cannot be explained scientifically or rationally. This receives evidence from the fact that people voluntarily undergo privations and make sacrifices – they renounce part of themselves as an act of abnegation – for this 'something greater than themselves' (1897a/t.1951a:335). Hence we feel, he says, 'that our conduct is guided by a sentiment of reverence' which stands far beyond ourselves (1897a/t.1951a:335). In this way mankind has been forced to imagine a world beyond the present and to 'people it with realities of a different order' (ibid.). From a number of sources we know that he is convinced that this transcendent force is society. But that does not, so far as I know, appear in *Le Suicide*. Durkheim admits that the definite form in which we clothe these ideas is without scientific value, but surely he held that the general idea itself was 'scientific'. A substratum, an infrastructure, indeed exists which is viewed in transcendental terms – he would call it part of social reality.

Two of many issues are at stake:

1 Is society as a transcendental force an adequate theory for the origin of religion?
2 How does such a force relate to the cult of the individual?

Today's students of religion would, I think, reject the theory as being too vague and impossible to prove. It assumes that there exists some inner sentiment or need, innate and universal in men and women. But apart from that the past has witnessed too many theories which have tried to account for the origin of religion and they have all been shown to be flawed. Such searches have now been abandoned. Further, any highly abstract theory does not necessarily lead to religion or a specific religion. Too many other factors have to intervene which then make the original notion of doubtful value.

One interesting facet of Durkheim's argument is the introduction of the notion of transcendence – interesting because so far as I know it appears nowhere else in his works, and because it is not generally associated with liberals, freethinkers and supporters of the cult of the individual in its various forms. It can be argued that, on Durkheim's terms, transcendence is at the base of the cult of the individual in so far as society is also at its base. But by and large this is not a position favoured by most humanists. It was the anti-liberal, anti-modernist thinker, Rudolf Otto (1869–1937), who called his readers back to the notion of *Das Heilege* in an attempt to negate trends to humanize the religion of his day in which a completely humanistic and 'scientific' approach to religion had become à la mode (see Pickering 1995). Strangely enough Otto greatly influenced Karl Barth, who on theological grounds openly opposed Hitler, whereas many liberals were sucked into the effervescence that accompanied Hitler's rise to power. Humanistic liberalism in Germany was then eclipsed.

Conclusion

I opened the essay by noting that the last sections of *Le Suicide* were seldom commented on. In a more pluralistic society than that in which Durkheim lived it is not difficult to see why commentators prefer to push under the table Durkheim's concluding remarks. Probably that which the modern liberal mind rejects most is Durkheim's dogmatic moral attitude in condemning suicide. But we should recall, as we have just said, that his moral vision was within *la vie serieuse*. He wanted a stable, moral, just society in which inevitably suffering and self-denial would exist. He was convinced, rightly or wrongly, that high levels of suicide would undermine such a society and introduce hedonism on which a moral acceptance of suicide would be built – the one giving rise to the other and vice versa.

But as always he falls back on religion in trying both to explain many social phenomena and at the same time offering salvation. Society at large today is not concerned about the former: whether it can realize the latter from within itself and without an external or transcendental authority remains an open question.

Notes

1 See *Oxford Dictionary of the Jewish Religion* (1997) New York and Oxford: Oxford University Press. Today it is frequently argued that those who commit suicide are of an unsound mind. But would that apply to those who committed suicide in concentration camps or just before arrest by the Nazis? Suicide was always acceptable in the face of persecution. It should be noted that Josephus saw suicide as an impious act against God but he approved of the mass suicides in the seige of Masada by the Romans in 72–3 BC. It would appear that early Christians accepted the Jewish position.

2 It is interesting that in one of the most recent books on Durkheim's *Le Suicide*, there is but the scarcest of reference to Bayet (see Lester 1994).

3 J. D. Douglas in his book, *The Social Meanings of Suicide* (written in 1966) supported Bayet in his criticism of Durkheim (see Douglas 1967:60–2n.88, 89, 90).

4 Buddhism of course gives much weight to suffering in its doctrines, but Durkheim did not classify Buddhism as a religion, but rather as a system of morals (1912a:43–4/t.1915d:31–21).

Bibliography

Bayet, A. (1922) *Le Suicide et la morale*, Paris: Alcan.

Bertrand, L. E. (1857) *Traité du suicide considéré dans ses rapports avec la philosophie, la théologie, la médicine, et la jurisprudence*, Paris: Baillière.

Douglas, J. D. (1967) *The Social Meanings of Suicide*, Princeton, NJ: Princeton University Press.

Durkheim, E. (1893b) *De la division du travail social: étude sur l'organisation des sociétiés superiéures*, Paris: Alcan.

(1902b) *De la division du travail social: étude sur l'organisation des sociétiés superiéures*, 2nd edition, Paris: Alcan.

(1895a) *Les Règles de la mèthode sociologique*, Paris: Alcan.

(1901c) *Les Règles de la mèthode sociologique*, 2nd edition, Paris: Alcan.

(1897a) *Le Suicide: étude de sociologie*, Paris: Alcan.

(1899c) 'Contribution to 'Enquéte sur l'introduction de la sociologie dans l'ensignement secondaire', *RIS* 7:679.

—(t.1951a) by J. A. Spaulding and G. Simpson, *Suicide: A Study in Sociology*, edited with an introduction by G. Simpson, Glencoe, IL: Free Press (London: Routledge and Kegan Paul, 1952).

(1901a(i)) 'Deux lois de l'évolution pénale', *Année Sociologique* IV:65–95.

(1912a) *Les Formes élémentaires de la vie religieuse. Le sytème totémique en Australie*, Paris: Alcan.

Garrisson, G. (1883) *Le Suicide en droit romain et en droit française*, Toulouse.
(1885) *Le Suicide dans l'antiquité et dans les temps modernes*, Paris: Rousseau.
Halbwachs, M. (1930) *Les Causes du suicide*, Paris: Alcan.
— (t.1978) by H. Goldblatt, *The Causes of Suicide*, London and Henley: Routledge and Kegan Paul.
Lester, D. (ed.) (1994) *Emile Durkheim:* Le Suicide *100 Years Later*, Philadelphia: Charles Press.
Pickering, W. S. F. (1995) *Locating the Sacred: Durkheim, Otto and Some Contemporary Issues*, Leeds: British Association for the Study of Religions, Occasional Paper 12.

7

THE MORAL DISCOURSE OF DURKHEIM'S *SUICIDE*

William Ramp

Introduction[1]

Durkheim's *Suicide* is firmly ensconced in sociological literature as an exemplar of the scientific method applied to social phenomena, and of a sociological approach to suicide. While not all agree on its methodological soundness or theoretical fertility, it is still seen as a watershed in the history of sociology, and as a touchstone and benchmark for subsequent work in the philosophy and methodology of the social sciences, and in the sociology of suicide. This status has had certain interpretive consequences. Commentators have discussed several possible influences on Durkheim's theoretical perspective, method and substantive descriptions: his sources, his familiarity with other work on the topic, and literary, philosophical and methodological precedents for his choice of topic and approach (e.g. Lukes 1973; Morrison 1998). Despite this work, however, certain elements of the intellectual, cultural and even political context in which Durkheim wrote remain to be fully examined. Such study is needed to provide a more nuanced view of *Suicide* as a specific and finely tuned intervention, not only into discussions of social science methodology or the aetiology of suicide, but also into broader questions of the nature of modernity and of forms of moral responsibility appropriate to it. The following discussion does no more than to suggest some avenues for such exploration, and to indicate some of their possible implications for an appreciation of Durkheim's work. Specifically, it proposes that *Suicide* has a significant moral and pedagogical dimension; indeed, that its very emphasis on scientific method may have had a rhetorical effect, repositioning the topic (of suicide, and more generally, of the consequences of 'civilization') on new ground. From Durkheim's point of view, one might suggest that such ground not only made suicide available to social science, but also located it in terms of a moral discourse which sought to transcend essentialism and personalism while still making authoritative claims on its hearers.

Why suicide? *Le Suicide* in its discursive context

The status of *Suicide* as a methodological classic is reinforced by Durkheim's own description of it in his preface, where he refers to it as a 'concrete and specific' illustration of 'methodological problems' addressed in the *Rules of Sociological Method* (Durkheim 1897a/t.1951a:37). This statement has often been taken at its abstract face value, but the preface also speaks concretely to Durkheim's efforts to legitimate sociology as a discipline and an element in a new, republican political culture. It also begs a question about the subject-matter: why suicide? To answer this question, let us consider briefly the context in which *Le Suicide* constituted an intervention.

Le Suicide in its time was part of, and addressed, a prolific nineteenth-century literature on 'problems of modern life': excessive individualism, isolation, neurasthenia, a decline in traditional moral regulation (see Giddens 1971; Lukes 1973:192–9, 219–24; Nye 1982, 1984, 1985; Forth 1996; Hawkins 1999). And as Lukes (1973:192), Hacking (1991), Douglas (1967, 1971), Karady (1983:93–4) and others have pointed out, both its concerns and its method were anticipated by moral statisticians as early as the Belgian, Quételet. This literature accompanied the growth of professions, disciplines, policies and discourses increasingly concerned with issues of crime, mental and physical illness, sexual aberration, lack of sanitation, and industrial unrest. Foucault (1991; see also Gordon 1991) has attempted to argue that these disparate subjects, and the academic and professional disciplines that developed around them, shared a developing administrative orientation he terms 'governmentality'. It was a concern, less for legitimating forms of sovereignty and preserving public order, than for enhancing the health, productivity and self-responsible social integration of individuals and populations, in terms of quasi-scientific theories of human behaviour and social development. Such theories reflected and promoted a two-sided development in modern liberalism. On one hand, they encouraged a minimalist economy of prudent state intervention. On the other, they eclipsed older doctrines about the 'rights' of both states and individuals in favour of an administrative orientation toward social amelioration which privileged the executive role of secondary institutions and professional agencies, as well as of the state. As Gordon (1991:33) notes sardonically, 'In the France of 1900, this conjunction expresses the political rationale of a regime which accepts the role of organized labour, while organizing armed force to suppress workers' meetings: a political incorporation of the class struggle.'

The populations who were the subjects of these theories and strategies became objects of various policing strategies which carved them up on the basis of typologies of sexuality, race, health, occupation, criminality and the like; treating them (and encouraging them to treat themselves) as objects both of study and of pedagogical or corrective/punitive intervention. At the same time, such populations were increasingly atomized, as individuals were called upon to exercise, in private, forms of moral self-surveillance and self-regulation, and as family units were urged to accept and propagate the ministrations of experts in medicine, psychology, sexual behaviour and domestic science.

In France, the end of the eighteenth century had seen the beginning of a shift from a moral discourse on suicide to a growing concern with suicide rates, expressed, for example, in De Guerry's *Statistique Morale de la France* of 1835 (Douglas 1967:171; see also Giddens 1971b:36–7). By 1842, Quételet was investigating the extent to which moral phenomena could be said to resemble physical phenomena: his answer being that large numbers served to cancel out individual peculiarities and to reveal the institutional and general features of society in the figure of the 'social man', a fictitious being conforming to the median results of statistical analysis. In France, Bertillon's statistical experimentation inspired Durkheim's later adoption of replicative analysis (Douglas 1967:11–25). These efforts spawned a fascination for 'numbers' which, as Hacking (1982; see also Lukes 1973:192) has illustrated, grew and fed on itself. But this fascination developed in concert with other concerns: a sense of a growing 'moral crisis' in European society, and a concern for 'health', both in individuals and populations, as an antidote to social breakdown.

By the 1850s, French social commentators were linking industrialization and the expansion of urban, commercial life to the development of 'égoïsme' and 'l'odieux individualisme' (Lukes 1973:196), both defined in terms Durkheim later applied to anomie, as consequences of moral paralysis. On the left, pathological individualism was taken to be at the root of social disorder, apathy and exploitation; on both sides of the political spectrum, there was talk of a 'general malaise', of the possibility of social dissolution, and (especially on the right) of a 'national decadence', one sign of which was taken to be a falling birth rate (Lukes 1973:193–9) – it is interesting to note, as Lukes does, that Durkheim authored a paper on birth rates and suicide in 1888. There was a felt sense that the decline of those traditional moral controls associated with pre-revolutionary social formations had left a vacuum. If one were anticlerical, this vacuum was to be filled by a new, secular morality, answerable in the abstract to reason and in practice to a science of normalcy or health. If one were a Catholic traditionalist, it would be addressed by a revival of Christian moral education and the social authority of the Church.

It is particularly interesting to note the role played in this discussion by motifs of health and degeneracy (Nye 1982, 1984, 1985, Hawkins 1999). On the right, social anarchy, and political anarchism (tagged as a form of 'intellectual proletarianization': see Forth 1996), were likened to forms of 'hysteria' arising from excessive individualism on one hand and the formation of 'crowds' on the other. The mass popularity of romantic literature was blamed for a degenerate aestheticism leading to a suicide 'mania' (Douglas

1971:123, 145n.). Durkheim himself took the supposedly increased incidence of pessimistic philosophical systems in the nineteenth century as an index of the extent to which 'le courant pessimiste est parvenu à un degré d'intensité anormal', going on to note that, '[l]'anarchiste, l'esthète, le mystique, le socialiste révolutionnaire, s'ils le désespèrent pas de l'avenir, s'entendent du moins avec le pessimiste dans une même sentiment de haine ou de dégoût pour ce qui est, dans une même besoin de détruire le réel ou d'y échapper' (Durkheim 1897a/t.1951a:370). Elsewhere, he noted that 'la neurasthénie sous toutes les formes' had become almost a mark of distinction 'dans nos sociétés raffinées' (Durkheim 1897a/t.1951a:181). 'Hyper-civilization' was said to produce a nervous system delicate and sensitive to 'irritation' and depression (Lukes 1973:219). The popular organicist discourses of 'solidarity', in both its traditionalist and left-wing variants, linked solidarity to national health, and social fragmentation to degeneracy and corruption (see Swart 1964; Nye 1982, 1984; Pick 1989; Donzelot 1991; Ewald 1991:209; Kushner 1993).[2]

In this context, suicide constituted a particularly resonant issue. Anticipating Durkheim's characterization of anomie, Brierre de Boisment discussed links between suicide and reversals of fortune (Douglas 1967:14); and more generally, suicide was commonly characterized as a social, not just an individual phenomenon, subject to statistical analysis, as early as the 1840s. It was variously linked to such factors as urbanization and social change, religious affiliation, race and heredity, and climate (Lukes 1973:191–3). There was (an occasionally contested) general agreement that rates of suicide were climbing because moral controls were decreasing in strength. Durkheim's Czech contemporary, Masaryk (1970[1888]), produced a monograph on suicide which linked it to 'civilization' and its products, anarchy and 'decay', used statistical analysis, and stressed the importance of moral integration as a solution. Durkheim himself was aware that his work was an intervention in a well-established discussion, as his frequent references to Morselli, and his extensive bibliographies of the existing suicide literature show (e.g. 1897a/t.1951a:52–3). As an issue, suicide spoke to a domesticated, post-1848 version of republican individualism. At the intersection of republican culture, of the modern economy, and of the newly developing moral professions stood the figure of the self-responsible individual. An ultimate act of self-sovereignty in a culture of individualism, suicide starkly and in the most extreme fashion illustrated the prerogatives once exercised by kings over the bodies of their subjects and now internalized – in a democratic age – as the right of the individual to rule and dispose of its body. But at this extreme, self-sovereignty was also a symbolic challenge to the moral integrity, productivity and welfare of the population: the reproductive base of national societies. Thus, suicide in nineteenth-century popular discourse became a new kind of moral issue. No longer a matter of mortal sin or individual tragedy, suicide became a *moral disease*, a potential contagion to which some members of the population might be particularly disposed through some moral, mental or physical 'weakness', or to which society as a whole might be prone due to the destabilizing effects of modern life: the artificiality of urban society, the irritation imposed on the physical and moral constitution by industrialization and the development of mass society, the loss of tradition or traditional forms of community.

Thus suicide fitted well into the popular concern among republican French intellectuals for the development of a *morale laïque* (Stock-Morton 1988); a modern science of morals married to a secular programme of moral education and social improvement. This concern, evidenced in the *solidarisme* of Bourgeois and others, was often articulated in terms of a mix of Kantian idealism (stressing the importance of individual autonomy against blind adherence to a creed or to traditional institutions) and positivism (stressing the development of a 'moral science'). Such a 'republican scientism' fitted a need for a practical philosophical and moral programme to counter the claims of Catholic traditionalism and radical socialism, and a perceived public demand for a new response to social change, involving a resolution of industrial conflict and also of conflicts between warring social élites (Karady 1983:93–4).

Suicide as a moral project

Durkheim himself claimed to have chosen the topic because few subjects were 'more accurately to be defined' (or had generated so much statistical data), *and* because suicide was instructive concerning 'causes of the general contemporary maladjustment being undergone by European societies and concerning remedies which may relieve it' (1897a/t.1951a:36, 37). A third reason emerges subsequently in the study itself: suicide is taken not only to be a mirror of the social malaise, but to be itself a singular threat to the moral order. Durkheim's venture into the territory appears in this light to be far less innovative, original or unique than it has been made out to be by those who have raised it to the status of a 'classic' in this century. *Le Suicide* clearly had a ready-made audience, and it was pitched to address some of the dominant concerns of its day. The distinctiveness of Durkheim's approach is reflected in its theoretical rigour (Giddens 1971b:38; Lukes 1973:192), but for our purposes it is also to be seen in the ways Durkheim used his methodology – as much as a *rhetorical* device as anything else – to position the discussion of suicide on ground that clearly necessitates a distinctive *sociological response* to a *moral problem*. And, as we shall discuss shortly, the profoundly interesting thing about *Suicide* is the extent to which Durkheim's elaboration of that response both links *and* distances his version of sociology from the developing governmentalist discourses and practices to which Foucault (1991), Pasquino (1991) and Donzelot (1991) have drawn our attention (and this despite Durkheim's reputation among Foucault and his followers as little more than an example, with Leon Bourgeois, of a 'solidarist' exponent of such governmentality).

Durkheim, as we know, delineated three distinct 'types' of suicide, with a fourth type (fatalistic suicide) being relegated to a footnote that has raised questions among commentators ever since. These types designated social conditions affecting suicide *rates*, not motivations for individual acts. But it is worth noting that Durkheim's more specific images of the types of suicide are often couched in subjectively vivid and evocative terms: unhappily married women, overwhelmed and disorganized widowers, loyal military officers bound to a code of death before dishonour, states of 'exaspération et de lassitude irritée', the constantly renewed torture of 'une soif inextinguible' (see, e.g. Durkheim 1897a/t.1951a:188, 212, 238–9, 247, 357). At times, his use of the pronoun *nous* has a similar effect, drawing us subjectively into the text. The contrast between these evocative passages and the starkness of the statistical analysis accounts for much of the rhetorical power of *Suicide*. In each instance, Durkheim identified the types of suicide with specific social pathologies attending either of the two polar types of solidarity. Thus, altruistic and fatalistic suicide are pathologies of mechanical solidarity; egoistic and anomic suicide, of organic solidarity. The latter two types, then, are the particular diseases of modern life, each symptomatic of an excessive development of some aspect of modern social organization in the form of *suicidogenic currents, elements of a 'collective melancholy'*. Durkheim's descriptions of these currents are often organized in terms of explicit parallels between personal and social malaise (see, e.g. Durkheim 1897a/t.1951a:213–14, 332 table, 364–6).

On the strength of such statements, and Durkheim's appropriation of evocative references to suicide as 'la rançon de la civilisation' (Durkheim 1897a/t.367), it would be easy to interpret *Suicide* as an essay on the pathology of progress expressed in personal life, had not Durkheim himself explicitly denied this interpretation (Durkheim 1897a/t.1951a:366–67). Suicide, he argues, does not correlate with 'progress' *per se*, but with abnormal and pathological perturbations, sudden changes in social life or social organization that lead to the excessive development of suicidogenic currents while at the same time retarding the *social* forces which counterbalance them. Thus, the sudden rise in suicide rates in the nineteenth century, Durkheim hypothesizes, relates to a relatively sudden development of an imbalance in the organization of industrial life (1897a/t.1951a:254–8).[3] At the same time, he suggests that particular 'moral constitutions' are more susceptible to such pathologies, their peculiar characteristics mirroring and exacerbating certain collective tendencies to suicide (1897a/t.1951a:363–4). Moral constitutions are best described as collective tendencies towards particular moral orientations; these may be general across a given society, found in specific sectors, or developed to a higher degree in particularly vulnerable groups (as in the tendency to altruism found in military circles). However, the term 'constitution' was also commonly used in relation to the psychological tendencies of individuals, and indeed, Durkheim includes in *Suicide* a chapter (Book Two, Chapter 6) dealing with 'individual forms' of the different types of suicide, in which he refers to personal characteristics of sufferers and gives phenomenological descriptions of suicidal acts. This begs the question whether Durkheim's usage does not portend a slip into a psychology of suicide. The answer has to be 'no', unless it be a collective psychology. Suicidogenic currents are both social and socially constructed phenomena (Hawkins 1999), and are to be investigated as such. To take the phenomenological description of individual suicides to be a theoretical maxim leads directly down the wrong path in any attempt to interpret *Suicide*.[4] The discussion of 'individual forms' of suicide indicates a way of moving from a discussion of types to an examination of individual cases, but not the reverse.[5] This interdiction, however, is not entirely satisfactory. The examples Durkheim gives of the different types of suicide gain their power at least in part from a kind of phenomenological resonance – from our ability to imagine ourselves in such circumstances.

Durkheim proposes that the deadly conjunction of vulnerable moral constitutions and exacerbative social circumstances needs to be remedied. It is achieved by the development of a stable framework of occupationally based 'corporations', in terms of which industrialization and the market are to be regulated. Individuals are thus tied back into a framework of moral regulation and the vitality of the social bond. Corporatism, however, was not Durkheim's only response to the phenomenon of suicide. In *Suicide*, he also made recommendations that are profoundly *moral* in nature; that attach directly to the individual's conduct. To understand these, we must recollect Durkheim's remarks on the social constitution of individual identity. To a modern consciousness, suicide, regardless of motivation, signifies an ultimate expression of individual autonomy, but for Durkheim, individual identity and autonomy were categories bestowed by society. Thus, one betrays society in asserting the right to dispose of one's life. Durkheim notes historical instances in which suicide was treated as a form of insubordination, or as something for which permission needed to be sought (Durkheim 1897a/t.1951a:329–30). In a contemporary context, in a civilization dominated by what Durkheim calls the 'cult of the dignity of the person' (Pickering 1984:482, see also 54, 492–3), the sacredness of the individual personality overrides the right to self-destruction (Durkheim 1897a/t.1951a:333). Thus, at the level of individual casuistry, suicide – as sacrilege against the self (Pickering 1984:424) – is to be made a subject of moral expiation. Durkheim abjures the idea of making suicide attempts subject to criminal prosecution, but he resurrects an idea long familiar to traditional Christianity: that the suicide be denied the right to burial with honour, because the suicide has taken a life that is, in some ultimate sense, not merely his or her own to dispose of (Durkheim 1897a/t.1951a:371, see also 327, 332–3). This suggestion is pregnant with symbolic meaning. One who has committed suicide is to be symbolically cast out of the collective by being denied full status in the community of the dead. The suicide has unlawfully taken from and violated the collective by destroying something sacred to it: in return the suicide is to be ritually expelled from full membership in the communal memory.

Read in this light, *Suicide* can be seen as an exercise in moral pedagogy or even moral exhortation. The evocative imagery to be noted in the phenomenological description of motives or states of mind is a device to get us to identify with what Durkheim is saying, just as the statistical analysis conversely shocks us out of the mistake of *personalizing* the issue as an individual one, as a consequence of identifying with its phenomenological impact. Anomic despair, egoistic ennui, the rigid code of honour of the military suicide: Durkheim's evocations of these serve not only to illustrate types, but also to make poignant the symptoms of the pathology as we might experience them. There are two sides to Durkheim's approach to suicide, but not two approaches. For Durkheim, suicide is at once and inseparably a social problem *and* a moral problem. As a social problem, suicide is to be mapped, categorized and analysed, and solutions to it are to be conceived of as *social* solutions: thus, for example, Durkheim does not propose that all instances of suicide can be entirely prevented, because the eradication of (all) individual cases is not the central aim. At the same time, *because society is a collective, moral entity*, suicide can be defined as a social problem only in the sense that it also, potentially, constitutes a *moral* one. An excessive suicide rate signals the existence of a social pathology and the potential for social decomposition (a social analogue to individual suicide); at the same time, any *individual* case of suicide, especially in its modern interpretation as an attack on the sacredness of the person, strikes a symbolic blow at the morality governing personhood. Thus, in relation both to the person and to society, suicide must be responded to as a moral symbol.

To say that *Suicide* is an exercise in moral pedagogy might seem to contradict Durkheim's own assertion (1897a/t.1951a:372–84) that education is *not* a solution to the problem of suicide. Durkheim pointed out that any system of education is only the 'image and reflection' of the larger society of which it is part, and thus that it cannot but reflect precisely those moral orientations which, in combination with specific social circumstances, lead to the development of suicidogenic currents. To deal with this objection, we need to be clear about what kind of pedagogical exercise *Suicide* is, and is not. It clearly does not recommend a specific set of educational programmes for the schools and public service agencies of the nation. But at another level, *Suicide* can indeed be described as an attempt at *moral enlightenment* in its treatment of the topic of suicide. It is, first, an exercise in *enlightenment* in the sense that it addresses our collective self-understanding, demonstrating that suicide is a social phenomenon which raises core issues about the meaning of social life. The idea of enlightenment involves a kind of *metanoia*, a turning-away from that which is false or misleading in favour of a position from which the struggle for true knowledge and for moral and practical autonomy may be engaged. Durkheim sets out not only to make certain substantive points about suicide as an empirical subject of research, but more importantly to demonstrate a way of understanding suicide that will enhance collective self-awareness as well as our moral and practical ability to shape our collective destiny. Second, *Suicide* is a *moral* exercise in two senses: it demonstrates that the moral constitution of society – its collective moral orientations – are directly related to the social prevalence of certain types of suicide. And it demonstrates how suicide in itself poses a central moral problem for contemporary individualism by at once expressing and fundamentally challenging collectively-cherished ideals concerning the sacredness of individual personhood.

Thus, Durkheim's response to suicide is not simply that of a scientist solving a problem of research: he tackles a profoundly moral question from a moral standpoint. And one might suggest that it is our problem, not his, to have difficulty seeing these as parts of a single enterprise. Durkheim's moralism on the subject of sanctions to be applied in individual cases of suicide is directly related to his sociological examination of suicide as a social phenomenon. His treatment of the modern increase in both egoistic *and* anomic suicide rates implies that such increases are *anomic in their effects*: the way in which such increases are perceived may threaten the moral framework of modern life. The impulse to suicide is social, dependent upon states of 'social unhappiness' and appearing as a trans-individual 'force' to which some are fatally susceptible. But suicide is an *excessive response* to excesses in such states, and, *unless checked symbolically, sends a signal that legitimates both forms of excess*. Durkheim characterizes both egoistic and anomic suicide similarly as partaking in the modern 'disease of the infinite': one exhibiting emotional over-excitement and the other, intellectual over-nourishment. An increase in suicide signals that excess of either kind – social pathologies institutionalized in the modern economy – has overwhelmed traditional forms of regulation as a vehicle of social meaning. Suicide thus becomes a sort of collective representation of moral pathology both for the scientist studying it and, more tellingly, for those left behind and wounded by the loss (in this sense, Durkheim anticipates contemporary concerns about suicide 'epidemics' in closely knit small communities or among peer groups). Abnormal rates of suicide can be anomic both causally and consequentially, and must be responded to in a way that reinforces the codes of social life: not merely by social reintegration *but also* by an accompanying strengthening of moral life, particularly in the economic sphere.

In this light, then, *Suicide* is more than an occasion for an academic exercise in theory or method. The choice of suicide as a topic is Durkheim's occasion for intervening, as a sociologist, *but also as a moralist*, in a *moral* debate that he did not invent or begin, and that did not end with his contribution. But if *Suicide* reflects its context, it also transcends it. Durkheim did not propose the elimination of suicide as a practical possibility, nor did he suppose that social happiness was a practical or even a proper goal of public policy or professional intervention. For Durkheim, any society is necessarily a structure of limits, without which no meaningful order is possible or conceivable. Specific forms of social organization, and specific moral and definitional boundaries, give rise to specific pathologies: forms of excess. Social limits and categories may be either excessively adhered to, or excessively transgressed. The transgression of limits may take individual forms, but transgression is itself a *social* force – a current. Any society is, by definition, haunted by a dark side – a side kept under control during times of stability, but unleashed in times of rapid change. Any attempts to control suicidogenic currents, *especially attempts undertaken by particular social agencies, from above, in an atmosphere of panic, would themselves run the risk of promoting excess and social destabilization: an excessive imposition of state or professional power, or an excessive concentration on the individual elements of suicide at the expense of the larger pathology*.

Conclusion: reading *Suicide* today

In this light, one must both agree and disagree with Jacques Donzelot's (1991) assessment of Durkheim as just another voice in the 'governmentalist' chorus of late nineteenth-century French political and professional life. Durkheim's references to social pathology, as well as his 'solidarist' remedies to the suicide problem, would seem to place him squarely in that chorus. But it needs to be remembered, first, that Durkheim's elaboration of the normal–pathological distinction was less a diagnostic exercise than an attempt to understand social phenomena in terms of a classificatory emphasis on category and typicality. It was also a causal theory of 'conditions' in terms of which the extraordinary (e.g. variations from type) could be identified and explained. Second, while Durkheim did indeed promote the development of solidarist frameworks for the management of both self and social relations, he did so from a standpoint in which both are conceived of as *moral* tasks, collectively engaged in by all who acknowledge themselves to be part of the *ecumene*. In his work, these tasks are held together by an idea of 'moral citizenship' – for lack of a better term – and by a concept of pedagogy as a moral enterprise. They are not yet mere administrative techniques for the management of populations and individuals by a cadre of professional care-givers, advisors and disciplinarians. Durkheim in fact explicitly warns against the 'ineffective' expansion of the state and the multiplication of state agencies to organize the lives of individuals. His discussion of occupational corporations – part of a broader proposal to reinvigorate a tier of secondary institutions and organizations intermediary between state and individuals – is not phrased as merely a social management exercise. Rather, such corporations are also intended as agents of social justice and a means of making moral awareness practically relevant and meaningful to their members. While these corporations would still be 'subject to the action' of the state, that body itself, as Durkheim indicates elsewhere (Durkheim 1950a/t.1957a:42–109), would have both managerial and moral tasks, one of which would be to defend the rights of individuals against encroachment by secondary institutions and organizations.

Durkheim, then, is advocating neither the institutional control of populations by professionals, nor the professional use of psychological techniques to engineer individual self-management. Another way of putting this might be to say that Durkheim had not yet separated the issue of sovereignty (in this instance, the collective authority of the moral, or a shared sense of moral responsibility) from that of governance (in Foucault's sense, of administrative techniques for enhancing order, happiness and productivity). His allowance that a certain level of necessary 'unhappiness' must attend the benefits of civilization, for example, is not simply a statement about the limits of normalizing social intervention. It can also be taken as a warning about the moral perils of transgressing those limits. In this light, it is worth noting that in the early twentieth century, the Third Republic moved increasingly to the employment of harsher and more individualized forms of social surveillance and segregation, justified on biological reductionist grounds (Nye 1984; Hawkins 1999).

Durkheim thus charted a difficult third way between reactionary moralism and what we might term medico-administrative social policing. If he can be read, as Donzelot reads him, as an exponent of a liberal form of governmentalism, it must also be noted that, from a contemporary 'social services' or 'corrections' standpoint, much of what he had to say about suicide may quickly be dismissed as difficult to put into practice by professionals. This is precisely because it does not lend itself to the sort of professionalized (and often state-sponsored) intervention into individual cases that Durkheim himself decried. If *Suicide* can be said to be motivated by an interest in moral enlightenment, that interest is not merely in a liberal conception of enlightenment tempered by a sense of moral responsibility, but in discerning the very basis of moral discourse and moral action. (In this light it is a pity, if sociologically understandable, that Durkheim was unable to bridge the great cultural and political divide in nineteenth-century French intellectual life between secular republicanism and French Catholicism. Though his discussions of the social and religious origins of science and logic, and of the moral dimensions of knowledge and enlightenment, lie solidly within the republican enterprise of *morale laïque*, they also break the cultural confines of *fin-de-siècle* republican scientism. What sort of dialogue might have resulted if conditions had been right for a full and creative engagement with those few Catholic voices then able to transcend the xenophobic triumphalism of the institutional Church and its nationalist allies.[6])

Durkheim attempted an ambitious moral theory of society organized around one of the most symbolically troubling features of modern life. Alongside its methodological and theoretical achievement, *Le Suicide* must also be seen as a unique *moral* statement, proposing a relentlessly *sociological* morality, as much attuned to the consequences, social meanings and causes of self-destruction as to its causes.[7] The moral discourse of *Suicide* has been overshadowed by issues of methodology, causality and practical application, perhaps because questions of individual motivation have gained prominence in both professional and popular discussions of suicide, while social explanations have often been relegated to the study of 'factors' in individual decisions. One wonders if Durkheim might tie this development to precisely the excessive individualism, combined with an 'inflation and hypertrophy of the state', that he decried in *Suicide* (1897a/t1951a:389). It is a condition in which the individual and the personal become at once signifiers of self-sovereignty *and* objectified avenues to the atomizing control of populations by an expanded professional and governmental apparatus. One can only wonder, not because Durkheim is no longer here to give an opinion, but because, within the horizon of interpretation (Jauss 1982, 1989) in which we now read him, he cuts an ambiguous figure. It is possible to read his work both as an example of the discourse of governmentality – a proposal to manage suicide as a 'social problem' – and as a moral critique of precisely such proposals to the extent that they abandon a concern for the sovereignty of the moral sense. Whether the latter critique is prophetic or nostalgic remains to be determined.

Notes

1 This chapter is developed from a paper delivered at the conference, 'Durkheim's *Suicide*: a Centennial Conference', Maison Française, Oxford, 12–13 December 1997. I wish to thank W. S. F. Pickering, and other participants at the conference, for their most helpful suggestions, and also L. G. Beaman for a careful reading of the manuscript of this chapter.

2 Hawkins (1999) notes that there were several variations on the theme of 'degeneracy'. Many involved some sort of explicit evolutionary framework, but degeneracy was variously seen as a 'throwback' phenomenon or as a companion of evolutionary sophistication; as a feature of individual biology or of the evolution of society; as hereditary or as a product of circumstances. In popular North American eugenicism of the early twentieth century, such different models and theories were often employed indiscriminately as part of a unified discourse.

3 As Hawkins (1999) notes, Durkheim was not a typical 'degeneracy theorist'. He subsequently repudiated a suggestion, made in *The Division of Labour*, that crime could be considered a pathology, and he did not argue that 'degeneracy' was an individual pathology, an inevitable consequence of civilizational evolution, or an evolutionary reversal. Rather, he noted the innovative social role of 'neurasthenics'

(1897a/t.1951a:76–7) and, generally speaking, located the development of suicidal currents in the phenomenon of rapid social change.

4 A comment made by Bill Pickering at the centennial conference on Durkheim's *Suicide*, Oxford, December 1997.

5 A point made by Mike Gane (1997). My entire discussion here of the various distinctions, parallels and relations Durkheim made between individual suicides and suicide as a social phenomenon is heavily indebted to discussions between Gane and Christie Davies, Mark Neal, W. Watts Miller, Mike Hawkins and W. S. F. Pickering at the centennial conference on Durkheim's *Suicide*, Oxford, December 1997.

6 Durkheim's attitudes toward Protestant and Catholic Christianity are discussed in Pickering (1984:421–75) and Jones (1998). Meštrović (e.g. 1985, 1988) makes suggestions about Durkheim's concept of anomie in relation to the Christian concept of sin, and about Durkheim's attitude toward the reformed tradition in Protestant Christianity. Several writers have seen elements of Durkheim's thought as responses to his Jewish heritage, though all such hypotheses must now be judged in light of Strenski's (1997) stringent critique of such supposed links.

7 For a recent discussion which highlights the moral dimension of Durkheim's sociological enterprise, in its confrontation with modernity (especially modern individualism and liberalism), see Watts Miller (1996).

Bibliography

Allport, F. H. (1925) 'The Group Fallacy in Relation to Social Science', *Journal of Abnormal and Social Psychology* 19:60–73.

Alpert, H. (1939) 'Emile Durkheim and Sociologismic Psychology', *American Journal of Sociology* 45:64–70.

Donzelot, J. (1991) 'The Mobilization of Society', in G. Burchell, C. Gordon and P. Miller (eds) *The Foucault Effect: Studies in Governmentality*, Chicago: University of Chicago Press.

Douglas, J. (1967) *The Social Meanings of Suicide*, Princeton, NJ: Princeton University Press.

(1971) 'The Sociological Analysis of the Social Meanings of Suicide', in A. Giddens (ed.) *The Sociology of Suicide: Selected Readings*, London: Frank Cass.

Durkheim, E. (1893b) *De la division du travail social: étude sur l'organisation des sociétiés superiéures*, Paris: Alcan.

— (t.1984a) by W. D. Halls, *The Division of Labour in Society*, with an introduction by L. Coser, London: Macmillan.

(1895a) *Les Règles de la méthode sociologique*, Paris: Alcan.

— (t.1982a) by W. D. Halls, *The Rules of Sociological Method*, edited with an introduction by S. Lukes, London: Macmillan.

(1897a) *Le Suicide: étude de sociologie*, Paris: Alcan.

— (t.1951a) by J. A. Spaulding and G. Simpson, *Suicide: A Study in Sociology*, edited with an introduction by G. Simpson, Glencoe, IL: Free Press (London: Routledge and Kegan Paul, 1952).

(1950a) *Leçons de sociologie: physique des mœurs et dudroit*, foreword by H. N. Kubali, introduction by G. Davy, Paris: Presses Universitaires de France.

— (t.1957a) by C. Brookfield, *Professional Ethics and Civil Morals*, London: Routledge and Kegan Paul.

Ellwood, C. A. (1925) 'The Relations of Sociology and Social Psychology', *Journal of Abnormal Psychology and Social Psychology* 19:3–12.

Ewald, F. (1991) 'Insurance and Risk', in G. Burchell, C. Gordon and P. Miller (eds) *The Foucault Effect: Studies in Governmentality*, Chicago: University of Chicago Press.

Follett, M. P. (1965[1918]) *The New State*, Gloucester, MA: Peter Smith.

Forth, C. E. (1996) 'Intellectual Anarchy and Imaginary Otherness: Gender, Class and Pathology in French Intellectual Discourse, 1890–1900', *The Sociological Quarterly* 37:645–71.

Foucault, M. (1991) 'Governmentality', in G. Burchell, C. Gordon and P. Miller (eds) *The Foucault Effect: Studies in Governmentality*, Chicago: University of Chicago Press.

Gane, M. (1997) 'On the Relation between the *Rules* and *Suicide*', paper presented at the Centennial Conference on Durkheim's *Suicide*, Maison Française, Oxford, 12–13 December (revised as chapter 3 in this volume).

Gehlke, C. E. (1968[1915]) *Emile Durkheim's Contribution to Sociological Theory*, New York: AMS Press.

Giddens, A. (1971a) 'Introduction', in A. Giddens (ed.) *The Sociology of Suicide: Selected Readings*, London: Frank Cass.

(1971b) 'The Suicide Problem in French Sociology', in A. Giddens (ed.) *The Sociology of Suicide: Selected Readings*, London: Frank Cass.

Gordon, C. (1991) 'Governmental Rationality: An Introduction', in G. Burchell, C. Gordon and P. Miller (eds) *The Foucault Effect: Studies in Governmentality*, Chicago: University of Chicago Press.

Hacking, I. (1982) 'Biopower and the Avalanche of Printed Numbers', *Humanities in Society* 5:279–95.

(1991) 'How Should We Do the History of Statistics?', in G. Burchell, C. Gordon and P. Miller (eds) *The Foucault Effect: Studies in Governmentality*, Chicago: University of Chicago Press.

Hawkins, M. (1999) 'Durkheim's Sociology and Theories of Degeneration', *Economy and Society* 29(1):118–37.

Hinkle, R. C. (1960) 'Durkheim and American Sociology', in K. H. Wolff (ed.) *Emile Durkheim, 1858–1917*, Columbus: Ohio State University Press.

Jauss, H. R. (1982) 'Literary History as a Challenge to Literary Theory', in Jauss, *Toward an Aesthetic of Reception*, Minneapolis: University of Minnesota Press.

(1989) 'Horizon, Structure and Dialogicity', in Jauss, *Question and Answer: Forms of Dialogic Understanding*, edited and translated by M. Hays, Minneapolis: University of Minnesota Press.

Jones, R. A. (1998) 'Religion and Science in the *Elementary Forms*', in N. J. Allen, W. S. F. Pickering and W. Watts Miller (eds) *On Durkheim's* Elementary Forms of Religious Life, London: Routledge.

Karady, V. (1983) 'The Durkheimians in Academe', in P. Besnard (ed.) *The Sociological Domain: The Durkheimians and the Founding of French Sociology*, Cambridge: Cambridge University Press.

Kushner, H. L. (1993) 'Suicide, Gender, and the Fear of Modernity in Nineteenth-Century Medical and Social Thought', *Journal of Social History* 26:461–90.

Lukes, S. (1973) *Emile Durkheim, His Life and Work: A Historical and Critical Study*, London: Allen Lane.

MacDougall, R. (1912) 'The Social Basis of Individuality', *American Journal of Sociology* 18:1–20.
Masaryk, T. G. (1970[1888]) *Suicide and the Meaning of Civilization*, translated by R. Weist and R. Batson, Chicago: University of Chicago Press.
Merton, R. K. (1934) 'Recent French Sociology', *Social Forces* 7:537–45. Reprinted (1965) in R. Nisbet (ed.) *Emile Durkheim*, Englewood Cliffs, NJ: Prentice-Hall.
(1957a[1948]) 'The Bearing of Empirical Research on Sociological Theory', in R. K. Merton, *Social Theory and Social Structure*, Glencoe, IL: Free Press.
(1957b) 'The Bearing of Sociological Theory on Empirical Research', in R. K. Merton, *Social Theory and Social Structure*, Glencoe, IL: Free Press.
(1957c[1938]) 'Social Structure and Anomie', in R. K. Merton, *Social Theory and Social Structure*, Glencoe, IL: Free Press.
(1967) 'On the History and Systematics of Sociological Theory', in R. K. Merton, *On Sociological Theory*, New York: Free Press.
Meštrović, S. (1985) 'Anomia and Sin in Durkheim's Thought', *Journal for the Scientific Study of Religion* 24:119–36.
(1988) *Emile Durkheim and the Reformation of Sociology*, Newark, NJ: Rowman and Littlefield.
Morrison, K. (1998) 'Durkheim and Schopenhauer: New Textual Evidence on the Conceptual History of Durkheim's Formulation of the Egoistic-altruistic Types of Suicide', *Durkheimian Studies/Etudes Durkheimiennes* 4, new series:115–23.
Nye, R. A. (1982) 'Heredity, Pathology and Psychoneurosis in Durkheim's Early Work', *Knowledge and Society: Studies in the Sociology of Culture Past and Present* 4:103–42.
(1984) *Crime, Madness and Politics in Modern France: The Medical Concept of National Decline*, Princeton, NJ: Princeton University Press.
(1985) 'Sociology and Degeneration: The Dark Side of Progress', in E. Chamberlin and S. L. Gilman (eds) *Degeneration: The Dark Side of Progress*, New York: Columbia University Press.
Parsons, T. (1935) 'The Place of Ultimate Values in Social Theory', *International Journal of Ethics* 45:282–316.
(1938) 'The Role of Theory in Social Research', *American Sociological Review* 3:13–20.
(1949[1937]) *The Structure of Social Action*, New York: Free Press.
Pasquino, P. (1991) 'Theatrum Politicum: The Genealogy of Capital – Police and the State of Prosperity', in G. Burchell, C. Gordon and P. Miller (eds) *The Foucault Effect: Studies in Governmentality*, Chicago: University of Chicago Press.
Pick, D. (1989) *Faces of Degeneration: A European Disorder, c. 1848–c. 1918*, Cambridge: Cambridge University Press.
Pickering, W. S. F. (1984) *Durkheim's Sociology of Religion: Themes and Theories*, London: Routledge and Kegan Paul.
Ritzer, G. and Bell, R. (1981) 'Emile Durkheim: Exemplar for an Integrated Sociological Paradigm?', *Social Forces* 59:966–95.
Selvin, H. (1965) 'Durkheim's Suicide: Thoughts on a Methodological Classic', in R. A. Nisbet (ed.) *Emile Durkheim. With Selected Essays*, Englewood Cliffs, NJ: Prentice-Hall.

Simpson, G. (1933) 'Emile Durkheim's Social Realism', *Sociology and Social Research* 18:3–11.

(1966[1951]) 'Editor's Preface', in E. Durkheim, *Suicide*, translated by J. A. Spaulding and G. Simpson, New York: Free Press.

Small, A. (1901–2) Review of Emile Durkheim's *De la division du travail social*, *American Journal of Sociology* 7:566–8.

Stock-Morton, P. (1988) *Moral Education for a Secular Society: The Development of Morale Laïque in Nineteenth-Century France*, Albany: State University of New York Press.

Strenski, I. (1997) *Durkheim and the Jews of France*, Chicago and London: University of Chicago Press.

Swart, K. (1964) *The Sense of Decadence in Nineteenth-Century France*, The Hague: Martinus Nijhoff.

Watts Miller, W. (1996) *Durkheim, Morals and Modernity*, London: UCL Press.

Wilson, E. M. (1934) 'Emile Durkheim's Sociological Method', *Sociology and Social Research* 18:511–18.

8

THE FORTUNES OF DURKHEIM'S *SUICIDE*

Reception and legacy

Philippe Besnard

In a letter to his nephew Marcel Mauss written in November or December 1896 even before he finished *Suicide*, Emile Durkheim wondered about how the book would be received:

> Will it make converts? I don't know. Though it seems to me I've been gaining more ground than I've been losing, I'm still sceptical. I'm afraid of being between two chairs, the specialists not finding me enough of a specialist and the philosophers and literati preferring more entertaining science.
>
> (Durkheim 1998a:48)

'Specialists' on one side, 'philosophers and literati' on the other – this dichotomy may serve as a guide in our study of the work's earliest reception.

Earliest reception

In the letter quoted above, Durkheim was not being sincere; in fact he was counting heavily on *Suicide* to make converts to sociology. And its immediate reception as he perceived it in the letters of thanks he received was not at all up to his expectations. This even threw him into a slight *post partum* depression. As he wrote to Mauss in July 1897:

> You must of course keep this entirely to yourself, but I feel deeply discouraged. I thought my *Suicide* was going to dissipate any equivocations, establish an entente. But I don't foresee this happening at all. I still sense the same reservations in what people have written me; what seemed to me the most convincing proofs do not seem to be having their effect. This one contests one thing, that one

> another. I see that I can do nothing against the reigning opinion. Under these conditions, what is the use of the *Année sociologique*? It is already giving me sleepless nights, and for what?
>
> (Durkheim 1998a:77)

The next letter, which may be dated July 15, is more explicit, perhaps in response to an alarmed answer from his nephew:

> I have the impression – well-founded or not matters little – that my *Suicide* is going to be a mere waste of effort. I feel the same doctrinal resistance I thought I had slightly driven back re-forming against it. I had a thoroughly ridiculous letter from Sorel; and Bouglé, whom I thought I had seen definitively coming over to me, continues to flutter about like a butterfly. Simiand's letter was fairly padded. Lapie seems to have decided in favour, even quite frankly so. In fact, my real ambition is to see a few talented young men such as these, proceed not to follow me servilely, but to make frank use of my results; the opposite impression, founded on the facts just mentioned, has been painful to me. It may be that I exaggerate, that I'm mistaken. The future will decide. I can only express my present feeling. . . . In order to work joyfully, I must see that my work serves someone and something.
>
> (Durkheim 1998a:78)

A third letter clarifies the reasons for his disappointment:

> Perhaps my impression is due after all to a fit of intellectual megalomania. For some time now it has seemed to me that things have been going as smooth as velvet, that multiple new perspectives were opening up; so I had somewhat been expecting – while dreading disappointment by the facts – that the erstwhile encountered resistances might continue to diminish – significantly. It is quite possible that I was wrong about where I stand, and in that case the best thing to do is to acknowledge it.
>
> (Durkheim 1998a:81)

Responses from collaborators on the Année sociologique

We can only conjecture about the content of the letters Durkheim refers to (all letters addressed to him have been lost), but we do have indirect indications about what was in some of them – those that counted the most with him because they were written by future collaborators on the *Année sociologique*, the very men he was working to convince and recruit. When *Suicide* was published at the end of June 1897, the *Année*'s editorial team had already been formed and the division into sections had just been decided on, but discussion continued, not only about how to organize the work but also on the theoretical orientation that should be given to the new discipline. Debate was particularly arduous with three young *agrégés*[1] in philosophy, Clestin Bouglé, Paul Lapie and Dominique Parodi. Lapie and Parodi, who had less affinity for sociology, were also the ones most favourably impressed by Durkheim's book, whereas Bouglé seems to have been as reserved as Durkheim suspected, as attested to in Lapie's letter to him of 9 July 1897:

> I read Durkheim's book with great pleasure. What do you call scientific 'narrow-mindedness'? I find in it a great deal of conscientiousness and much ability in the interpretation of facts. Basically, it is not so distant from social psychology; there are some pages evidently inspired by our correspondence and by the desire to make concessions to us. . . . I know, of course, that he insists that the motives driving social man are unconscious; but whether his egoism, altruism, or anomie are more or less conscious, they are nonetheless psychological causes. That is what I have just written to him.
>
> (quoted in Besnard 1983:66)

For his part Parodi wrote to Bouglé: 'I have read *Suicide* with much interest. Here, at last, is a true sociology book and one that goes beyond the eternal questions of method' (1983:68).

But the young men of more confirmed sociological vocation manifested much less enthusiasm, and the first of these was Bouglé. Durkheim wrote him a long letter on 6 July handling several delicate subjects at once: an outline for the first section of the *Année*; a response to objections on relations between social and individual as presented in *Suicide*; a request for a review of the book for the *Revue philosophique* because 'for other reasons' Richard and Tarde could not be approached. Before closing Durkheim wrote:

> I have just this moment received a letter from Lapie, from which it transpires that the agreement between us on the great controversy is as complete as may be and I am most pleased. I fancy that, apart from some questions of form, we two have come to something similar, have we not?
>
> (Durkheim 1998a:46)

Durkheim strongly suspected this was not so (in his felicitous phrase to Mauss a few days later, Bouglé 'continue à papillonner'). Confirmation came with Bouglé's contribution to the *Année*: the first work reviewed – and for the most part lauded – in the 'General sociology' section for which he was responsible was Tarde's *L'Opposition universelle*. Moreover, Bouglé refused to review *Suicide* for the *Revue philosophique*. The task was performed instead by Paul Fauconnet, a young *agrégé* in philosophy whom Mauss had asked to participate in the *Année*.

The reviews of *Suicide* by Fauconnet (1898), Simiand (1898), and Richard (1898), all of whom were already members of the *Année* team, hardly express unmitigated admiration. Fauconnet, in the discussion following a long analysis of the content of Durkheim's work, was the one to show the least reservations – or at least they were formulated in such an indirect way that they could not be clearly identified as such, especially since he included Durkheim's responses to them without saying whether he had been convinced by them.

We meet with quite a different tone in the *Année sociologique* itself. There the task of reviewing Durkheim's work logically fell to Gaston Richard, in charge of the section entitled 'Criminal sociology and moral statistics', and his review was largely negative. He grants the book only one merit, that of packing off socialists and economists together with a 'certificate of incompetence'. The criticisms, though varied, appear structured around a defence of Tarde and his sociology: Durkheim's proposed definition of imitation is too restrictive; 'suicidogenic currents' is a dangerous metaphor; the varieties of suicide should be linked not to any such currents but rather to 'psychological types'. Everything in the conclusion shows how much closer Richard feels to Tarde than Durkheim:

> With the suicidogenic current eliminated and the individual factor reestablished, nothing prevents us from bringing together the two so fertile points of view presented here without much reason as if they were the two terms of an antithesis, by which I mean individual action and collective action. I see these as two factors of all social life and cannot understand what the sociological explanation gains in clarity or strength from denying one of them.
>
> (Richard 1898:405)

Suicide was of course not a fashion, Richard admitted – a concession to Durkheim's refutation. 'Nevertheless, no one commits suicide if he is not more of an imitator than the average man' (1898:406). If modern suicide exists, he explains, it takes the form of an imitation (custom, relic, or 'inoculation') of primitive altruistic suicide.[2]

Simiand's review of *Suicide*, published in the section entitled 'L'Année sociologique 1897' of the *Revue de métaphysique et de morale*, does not show the same sympathy for Tarde. His critical discussion, though shorter than the summary, is nonetheless incisive: he considers it a waste of time to devote a chapter to refuting Tarde's theory of imitation. He also formulated three 'reservations on method' (which clearly anticipate his future methodological concerns). First, how can one purport to formulate an objective definition of suicide when that definition does not correspond to the official statistics used? Second, there is no initial critique of the value of the statistics for the different countries and periods; suicide statistics are necessarily inexact, but the degree of inexactitude can vary. Lastly, Durkheim's results or 'laws' were founded on too narrow an empirical base.

But Simiand's most devastating criticism was of the conception of social facts presented in *Suicide*: 'Sociology may be founded as a science at much lesser cost.' Instead of claiming, as Durkheim had, that collective tendencies were 'forces as real as cosmic forces', it would be better to say 'as far from real', for 'science does not need to work with 'realities'. He rejected what he deemed a 'metaphysics of sociology', a 'sociological realism' (Simiand 1898:649–50). But this radical critique did not prevent him a few pages later, in his review of the first volume of the *Année sociologique*, from expressing the wish that this encounter between members of a group of men not be 'limited or ephemeral', for it justified the hope 'that sociology may one day have its place among the sciences' (1898:653). We see that while he identified himself completely with the *Année* project, Simiand's attitude towards Durkheim was far from reverential.

Philosophers and literati

As we have seen, it was Lapie and Parodi, the two young *Année* collaborators of the most philosophical – and least sociological – bent, who were most favourably impressed by Durkheim's new book. This disciplinary division is in fact perceptible generally in the work's first reception.

Contrary to what Durkheim pretended to fear, philosophers did not find his demonstration dull. Instead, they were impressed by the 'statistical results, in many cases established through long and patient research; the combinations, calculations, percentages produced from those results, . . . reproduced with complete scientific honesty'. These lines are taken from an anonymous review published in the November 1897 supplement to the *Revue de métaphysique et de morale* that opens thus: 'Here is a work that would probably have spared readers of the *Règles de la méthode sociologique* a number of regrettable misunderstandings if they had known of it earlier' (Anon. 1897:2).[3]

The review in the *Année philosophique* was, it is true, not nearly as laudatory. After a summary of the work, Pillon, the usual reviewer, criticized the central thesis of the work in a few lines of Tardian inspiration:

> The causes he calls social were, at the beginning, only individual psychological causes whose influence became generalized; they can only be combatted through an ever more extended influence of other individual psychological causes.
>
> (Pillon 1898:524)

(It should be noted that as director of the *Année philosophique*, published by Alcan since 1891, Pillon was perhaps not kindly disposed to the new *Année sociologique.*)

Two years later, E. Goblot, reviewing Volume 5 of the *Annales de l'institut international de sociologie*, used *Suicide* as an example of genuinely scientific proceeding in the context of a critique of organicism: 'In his study of suicide M. Durkheim has offered an example of what scientific research in sociology is.' The very reservations that a philosopher of science might express became strong points:

> We might think that suicide is an eminently individual deed; well, it is influenced by the social milieu, and it is from this point of view that M. Durkheim has studied it. We might also think that this influence is exerted in the form of motives, and that the problem thus becomes psychological again rather than sociological, and M. Durkheim does come up short before the problem thus posed. But on the point that he set out to study . . . he has made discoveries. And it is through discoveries that sciences move forward.
>
> (Goblot 1900:742)

These few responses from 'pure' philosophers suggest that with *Suicide* Durkheim had gained some of the credit he had lost with them; they had not much liked his methodological manifesto (Paoletti 1995). Mauss seems to have had this in mind in 1938 in a note on the relations between Durkheim and Lucien Herr: 'There may have been a moment of hesitation between the two . . . after the *Règles de la méthode*. . . . In any case, the publication of *Suicide* reconciled the two men's thought' (Mauss 1997:742).

What of the literati? One of the first reviews appeared in the *Revue socialiste* for November 1897. It was signed by a regular collaborator, Pierre Deloire, and was only a page long. Deloire criticizes the corporatist solution recommended by Durkheim, reproaches him with relying too heavily on statistics, which meant he had studied only the 'external manifestations' of 'social feelings', and for not speaking of the 'robbery incessantly committed by employers when they overwork their employees'. But the originality of this short analysis was to present all four types of suicide without leaving out fatalistic suicides 'caused by the ennui of invariable equilibrium' (Deloire 1897:635). Though this review is devoid of enthusiasm, it comes just before one by Henri Genevray that demolishes – from a thoroughly Durkheimian perspective – Tarde's *L'Opposition universelle.*

In the 20 April 1898 issue of the *Revue bleue*, a 'political and literary' journal, we find a text on *Suicide* by an unlikely author, the literary critic and Académie Française member, Emile Faguet – a 'man of letters' in the full sense of Durkheim's expression. The article is quite friendly overall, though Faguet does not accept including sacrifice in the definition of suicide. He is particularly interested in the effect of mutuality in marriage, explaining that the married woman without children is even more isolated than the single woman because the husband, far from being 'company', is in fact '*an isolator*'. Faguet brings all the social factors of suicide down to one – individual isolation – which must be combatted through association.

A few years later, on 21 July 1909, a man of letters and politician Maurice Barrès (whose novel *Les Déracinés* came out the same year as *Suicide*) would cite Durkheim's work in a speech to the Chamber of Deputies to show the importance of religion for social cohesion: 'Uncontestably, religion has a prophylactic effect on suicide' (quoted in Winock 1997:103).

'Specialists': silence from the medical profession and the Italian reaction

In the medical press Durkheim's book was met with virtually total silence even though throughout the century suicide had been a major object of investigation among alienists. We find no review of it in the *Annales médico-psychologiques*, the *Revue psychiatrique*, the *Gazette des hopitaux*, or even the *Bulletin acadèmique de médecine*, though it regularly reviewed recent publications. Nothing in the *Annales d'hygiène publique et de médecine légale* either, despite the fact that in 1897 it had published two articles on suicide. The *Gazette médicale de Paris* listed the work without comment in its annual recapitulative bibliography. Across the Channel, a single anonymous, purely descriptive notice appeared in 1898 in the *Journal of Mental Science*, but at a colloquium on suicide organized by the British Medical Association at Edinburgh in 1899 Durkheim's book was not even mentioned (Berrios and Mohanna 1990).

The *Archives d'anthropologie criminelle* could hardly ignore the book. The analysis of it by C. Tournier, a regular contributor to the bibliography section, follows 'this quite remarkable book' 'step by step' while expressing doubts about Durkheim's minimization of the 'individual factors involved in suicide' (Tournier 1898:335).

Durkheim was expecting a response from Tarde, the primary target of his book (Besnard 1995). But Tarde ultimately gave up the idea of publishing that response, even though he had already written a significant part of it. We have seen how often reference is made to Tarde in the first reception of the book (especially in Richard's and Pillon's reviews). But his thinking is perhaps best represented in the response of an Italian author named Gustavo Tosti. Tosti, who lived in New York, was in regular correspondence with Tarde and devoted a long piece to him in the September 1897 issue of *Political Science Quarterly*. While he seems to have been an amateur sociologist – we find no trace of him in later literature – he was a skilful dialectician, and his discussion of Durkheimian sociology is quite strong – and better, it seems to me, than Tarde's analysis.

Tosti first published a text in the January 1898 issue of the *American Journal of Sociology* entitled 'Suicide in the Light of Recent Studies' which was in fact concerned exclusively with Durkheim's book; then another, shorter but no less incisive account in the *Psychological Review*.

The *AJS* review begins with a perfidious remark to which Durkheim must have been quite sensitive: his doctrine is presented as 'the manifestation of a solitary thought in the contemporary movement of social studies' (Tosti 1898a:464). The argument in what follows is typically Tardian: Durkheim thought he had refuted Tarde, but the effect of his book is the opposite of the one he was aiming at: 'His desperate attempt to prove the positive character of his conception of society is a complete failure.' The book that claims to demonstrate 'the alleged independence of the social phenomenon from the action of individual factors . . . ends in the best verification of the opposite conception of social fact as resulting from the combined studies of Tarde and Baldwin' (1898a:477).

Tosti is willing to accept that society is a different order of reality from that represented by each individual taken separately:

> We find in collective or social life the production of forces or powers not given in the individual organism. Even from the Tardian sociological standpoint, it is not permitted to deny the peculiar distinctive character of the social fact versus its elements, i.e. the individuals.
>
> (1898a:473)

But to his mind we cannot simply ignore the law of intercerebral action – imitation – which is the only intelligible process by which elements (individuals) may be combined. Durkheim fails to explain how 'social forces . . . are incorporated by the individual' (1898b:426).

Tosti reproached the author of *Suicide* with 'completely overlook[ing] the fact that *a compound is explained both by the character of its elements and by the law of their interaction*' (1898a:474, Tosti's emphasis) – a remark which elicited an immediate reaction from Durkheim. In his letter dated 6 February and published in the May issue (where he used the word 'combination' in place of Tosti's 'interaction'), Durkheim cites passages from *Suicide* to prove how great a role he attributed to individual factors. Tosti retorted very effectively in the July issue (1898c).

In his reply to Tosti, Durkheim had indicated that he was also responding to another Italian critic cited by him: the statistician Augusto Bosco (likewise in contact with Tarde), who had reviewed the book in the *Rivista italiana di sociologia* and whom we may put in the category of 'specialist'. Bosco's review, which appeared in November 1897, is at best lukewarm: 'I don't believe that the author has succeeded in the demonstration he set out to perform and which is the main objective of his book' (Bosco 1897:377).

Bosco's criticisms were many and cannot be reduced to the general argument Tosti derives from them. Bosco could not follow Durkheim in his thorough rejection of the idea that race has an influence; meanwhile Durkheim's interpretation of seasonal variations in suicide seemed to him more ingenious than valid because the intensity of public life is greater in winter. He also reproached Durkheim with not taking into account the problem of recording suicides: Catholics might well dissimulate suicides more often than Protestants; the increase in suicides might be due to better techniques of registering them. Finally, Durkheim's demonstration of suicide among soldiers did not seem credible to him. Bosco did grant the work certain merits, however, citing in particular the differential effect of marriage by sex and correctly reproducing the divorce-marriage-suicide relation. Yet even to this statistician it seemed that statistical research on the relation between marital status and suicide had to be enriched, namely by observing individual cases, as Brierre de Boismont had done.

Durkheim's most illustrious critic (by today's standards) was Vilfredo Pareto. His review of *Suicide* – a rare occasion for dialogue between two founders of sociology – appeared in the first volume of a new journal, the *Zeitschrift für Sozialwissenschaft*, and except for the minimal kindness of its first sentence – 'This is a well-written book that will prove of interest to the reader' – it was devastating: 'Throughout the book the reasoning is, unfortunately, not at all rigorous . . . To note all the errors one would have to write a book just as long or longer' (Pareto 1898:78).

Pareto targeted the book's first demonstration – perhaps the strangest, it is true – concerning the near invariability of suicide rates within a given society; a constancy suggested to be even stronger than that for mortality in general.[4] Obviously this was false, and Pareto remarked that Durkheim had chosen years that served his demonstration. He was also surprised to see that a book published in 1897 should not look into statistics any later than 1869 to assess the development and variations in the suicide rate in France. After giving one last example of what he called 'a priori proof' – suicide among soldiers – Pareto concluded that Durkheim 'seems to offer metaphysical abstractions as causes for real phenomena' (1898:80). His critique is that much harsher because it too comes from the 'experimental method' perspective.

Suicide in the purgatory of delayed recognition

The first critical reception, hardly enthusiastic as we have seen, was not compensated for by any sales success; nor did *Suicide* slowly but surely become a classic. On the contrary, the book went unrecognized – we might even say forgotten – for nearly half a century after its publication.

We have a few general indicators about this state of affairs. First, there were few re-editions. The first (1897) edition probably ran 1000 copies

(1500 at the most), and it was not republished until 1912, the same year of *Les Formes élémentaires de la vie religieuse*. *Les Règles de la méthode sociologique* was then in its sixth edition and the *Division du travail* in its third. The gap between *Suicide* and Durkheim's other works widened between the two world wars: during this period *Rules* and *Division* were republished three times; *Formes* twice; but *Suicide* only once, on the occasion of the publication of Halbwachs' *Les Causes du suicide* in 1930. In the 1940s and 1950s only *Rules* was republished. It was not until the 1960s, with the Presses Universitaires de France's project to republish all four of Durkheim's works, that *Suicide* attained second place in sales, just behind the *Rules*. From then on it would be republished numerous times (Besnard 1993).

In his study of references to Durkheim's books in the *American Journal of Sociology* and the *American Sociological Review*, Paul Vogt (1993) made approximately the same observation: *Suicide* was hardly cited until the beginning of the 1950s, and it was cited less frequently than *Division*.

Clearly, then, *Suicide*'s career does not describe a straight line. But it is important to go beyond these rather coarse-grained indicators and examine the literature in which we might expect to find references to *Suicide* – that produced by the Durkheimians, first of all; then writings in the sociology of suicide.

Suicide *eclipsed among the Durkheimians*

Let us consider first what may be called the common exposition of Durkheim's works: introductions to, popularizations and in some cases discussions of Durkheimian sociology produced in France between 1910 and 1940. We are especially justified in considering such texts given that one fundamental characteristic of the Durkheimian enterprise was to get the discipline of sociology established, institutionalized.

The Durkheimian Georges Davy played a major role in introducing and disseminating Durkheim's thought. He wrote the first book on Durkheim (Davy 1911) at a time when he was both collaborator and close friend. Davy's book is divided into two parts: a study of Durkheim's sociological system and a selection of excerpts from his work. Of the 150 pages of excerpts, only 29 are from *Suicide* (though at the time it was Durkheim's most recent book; *Les Formes élémentaire de la vie religieuse* had not yet been published). Of the 29 pages from *Suicide*, 14 are on the nature of social phenomena and 9 discuss occupational groups – there is thus virtually nothing on Durkheim's study of suicide itself. More striking still, in Davy's presentation of Durkheim's work, which he sought to make as faithful as possible, references to *Suicide* are few and far between, and nearly all of them are from the chapter entitled 'The social element of suicide' where Durkheim presents his conception of collective consciousness. There is no presentation of his research and no mention of the types of suicide, either in this book or other texts of the same type that Davy wrote later, for example his 1920 article on Durkheim's work in the *Revue de métaphysique et de morale*. In his 'sociology' chapter for G. Dumas's *Traité de psychologie* (Davy 1924b), Davy refers to *Suicide* only to indicate Durkheim's refutation of the theory of imitation.

The second comprehensive presentation of Durkheimian sociology after Davy's in 1911 was Maurice Halbwachs': a major article entitled 'La doctrine d'Emile Durkheim', published the year after Durkheim's death (Halbwachs 1918). Once again it is striking to see that while 12 pages are devoted to the *Rules of Sociological Method*, 8 to the *Division of Labour in Society*, and 17 to the *Elementary Forms of Religious Life*, and while Halbwachs discusses many other writings by Durkheim, namely on morality, this article contains no precise reference – even in the notes – to *Suicide*. Halbwachs does not go beyond mentioning that Durkheim 'paid particular attention to the increase in suicide numbers', understood as a manifestation of the increase in egoism (Halbwachs 1918:402). It is particularly strange that Halbwachs, who would later write the *Causes du suicide*, should so keep the work dark.

In 1926 two books on Durkheim were published in France by non-Durkheimian authors. La Fontaine's mediocre work, *La Philosophie d'Emile Durkheim*, contains no mention of *Suicide*. But *La Méthode sociologique de Durkheim*, a strong, penetrating critique by René Lacombe, does include a discussion of *Suicide*, mainly on the theory of egoism.

The 1920 university reform in France, which accredited courses for the university degree both in sociology and morality and sociology while introducing the discipline of sociology into teacher training programmes, gave rise to a crop of textbooks and anthologies. These works are an excellent means of apprehending the predominant version of Durkheimism. In fact, many of them were written by Durkheimians – Marcel Déat's *Sociologie*, for example, written in 1925, is a presentation of the sociology of Durkheim and his school: yet there is not a word on *Suicide* in this book, which is not so much as cited. The same is true of René Maunier's *Introduction à la sociologie* (1929) – though the author was a collaborator on the new series of the *Année sociologique* – and Davy's textbook (1924a), though this is perhaps not surprising given that its main focus was political sociology. A major anthology edited by Bouglé and Raffault (1926) presents 22 texts by Durkheim, none from *Suicide*. An annotated bibliography by Bouglé and Déat entitled *Guide de l'étudiant en sociologie* (1921) cites *Suicide* only for its discussion of the theory of imitation.

This remarkable concealment of one of Durkheim's important books, observable in the explanatory or popularizing works of those closest to him, also characterizes non-Durkheimian authors, though to a lesser degree. In *Notions de sociologie appliquées à la morale et à l'éducation*, Hesse and Gleyse allude only briefly to *Suicide*, to show that man is a social animal and cannot live alone (Hesse and Gleyse 1922:7); the book does not figure in their list of recommended readings. It does appear, however, in the bibliography of

René Hubert's *Manuel élémentaire de la sociologie*, where it is summarized in a few lines (Hubert 1925:305) pertaining exclusively to the theory of integration. Same treatment in *Eléments de sociologie* (1925) by Charles Lalo, who in spite of his collaboration on the *Année sociologique* can hardly be considered a Durkheimian sociologist. *Suicide* is cited in Essertier's very thoroughgoing bibliography, *Psychologie et sociologie* (1927).

References to *Suicide* are to be found in the 1920s in writings of a former collaborator on the *Année sociologique* who had become a resolute opponent of Durkheimian sociology and whom we have already encountered: Gaston Richard. Predictably, these are all critical (Richard 1923, 1925, 1930). Richard affirms that 'Durkheim's theory on suicide is nothing more than an elaboration from statistical data collected by other scholars, especially Morselli' (1925:350) but also – and this is less expected – by Gabriel Tarde (1925:349). His general purpose is to expose a contradiction between *Suicide* and the *Rules* by showing that 'the pathology affecting solidarity diagnosed in *Suicide* stands in absolute contradiction to the optimistic, teleological assessment of criminality and the social function of the criminal' (1930:121). Richard even distorted Durkheim's analyses to make his point, affirming for example that Durkheim had demonstrated that suicide and homicide are 'analogous phenomena that follow parallel paths' (1930:118).

In one of his texts Gaston Richard notes in passing that *Suicide* is the least read and least well known of Durkheim's works (1923:129). The present investigation confirms his remark and enables us to clarify it: the common exposition of Durkheim in France eclipsed *Suicide*. And we may well speak of a case of collective repression, since the work's absence is more marked among authors close to Durkheim. In fact, *Suicide* was evoked only by writers far removed from his influence, or frankly critical.

The silence around *Suicide* in academic presentations of Durkheimism was such that breaking it must have seemed almost an act of provocation. This may be seen in a debate on how to teach sociology that took place on 18 June 1932 at the Institut Français de Sociologie (a scholarly society run by Durkheimians). In discussing a project proposed by Paul Fauconnet, Marcel Granet, then vice-president of the Institut, energetically criticized its encyclopaedic nature. In his opinion, the best way of showing what scientific knowledge about social facts was, and how it progressed, would be to treat a few, carefully chosen issues. And at the forefront of the examples he gave came suicide, a choice he explained first and foremost with reference to 'personal experience':

> For me as for others, it was neither the *Rules of Sociological Method* nor the *Division of Labour in Society* that shook me up and won me over; it was *Suicide*; and I think sociologists could be classified into those who readily take inspiration from *Suicide* and the others.
>
> (Granet 1932:104)

Granet's confession is not pure reconstruction. His first text, *Contre l'alcoolisme, un programme socialiste* (1911), is that of a socialist activist who was clearly influenced by *Suicide*, though he did not cite the book directly. This slightly qualifies the idea that the work was a relative failure among Durkheimians. However, Granet belonged to the second generation and only read the book a dozen years after it was published. It is also not surprising that the theme of suicide should be evoked in 1932, just two years after Halbwachs' book, the publication of which was itself accompanied by a reprint of Durkheim's work. As for Granet's idea of dividing up sociologists according to their regard for *Suicide*, it was clearly polemical, most likely expressing a tension within the Durkheimian group between those who were essentially 'academics' such as Bouglé, Fauconnet and Davy, and those who were first and foremost specialized 'researchers' like Granet himself and Mauss, who for his part expressed entire agreement with Granet's point.

Does this mean there are more traces of *Suicide* to be found in 'researchers'' works? With the exception of Halbwachs, who I shall come back to later, the answer must be no.

Marcel Mauss liked to mention his participation in the empirical and bibliographical investigations on which his uncle's study was based, namely the 25,500 suicide cases he examined. In fact, he referred very rarely to his uncle's book – only in scientific talks or other oral interventions, and then only on the subject of altruistic suicide (Mauss 1969, 2:124, 3:55). The most direct reference is in a paper entitled 'Effet physique chez l'individu de l'idée de mort suggérée par la collectivité' and it led to a remarkable *lapsus calami*. After describing cases observed in Australia and New Zealand of death due to the subject's 'believ[ing] himself, for precise collective causes, in a state close to death' (Mauss 1926:654) Mauss ends his presentation thus:

> To conclude, allow me to mention that these facts confirm and extend the theory of anomic suicide that Durkheim presented in a book which stands as a model of sociological demonstration.
>
> (1926:669)

We can only think he meant to say 'altruistic suicide'.

Among collaborators on the *Année sociologique* who used *Suicide*, mention should be made of Paul Lapie, a rather heterodox Durkheimian who had nonetheless been taken with the work, as we have seen. In *La Femme dans la famille* (1908), Lapie alludes to the theme of conjugal anomie or, more exactly, its empirical foundations. He cites the result Durkheim reached in *Suicide*, that men benefit more than women from the conjugal union, particularly that in places where divorce is widely practised, the immunity marriage confers on men is diminished whereas for women it is increased. He concludes, following Durkheim, that of the two sexes, it is woman who needs freedom. This marginal Durkheimian alone took up this highly suggestive conclusion from *Suicide*. He was also one of the few readers to have correctly restated Durkheim's result.

Still, Lapie did not use the term 'anomie', which we find instead in the writings of another *Année* collaborator, Louis Gernet, who like Granet was of the second generation. In his doctoral thesis, *Recherches sur le développement de la pensée juridique et morale en Grèce*, defended in 1917, Gernet uses 'anomie' in the sense it has in Durkheim's work: a sign that the word could be understood twenty years after the book was published.

These few traces do not amount to much, given the true Durkheimian heritage we supposedly find in Halbwachs; this leads us to an examination of sociological literature on suicide after Durkheim.

The sociology of suicide through the 1940s

Curiously, Durkheim's book also had difficulty making itself felt in this area of study.

In a book published in 1908 by Camille Jacquart, a Belgian author, entitled *Essais de statistique morale I: Le suicide*, we might expect to find a serious discussion of the French book published eleven years earlier. In fact Jacquart used his predecessor's study primarily as a source for French data; he reproached Durkheim with constructing 'a sociological theory on a scaffolding of metaphors' (1908:85). Moreover, Jacquart did not say a word about anomic suicide, which is rather surprising given that he meant to study the influence of industrial crises on suicide rates and that one of his general conclusions is that an abrupt change in a society's economic activity 'produces extraordinary excitement together with exaggerated needs and overreaching ambitions which, because they are not satisfied, in turn generate suicide' (1908:105). Signalling this book in Volume 11 of the *Année sociologique*, Durkheim (1910:515) wrote briefly: 'Adds nothing to known facts. Links increase in suicide to increase in industrialism and the resulting overstimulation of appetites.'

A year earlier, another Belgian author, Guillaume De Greef, in *La Structure générale des sociétés* (the first volume of which is entitled *La Loi de limitation*) had engaged in a long discussion of suicide (1907:149–60) in which Durkheim's name does not appear.

Le Suicide et la morale (1922) by Albert Bayet, who may be considered a late Durkheimian because he collaborated on the new series of the *Année sociologique*, contains no real discussion of Durkheim's theory of suicide – this in contrast to the psychologist Charles Blondel, who devotes an entire chapter to the theory in *Suicide* (1933).

But what of Halbwachs' *Les Causes du suicide*, which seems to refute the statement that *Suicide* had fallen into virtual oblivion? Halbwachs' book was published in 1930, at the same time Durkheim's was republished, and it was prefaced by Mauss. Every effort was made to accredit the idea that with this work a research tradition was being perpetuated; close scrutiny of it belies this. Halbwachs does of course check, correct, even refute certain aspects of Durkheim's empirical generalizations, but these pre-existed Durkheim's work. Derived from moral statistics, they were the generalizations that Durkheim had taken up, clarified and used to construct his theory. Halbwachs does not seem the least bit interested in that theory; he hardly discusses it, preferring, in general, to ignore it.

So it is that without really talking about it, Halbwachs rejects Durkheim's theoretical framework, namely the distinction between the two dimensions of the social bond – integration and regulation – from which the four types of suicide then derive. As early as page 7, presenting Durkheim's 'explanation' for suicide, Halbwachs cites only the sentence defining egoistic suicide: 'Suicide varies inversely with the degree of integration . . .'. The expression 'anomic suicide' appears only in connection with its possible difference from egoistic suicide. This is because Halbwachs implicitly rejects the distinction between them, described as 'psychological' and, while 'perhaps founded', in any case unverifiable (1930:312). In a few lines the central point of Durkheim's theory is cast aside.

In his empirical work, Halbwachs neglects or rejects anything that could possibly pertain to the Durkheimian theory of regulation. Not a word on conjugal anomie and its empirical foundations in his long chapter on suicide and the family. Only the chapter on the influence of economic crises seems to show some acknowledgement of anomic suicide, though the term does not appear. In fact, it is in this chapter that the author seems to want to do the most damage to Durkheim's theses: moments of sudden economic expansion ('fortunate crises') do not bring about an increase in suicide; that increase is the effect not of a disturbance in the collective order but of the decrease in 'general activity' characteristic of the period of depression that follows on such crises. It is precisely this point of disagreement that he emphasizes in his introduction (1930:15). In sum, though on many points, such as the protective influence of the family, political crises and war, Halbwachs confirms Durkheim's results, he is either silent on or seeks to refute anything having to do with anomie.

The word 'anomie' does finally make an entrance – in the conclusion, where it is mentioned twice (1930:497, 501). Here Halbwachs does discuss Durkheim's thesis (as it pertains to economic anomie), and once again his judgement is negative: nothing allows us to affirm that 'there is relatively more anomie now than in the past'; social life in our modern civilizations carries with it 'a kind of spontaneous discipline':

> 'No [other] society more pitilessly eliminates innovations to which it is unaccommodating, or more tyrannically regulates gestures and

> modes of thought and feeling. Nor is there any which does more to blunt human passions and channel them into one single mold.
> (1930/t.1978:322)[5]

Halbwachs' rejection of Durkheim's theoretical framework is particularly sharp concerning the theory of regulation but this is also true for integration. Not only did he not have any use for the notion of altruistic suicide, his general sociological interpretation of suicide (arising from the 'complexity of life', as merely suggested in his conclusion) may even be seen as reversing Durkheim's theory of egoistic suicide. According to Halbwachs, multiplying contacts between people increases opportunities for suicide. In times of war or political crisis, life is simplified and 'occasions for individual vexations' are reduced. An economic crisis, however, provokes 'all kinds of new relationships' between individuals and multiplies 'occasions for boredom, humiliation, disappointment, and suffering on account of others'. Explicitly distancing himself from Durkheim through these examples, Halbwachs even goes so far as to state a kind of general law: 'the diminution of collective activity has as its counterpart an increase of relationships or contacts between individuals, and conversely' (Mauss 1930/t.1978:319).

We could almost say Halbwachs would have written substantially the same book even if Durkheim had not written *Suicide* at all. It is difficult, then, to follow Mauss in his preface when he presents the two books as 'two moments of the same research' (Halbwachs 1930:v) or elsewhere when he cites this supposed filiation as an example of the way 'a science should progress' (1933:40).

Suicide's patent lack of success was not just a French phenomenon. It is striking that Ruth Cavan in her 1928 study of suicides in Chicago only mentions Durkheim's work once, in connection with the alcoholism–suicide relation. Her book is in fact the best-known example of American sociological literature on suicide written between the world wars, a literature with two salient traits: methodological recourse to ecological correlations and thematic emphasis on social and individual disorganization in the aetiology of suicide. The twofold orientation of this literature makes Durkheim's absence from it very odd since it seems particularly compatible with his anomic suicide. Let one example of the many available suffice: Mowrer's 1939 paper in the *American Sociological Review*, published a year after Merton's 'Social Structure and Anomie'. Mowrer purports to study the effect of disturbances in social equilibrium – in this case, economic depression – on personal disorganization, for which the indicator chosen is the suicide rate. Mowrer makes no mention of Durkheim's work.

In sociological suicide literature of the 1940s we find only two authors who refer to Durkheim: Lunden (1947), because he studied suicides in France from 1910 to 1940, and Potterfield (1949), who cites some of the results in *Suicide*, among other sources, in a discussion of the relation between suicide and homicide. It should be noted that Potterfield made no allusion to the work in a later article (1952) in which he nonetheless discusses the notion of social disorganization.

We cannot help being struck, then, by how little impact Durkheim's work had even in the particular area of suicide research – at least before *Le Suicide* was translated into English.

No echo in Chicago

We have seen through the preceding examination of two intellectual traditions in which we might reasonably expect to discern an influence just how fully Durkheim's *Suicide* was thrust into the purgatory of postponed recognition. It will therefore not be surprising to discover that at a more general level it was likewise quite forgotten.

Introduction to the Science of Sociology, by Park and Burgess (1921) was for a long time the authoritative textbook on the subject in the United States. It contains two texts by Durkheim, one from the *Elementary Forms of Religious Life* and one from the *Division of Labour in Society*. *Suicide*, on the other hand, is not even mentioned, even in the work's numerous and lengthy bibliographies, though these do include many other texts by Durkheim, especially articles. The first book exclusively on Durkheim's work, a thesis written by Gehlke in 1915 at Columbia University, showed little interest in *Suicide*; it is rarely mentioned, and discussed only in relation to the issue of professional groups (Gehlke 1915:172–3).

The names Park and Burgess lead us to the research theme of 'social disorganization', which became a veritable tradition of study in the United States between the wars, especially at the University of Chicago in the 1920s. Once again, Durkheim's theory of suicide might have prospered on this terrain – but it did not, not even in studies specifically focused on suicide, as we saw above with Ruth Cavan's book. We can assume that Halbwachs hardly drew attention to the theory of anomic suicide in the course he gave on suicide at Chicago in 1930. Actually, the major American suicide studies had already been published when Halbwachs came to the US.

The only sound in all this silence is to be found not in an empirical study, but rather a sort of textbook by Mabel Elliott and Francis Merril published in 1934 and entitled *Social Disorganization*, in which the authors survey sociological studies on 'social problems'. Their chapter on suicide is heavily based on Durkheim and his three types of suicide; elsewhere in the book they apply the notion of anomic suicide to suicides that follow-on a reversal of fortunes in the context of an economic crisis. Durkheim's presence may be explained by the authors' interest in France: the first edition of the book contains a chapter on contemporary French thought, designed, as the authors explain, to counteract the strange and 'lamentable' insularity of American authors (Elliott and Merril 1934, 735). We see to what degree this single, discreet appearance of anomie in the American universe of social disorganization resembles an accident when we look at another textbook, also titled *Social Disorganization*, published in 1948 by R. E. L. Faris, heir in the literal sense of the word to the University of Chicago tradition because he was the son of Ellsworth Faris and studied in the Chicago sociology department when it was at its apogee (1924–31). In Faris' chapter on suicide there is only one vague allusion to Durkheim, while there are many to Halbwachs. There is no change in this for the second edition of 1955. And anomie, whether Durkheimian or Mertonian, is entirely absent.

How *Suicide* became a classic

The Americans' rediscovery

The silence on *Suicide* is to be understood in the context of a general unfamiliarity with and misunderstanding of Durkheim's work in the world of American sociology at the time (Hinkle 1960). Not until the 1930s – particularly the end of the decade – did Americans show any real interest. Then the signs were many, namely Simpson's translation of the *Division du travail social* (1933) and Merton's long analysis of that work in 1934; the translation of the *Règles de la méthode sociologique* in 1938 (Durkheim 1895a). Three important theses on Durkheim were written at about the same time: Benoit-Smullyan's, defended at Harvard in 1938; Foskett's, defended at Berkeley in 1939, and Alpert's at Columbia, published in 1939 (Alpert made little use of *Suicide*). We know the importance of Parson's *Structure of Social Action* (1937) for the reception of Durkheim in the United States; it is, moreover, in this book that we find a positive re-evaluation of *Suicide*, conceived as a moment of transition in Durkheim's intellectual itinerary, the beginning of a movement away from morphological factors and an interest in the way collective consciousness penetrates individual consciousnesses. Parsons understood the conceptualization of anomic suicide as a sign of Durkheim's break with his earlier works.

Parson's book is the fullest expression of the return to the European (and particularly continental) founders effected by the members of Harvard's young department of sociology in the 1930s. Opened in 1931, the department was headed by Sorokin, a great scholar fully familiar with European sociology; it was at Harvard that Benoit-Smullyan's thesis was defended and Merton got his start. Elton Mayo was also there; in *The Human Problems of an Industrial Civilization* (1933) he was the first American sociologist to call attention to *Suicide*, putting particular emphasis on the notion of anomie, and thereby introducing the term into American sociology.[6] I have shown elsewhere that this reinvention of anomie at Harvard (in which Mayo, Merton and Parsons participated) was a way of distinguishing that department from the Chicago school with its traditional focus on social disorganization (Besnard 1985).

The return to Durkheim that began in the late 1930s in America was thus part of a broader movement, in which young sociologists desirous of becoming masters in their discipline dissociated themselves from what was the then American sociological tradition.

Suicide was rediscovered by theorists, by generalists rather than specialists working on particular social problems, though the latter might well have looked for theoretical inspiration in Durkheim. The process of innovation and diffusion was begun by young theorists reading European authors in the original, not from a particular sector of applied sociology. And this was the best way for the work to acquire 'classic' status.

The diffusion process had begun just before World War II, but the language obstacle had to be overcome before it could really take off. Publication of the English translation of *Suicide* in 1951 by Free Press had fairly speedy consequences: as early as the mid-50s, the number of references to the work in American sociology began to go up significantly.

Most sociological studies of suicide written in the 1950s refer to Durkheim (Strauss and Strauss 1953; Henry and Short 1954; Gibbs and Martin 1958; Powell 1958). Concurrently, new readings of the work, both theoretical (Dohrenwend 1959) and methodological (Selvin 1958), were undertaken.[7] In a 1955 ecological study of suicide in London, the British author Sainsbury, himself fully in line with the Chicago School, not only referred five times to *Suicide* but explained that his work owes much to Durkheim's pioneering study (Sainsbury 1955:89). Clearly Durkheim had fast become a required, even ritual reference, because in fact Sainsbury had not used his theory at all; Durkheim is strikingly absent, for example, from the author's presentation of the relation between divorce and suicide.

In this field as in others, American sociology set the tone for other 'national' sociologies. In France, rediscovery of Durkheim and *Suicide* did not begin until the early 1960s, first with the new edition of his four works published by the Presses Universitaires de France; later in various university courses on classic authors; finally in books introducing Durkheim's work. We should note the publication in 1966 of *L'Analyse empirique de la causalité*, an anthology of texts edited by Boudon and Lazarsfeld, which presents two excerpts from *Suicide*, as well as the article by Selvin cited above, which underlines the methodological relevance of this 'classic'. *Suicide* became the precursor of multivariate analysis, and more generally a 'founding text' of sociology. Raymond Boudon (1967) worked to formalize Durkheim's reasoning in several passages of *Suicide*, bringing out his innovative approach to the problem of causal inference (see also Isambert 1973). The relations between religion and suicide or length of day and suicide (Boudon 1969) became canonical examples. This return to Durkheim was not, however, unequivocal: at one point it appears as a means of distinguishing French sociology from American sociology; at another as a means of locating the roots of modern empirical research procedures in classical sociology. What is in any case particularly striking is the contrast between this Durkheim revival and the post-war years, when reconstructing French sociology had been understood to involve a total break with Durkheimism.

The primacy of egoistic suicide

Starting in the 1960s, references to *Suicide* became so frequent that they defy attempts to inventory them. But while it would be impossible to describe in detail here the career of Durkheim's theory in the sociology of suicide, we can indicate its main features, at least one of which is quite distinct: the book was received selectively, with marked preference given to Durkheim's theory of integration. This is clear in the influential work by Gibbs and Martin (1964) and in other works by the same Jack Gibbs. In fact, in several American readings of *Suicide*, from Johnson (1965) to Pope (1976) this preference is justified by reducing Durkheim's theory to 'a single cause of suicide' (to paraphrase the title of Johnson's article) and by identifying anomie with egoism.[8] Durkheim's theory of suicide actually became the theory of egoistic suicide. As we have seen, Richard and Halbwachs had set the example for such selective perception.

The privilege granted to egoistic suicide is still more marked – empirical works of this period presenting themselves as either extensions or tests of Durkheim's theses. The most notable exception to this is an early work: Henry and Short's *Suicide and Homicide*, published in 1954. Their study of the relation between the economic cycle and variations in annual suicide rates in the United States deliberately adopts a Durkheimian perspective. The results were the same as those already established by American studies between the wars, which of course did not refer to Durkheim: suicide rates increase in a depression and decrease in a time of prosperity. But Henry and Short also believed they had found support for the theory of anomie in the fact that fluctuations in the economic situation particularly affect suicide in high social status categories. In fact some of their other results could have been demonstrated to support the hypothesis of progressive anomie (Besnard 1987a:176). This interesting study had no real effect, however. Twelve years later, Pierce set out to validate Durkheim's hypothesis – against Henry and Short – by showing that the suicide rate (for men in the US) varied directly with the degree of change in public perception of the economic situation (measured by a stock-exchange index), regardless of the direction of this change. Pierce's study was not even criticized until fourteen years after it was published, by Marshall and Hodge (1981). Meanwhile, it had not even been mentioned by Hamermesh and Soss (1974), who made one of the first attempts to appropriate suicide as an object for economic reasoning. We see to what degree the Durkheimian theme of economic anomie was left by the wayside. It is true that given the number of refutations that had accumulated since Halbwachs, the hypothesis of an anomie of prosperity could hardly do well in the field of statistical study of suicide (Chauvel 1997).

Investigations into the social topography of suicide also appealed to the regulation side of Durkheim's theory. Already suggested by Henry and Short, this research path was taken, and opened, by Edwin H. Powell (1958), who believed a curvilinear relation could be observed between social status and suicide; the anomie hypothesis might be used to account for the frequency of suicide among the upper classes. When this relation was finally challenged (relatively late in the US due to a lack of adequate data), research took two new directions: study of the impact of downward social mobility on suicide – Breed's work (1963) was conceived with reference to Durkheim, while an earlier study on the same subject (Potterfield and Gibbs 1960) had been conducted without any reference to either anomie or Durkheim – and the rediscovery of fatalistic suicide.

Fatalism bloomed in 1967, the very year of Douglas' book (1967), in which Durkheim's theory is presented as a model of balance between two pairs of opposed forces, and Allardt's article (1967), which links fatalism with the forced division of labour. Fatalism was also just the thing to account for the frequency of suicide among the underprivileged classes (Maris 1967) and among blacks (Breed 1970). This led to a slight increase in interest in the 'regulation' dimension: in Rushing (1968) it was a matter of choosing between the anomic and the fatalist hypotheses; in Maris (1969) the two were combined in a rather vague explanatory model.

In the 1970s the notions of anomie and fatalism virtually ebbed out of sociological literature on suicide, finding refuge only in peripheral journals with few readers or outside the discipline.

Of all the components of Durkheim's work, the oblivion into which his theory of conjugal regulation fell – the idea that marriage benefits the man but not the woman – was the most complete, at first because the theory was not generally understood (see for example Cashion 1970), then because it has been shown that we are missing the data that would enable us really to test it (Besnard 1982, 1997). One of the rare studies in the sociology of suicide in the late 1970s that does allude to anomie – and rarer yet, to the conjugal and domestic variety – both thoroughly rejects and thoroughly fails to understand this Durkheimian theme (Danigelis and Pope 1979).

During the 1970s, moreover, *Suicide* ceased to be the work by Durkheim that most inspired American sociologists, and was dethroned by *The Division of Labour in Society*. Over the decade, all important American sociology journals published studies attempting to formalize and test Durkheim's model of social change (examples abound to demonstrate this new interest). And rather astoundingly, *The Division of Labour in Society* took the place of *Suicide* as a source of inspiration for studies seeking to account for variations in criminality (Webb 1972; Krohn 1978; Messner 1982) and even variations in suicide (Miley and Micklin 1972). Perhaps we should interpret the flagging interest in *Suicide* as a consequence of critiques of suicide statistics formulated during the 1960s (namely Douglas 1967 and Baechler 1975), though these were fragile and even refutable (Besnard 1976).

Since the 1980s, Durkheim's legacy in the sociology of suicide seems clearly dominated by the question of the relation between religion and suicide. We remain, then, concerned with egoistic suicide, and come back to the most common usage of the work. A regressive tendency, some will say, because the 'religion and suicide' industry has also reactivated a methodological approach that had been somewhat abandoned in the 1960s and 1970s – I refer to the use of ecological correlations. Durkheim has thus come to serve as a legitimating precursor in the matters of both subject and approach.

Because many of the numerous studies on this theme were published in major American sociology reviews, *Suicide* was thus thrust back to the forefront of the discipline (examples are Breault and Barkey 1982, Breault 1986 and Bainbridge 1989). All these studies involve calculating correlations between aggregate data at different levels: that of the country, for the most rustic, but more often (because this is essentially an American industry) that of territorial units in the United States such as counties or groups of counties, metropolitan areas, and, in some cases, states. The dependent variable is of course suicide; the independent ones are percentage of the population affiliated with the different religious denominations and/or overall religious affiliation. The most sophisticated studies make use of several control variables. The results of the studies are fairly contradictory, which leads to both new studies and methodological debate on the choice of territorial unit or the ecological fallacy problem.

Even on the (negative) relation between rates of religious affiliation and suicide, American sociologists of suicide are not unanimous. The results are even more uncertain when it comes to the differences between religious denominations, namely the great 'Catholic–Protestant' opposition. One of the most interesting studies (Pescolido and Georgiana 1989), which identifies 27 religious denominations, finds Catholics to be in the most favourable situation, and accepts the idea – though without offering empirical support for it – of a curvilinear relation between degree of integration and suicide (with Catholics situated at the bottom of the curve). The authors, who reread Durkheim with the help of Simmel, reformulate the notion of integration in terms of network theory. Moreover, this interpretation in terms of social support has received the widest acceptance. The most recent study (Ellison *et al.* 1997) observes no autonomous effect of Catholicism or religious affiliation, instead finding a negative relation between suicide and the degree of a territorial unit's religious homogeneity.

We may note that in this last study, the ecological approach is justified by the choice of independent variable – religious homogeneity – which is indeed a structural variable. This is no longer operative when what is being measured is the effect of belonging to this or that religious denomination. The reference to Durkheim seems that much more necessary in this sociological literature given that he is commonly presented as a proponent of using aggregate data. But this is to forget that the most thorough and fully developed demonstrations in *Suicide* are based on characteristics of people who have committed suicide taken at the individual level. This is obviously the case for the study of the effect of marital status, based as we know on Mauss' examination of 25,500 individual suicide files. And it is even true for the chapter on religion, though in this chapter Durkheim conforms much more to the ecological approach – first at the level of countries, then the German provinces, and finally the Swiss cantons, a precious laboratory because they combine religions and languages. But Durkheim did not settle for these data alone. His demonstration of the effect of religious affiliation is only complete, as Selvin noted (1958), because of the data on individuals, borrowed from statistics on German-speaking provinces or countries in which the suicide's religion was known.

A century later it is therefore rather amusing to see Kevin Breault, one of the most authoritative and productive representatives of the ecological approach applied to the religion–suicide link, throw in the towel, affirming there is no justification for the ecological study of suicide and adopting the formula 'no more aggregate studies' as one of the 'new rules of sociological method' (Breault 1994:24).

The same difficulty may be found in investigations into the effect of family and marriage on suicide. There, too, suicidological works have almost all established ecological or time-series correlations (Besnard 1997). It is true that we are missing one essential piece of information: whether or not those who committed suicide had children. Moreover, in cause-of-death statistics there is no trace of the intermediate situations (non-married couples) so common today. One of the reasons Durkheim's book is still so relevant is that in over a century we have not really progressed in this area: we have lacked and continue to lack necessary data. It can even be said that we have regressed, because Durkheim himself had already taken on the problem – with its own particular difficulties (Besnard 1973) – of assessing suicide rates among spouses and widows and widowers according to whether or not they had children. We should therefore not be surprised to see Durkheim's figures still being used in debates on gender-related social differences within the family (Besnard 1987b; Dubar 1987).

Starting in the 1970s, *Suicide* became a classic in the most ordinary sense of the term: a basic text for the teaching of sociology. In France, for example, the work was republished by the Presses Universitaires de France twice in the 1960s and three times in the 1970s, and it is second in sales only to the *Rules*. This has been the case since 1981, when both works were published in the Quadrige small paperback collection, but the gap between them is closing.

No visible trace of a decline in popularity from this point of view, then. But decline is inevitable. It seems to me we may perceive the first signs of it in the sociological literature proper of the 1970s. And the debate around 'religion and suicide' that has been raging since the 1980s should not delude us: it represents a shrinking of the work's legacy down to the object 'suicide' and even to one of the least original parts of the book (at least in terms of data and data analysis). A century after it was published *Suicide* may well have entered into a declining phase in the cycle of intellectual fashion.

Notes

This chapter was translated from French by Amy Jacobs.

1 *agrégé*: one who has passed the *agrégation*, a yearly national recruiting competition for teaching posts in secondary education.

2 Massimo Borlandi has written an in-depth study of the relations between Richard, Durkheim and Tarde (1997, unpublished). Gaston Richard returned to *Suicide* in 1903 in a brief textbook entitled *Notions élémentaires de sociologie* designed to complete his *Manuel de morale* – this, then, was the first time Durkheim's work was mentioned in a textbook. Richard's account is flat and biased; he takes the opportunity to reject Durkheim's interpretation of the relation between education and suicide: 'the specious hypothesis has been ventured that a taste for knowledge already denotes the dissolution of social and religious beliefs' (Richard 1903:39).

3 It is hard to know who wrote this review: Elie Halévy, Célestin Bouglé or Xavier Léon, editor in chief of the *Revue?*

4 Durkheim would use the same argument regarding homicide in a course he gave in 1908–9 (Durkheim 1975b, 2:298).

5 We find the same rejection of Durkheim's theory of anomie in Halbwachs' review of his own book for the *Année sociologique*: 'What then is the reason for this surprising increase in suicides that has continued for half a century? Is it only, as Durkheim believed, the state of disorder and deregulation (anomie) that result from the weakening of traditional ties? Is it not rather the increased complication of social life . . .?' (Halbwachs 1935:179).

6 This explains why Merton (1938:674) refers to Mayo rather than Durkheim when introducing the term 'anomie' in 'Social Structure and Anomie'. But in *Social Theory and Social Structure* (1949) he refers directly to *Suicide*, in particular to Durkheim's analysis of the religion–suicide relation, to show how an empirical generalization can be incorporated into a sociological theory.

7 The harvest of 1958 was particularly abundant as this was the centenary of Durkheim's birth.

8 On the divergent interpretations of *Suicide*'s theoretical framework and the strong tendency to indentify anomie and egoism, see Besnard (1987a:48–81).

Bibliography

Allardt, E. (1967) 'Durkheim e la sociologia politica', *Rassegna Italiana di Sociologia* 8(1):47–66.

Alpert, H. (1939) *Emile Durkheim and His Sociology*, New York: Columbia University Press.

Anon. (1897) Review of E. Durkheim, *Le Suicide*, *Revue de Métaphysique et de Morale* 5, November supplement, 2–3.

Baechler, J. (1975) *Les Suicides*, Paris: Calman-Lévy.

Bainbridge, W. S. (1989) 'The Religious Ecology of Deviance', *American Sociological Review* 54:288–95.

Bayet, A. (1922) *Le Suicide et la morale*, Paris: Alcan.

Berrios, G. and Mohanna, M. (1990) 'Durkheim and French Psychiatric Views on Suicide during the 19th Century: A Conceptual View', *British Journal of Psychiatry* 156:1–9.

Besnard, P. (1973) 'Durkheim et les femmes ou *Le Suicide* inachevé', *Revue Française de Sociologie* 14(1):27–61.

(1976) 'Anti- ou anté-durkheimisme? Contribution au débat sur les statistiques officielles du suicide', *Revue française de sociologie* 17(2):313–41.

(1979) 'La Formation de l'équipe de *L'Année sociologique*', *Revue Française de Sociologie* 20(1):7–48.

(1982) 'Durkheim and Sexual Anomie: A Comment on Tiryakian', *Social Forces* 61(1):284–6.

(ed.) (1983) *The Sociological Domain*, Cambridge: Cambridge University Press.

(1985) 'The Americanization of Anomie at Harvard', *Knowledge and Society* 6:41–53.

(1987a) *L'Anomie, ses usages et des fonctions dans la discipline sociologique depuis Durkheim*, Paris: Presses Universitaires de France.

(1987b) 'Les Sociologistes et le sexe. Réponse à Claude Dubar', *Revue Française de Sociologie* 28(1):137–44.

(1993) 'La Diffusion de l'édition française', in P. Besnard, M. Borlandi and W. P. Vogt (eds) *Division du travail et lien social. La thèse de Durkheim un siècle après*, Paris: Presses Universitaires de France.

(1995) 'Durkheim critique de Tarde: des *Règles* au *Suicide*', in M. Borlandi and L. Mucchielli (eds) *La Sociologie et sa mèthode.* Les Règles *de Durkheim un siècle après*, Paris: L'Harmattan. pp. 221–43.

(1997) 'Mariage et suicide: la théorie durkheimienne de la régulation conjugale á l'épreuve d'un siècle', *Revue Française de Sociologie* 38(4):735–58.

Blondel, C. (1933) *Le Suicide*, Strasbourg: Librairie Universitaire d'Alsace.

Bosco, A. (1897) Review of E. Durkheim, *Suicide*, *Rivista Italiana di Sociologia* 1(3):376–83.

Boudon, R. (1967) *L'Analyse mathématique des faits sociaux*, Paris: Plon.

(1968) *A quoi sert la notion de 'structure'?*, Paris: Gallimard.

(1969) *Les Méthodes en sociologie*, Paris: Presses Universitaires de France.

Bouglé, C. and Déat, M. (1921) *Guide de l'étudiant en sociologie*, Paris: Garnier.

Bouglé, C. and Raffault, J. (1926) *Eléments de sociologie, textes choisis et ordonnés*, Paris: Alcan.

Boudon, R. and Lazarsfeld, P. (eds) (1966) *L'Analyse empirique de la causalité*, Paris–La Haye: Mouton.

Borlandi, M. (1997) 'Quand Richard se professait durkheimien', unpublished.

Boz, P. (1897) 'La Démographie et la statistique dans les sciences morales et sociales', *Revue Socialiste* 26(151):85–92.

Breault, K. D. (1986) 'Suicide in America: A Test of Durkheim's Theory of Religious and Family Integration, 1933–1980', *American Journal of Sociology* 92(3):628–56.

(1994) 'Was Durkheim Right? A Critical Survey of the Empirical Literature on *Le Suicide*', in D. Lester (ed.) *Emile Durkheim* Le Suicide *100 Years Later*, Philadelphia: Charles Press, pp. 11–29.

Breault, K. D. and Barkey, K. (1982) 'A Comparative Analysis of Durkheim's Theory of Egoistic Suicide', *Sociological Quarterly* 23(3):321–31.

Breed, W. (1963) 'Occupational Mobility and Suicide among White Males', *American Sociological Review* 28(2):179–88.

(1970) 'The Negro and Fatalistic Suicide', *Pacific Sociological Review* 13(3):156–62.

Cashion, B. G. (1970) 'Durkheim's Concept of Anomie and Its Relationship to Divorce', *Sociology and Social Research* 55(1):72–81.

Cavan R. (1928) *Suicide*, Chicago: University of Chicago Press.

Chauvel, L. (1997) 'L'Uniformisation du taux de suicide masculin selon l'âge', *Revue Française de Sociologie* 38(4):681–734.

Danigelis, N. and Pope, W. (1979) 'Durkheim's Theory of Suicide as Applied to the Family: An Empirical Test', *Social Forces* 57(4):1081–106.

Davy, G. (1911) *Emile Durkheim. Choix de textes avec étude du système sociologique*, Paris: Louis-Michaud.

(1920) 'Emile Durkheim: l'œuvre', *Revue de Métaphysique et de Morale* 27:71–112.

(1924a) *Eléments de sociologie* I: *La sociologie politique*, Paris: Delagrave.

(1924b) 'La Sociologie', in G. Dumas (ed.) *Traité de psychologie*, vol. 2, Paris: Alcan, pp. 765–810.

(1973) *L'Homme, le fait social et le fait politique*, Paris: Mouton.

De Greef, G. (1907) *La Structure générale des sociétés* I: *La Loi de limitation*, Brussels: Larcier.

Déat, M. (1925) *Sociologie*, Paris: Alcan.

Deloire, P. (1897) Review of E. Durkheim, *Le Suicide*, *Revue Socialiste* 26(155):635–6.

Dohrenwend, B. P. (1959) 'Egoism, Altruism, Anomie, and Fatalism: A Conceptual Analysis of Durkheim's Types', *American Sociological Review* 24(4):466–72.

Douglas, J. D. (1967) *The Social Meanings of Suicide*, Princeton, NJ: Princeton University Press.

Dubar, C. (1987) 'A propos de l'interprétation du *Suicide* de Durkheim par Philippe Besnard', *Revue Française de Sociologie* 28(1):127–36.

Durkheim, E. (1893b) *De la division du travail sociale: étude sur l'organisation des sociétés supérieures*, Paris: Alcan.

— (t.1933b) *The Division of Labor in Society*, by G. Simpson, New York: Macmillan.

(1895a) *Les Règles de la méthode sociologique*, Paris: Alcan.

— (t.1938b) *The Rules of Sociological Method*, by S. A. Solovay and J. H. Mueller, Chicago: University of Chicago Press.

(1897a) *Le Suicide: étude de sociologie*, Paris: Alcan.

(1910) Review of C. Jacquart, *Essais de statistique morale* I: *Le suicide*, *Année Sociologique* 11:515.

(1975b) *Textes*, 3 vols, Paris: Minuit.

(1998a) *Lettres à Marcel Mauss*, Paris: Presses Universitaires de France.

Elliott, M. A. and Merril, F. E. (1934) *Social Disorganization*, New York: Harper.

Ellison, C. G., Burr, J. A. and McCall, P. L. (1997) 'Religious Homogeneity and Metropolitan Suicide Rates', *Social Forces* 76(1):273–99.

Essertier, D. (1927) *Psychologie et sociologie. Essai de bibliographie critique*, Paris: Alcan.

Faguet, E. (1898) 'Sur le suicide', *Revue Bleue*, 20 April 1898, reprinted in E. Faguet, *Propos littéraires*, 4th series, Paris: Société Française d'Imprimerie et de Librairie, 1907, pp. 321–34.

Faris, R. E. (1948) *Social Disorganization*, New York: Ronald Press.

Fauconnet, P. (1898) Review of E. Durkheim, *Le Suicide*, *Revue Philosophique* 45:422–31.

Fauconnet, P. and Mauss, M. (1901) 'Sociologie', *La Grande Encyclopédie* 30:165–76.

Genevray, H. (1897) Review of G. Tarde, *L'Opposition Universelle*, *Revue Socialiste* 26(155):636–7.

Gehlke, C. E. (1915) *Emile Durkheim's Contributions to Sociological Theory*, New York: Columbia University Press.

Gernet, L. (1917) *Recherches sur le développement de la pensée juridique et morale en Grèce*, Paris: Leroux.

Gibbs, J. P. and Martin, W. T. (1958) 'A Theory of Status Integration and Its Relationship to Suicide', *American Sociological Review* 23(2):140–7.

(1964) *Status Integration and Suicide*, Eugene, OR: University of Oregon Books.

Goblot, E. (1900) Review of *Annales de l'Institut International de Sociologie*, *Revue Philosophique* 49(1):99–103.

Granet, M. (1911) *Contre l'alcoolisme, un programme socialiste*, Paris: Librairie du Parti Socialiste (Cahiers du Socialiste, 11).

(1932) 'Intervention dans le "débat sur l'enseignement de la sociologie"', *Bulletin de l'Institut Français de Sociologie* 2(3):98–107.

Halbwachs, M. (1918) 'La Doctrine d'Emile Durkheim', *Revue Philosophique* 85, 353–411.

(1930) *Les Causes du suicide*, Paris: Alcan.

— (t.1978) by H. Goldblatt, *The Causes of Suicide*, London: Routledge.

(1935) Review of M. Halbwachs, *Les Causes du suicide*, and of E. Durkheim, *Le Suicide*, *Annales Sociologiques*, series C, 1:174–80.

Hamermesh, D. S. and Soss, N. M. (1974) 'An Economic Theory of Suicide', *Journal of Political Economy* 82(1):83–98.

Henry, A. F. and Short, J. F., Jr. (1954) *Suicide and Homicide: Some Economic, Sociological, and Psychological Aspects of Aggression*, Glencoe, IL: Free Press.

Hesse, A. and Gleyse, A. (1922) *Notions de sociologie appliquée à la morale et à l'éducation*, Paris: Alcan.

Hinkle, R. C. (1960) 'Durkheim in American Sociology', in K. H. Volff (ed.) *Emile Durkheim, 1858–1917*, Colombus: Ohio State University Press, pp. 267–95.

Hubert, R. (1925) *Manuel élémentaire de sociologie*, Paris: Delalain.

Isambert, F.-A. (1973) 'Durkheim et la statistique écologique', in *Une nouvelle civilisation? Hommage à Georges Friedmann*, Paris: Gallimard, pp. 93–110.

Jacquart, C. (1908) *Essais de statistique morale* I: *Le Suicide*, Bruxelles: Dewit.

Johnson, B. D. (1965) 'Durkheim's One Cause of Suicide', *American Sociological Review* 30(6):875–86.

Krohn, M. D. (1978) 'A Durkheimian Analysis of International Crime Rate', *Social Forces* 57(2):654–70.

Lacombe, R. (1926) *La Méthode sociologique de Durkheim*, Paris: Alcan.
La Fontaine, A. P. (1926) *La Philosophie d'Emile Durkheim*, Paris: Vrin.
Lalo, C. (1925) *Eléments de sociologie*, Paris: Vuibert.
Lapie, P. (1908) *La Femme dans la famille*, Paris: Doin.
Lunden, W. A. (1947) 'Suicides in France 1910–1943', *American Journal of Sociology* 52(2):321–34.
Maris, R. W. (1967) 'Suicide, Status, and Mobility in Chicago', *Social Forces* 46(2):246–56.
(1969) *Social Forces in Urban Suicide*, Homewood, IL: Dorsey Press.
Marshall, J. R. and Hodge, R. W. (1981) 'Durkheim and Pierce on Suicide and Economic Change', *Social Science Research* 10(2):101–14.
Maunier, R. (1929) *Introduction à la sociologie*, Paris: Alcan.
Mauss, M. (1926) 'Effet physique chez l'individu de l'idée de mort suggérée par la collectivité (Australie, Nouvelle-Zélande)', *Journal de Psychologie* 23:653–69.
(1933) 'La Sociologie en France depuis 1914', in *La Science française*, Paris: Larousse, pp. 36–40.
(1969) *Oeuvres*, 3 vols, Paris: Minuit.
(1997) *Ecrits politiques*, Paris: Seuil.
Mayo, E. (1933) *The Human Problems of an Industrial Civilization*, New York: Macmillan.
Merton, R. K. (1934) 'Durkheim's *Division of Labor in Society*', *American Journal of Sociology* 40:319–28.
(1938) 'Social Structure and Anomie', *American Sociological Review* 3(5):672–82.
(1949) *Social Theory and Social Structure*, Glencoe, IL: Free Press.
Messner, S. F. (1982) 'Societal Development, Social Equality, and Homicide: A Crossnational Test of a Durkheimian Model', *Social Forces* 61(1):225–40.
Miley, J. D. and Micklin, M. (1972) 'Structural Change and the Durkheimian Legacy: A Macrosocial Analysis of Suicide Rates', *American Journal of Sociology* 78(3):657–73.
Mowrer, E. E. (1939) 'A Study of Personal Disorganization', *American Sociological Review* 4(4):475–87.
Paoletti, G. (1995) 'La Réception des *Règles* en France du vivant de Durkheim', in M. Borlandi and L. Mucchielli (eds) *La Sociologie et sa méthode.* Les Règles *de Durkheim un siècle après*, Paris: L'Harmattan, pp. 247–83.
Pareto, V. (1898) Review of E. Durkheim, *Le Suicide*, *Zeitschrift für Sozialwissenschaft* 1:78–80, reprinted in V. Pareto, *Mythes et idéologies*, Genève-Paris: Droz, 1966, pp. 122–4.
Park, R. E. and Burgess, E. W. (1921) *Introduction to the Science of Sociology*, Chicago: University of Chicago Press.
Parsons, T. (1937) *The Structure of Social Action*, New York: McGraw-Hill.
Pescolido, B. A. and Georgianna, S. (1989) 'Durkheim, Suicide and Religion: Toward a Network Theory of Suicide', *American Sociological Review* 54(1):33–48.
Pierce, A. (1967) 'The Economic Cycle and the Social Suicide Rates', *American Sociological Review* 32(3):457–62.
Pillon, F. (1898) Review of E. Durkheim, *Le Suicide*, *L'Année Philosophique* 8:252–4.
Pope, W. (1976) *Durkheim's* Suicide: *A Classic Analyzed*, Chicago: University of Chicago Press.

Potterfield, A. L. (1949) 'Indices of Suicide and Homicide by States and Cities', *American Sociological Review* 14(4):481–90.

(1952) 'Suicide and Crime in the Social Structure of an Urban Setting: Fort North, 1930–1950', *American Sociological Review* 17(3):341–3.

Potterfield, A. L. and Gibbs, J. P. (1960) 'Occupational Prestige and Social Mobility of Suicides in New Zealand', *American Journal of Sociology* 66(2):147–52.

Powell, E. H. (1958) 'Occupation, Status, and Suicide: Toward a Redefinition of Anomie', *American Sociological Review* 23(2):131–9.

Richard, G. (1898) Review of E. Durkheim, *Le Suicide*, *Année Sociologique* 1:397–407.

(1903) *Notions élémentaires de sociologie*, Paris: Delagrave.

(1923) 'L'Athéisme dogmatique en sociologie religieuse', *Revue d'Histoire et de Philosophie Religieuses* 125–37, 229–61.

(1925) 'La Morale sociologique et la pathologie de la Société', *Revue d'Histoire et de Philosophie Religieuse* 5(4):340–68.

(1930) 'La Pathologie sociale d'Emile Durkheim', *Revue Internationale de Sociologie* 38(3–4):113–26.

Rushing, W. A. (1968) 'Income, Unemployment, and Suicide: An Occupational Study', *Sociological Quarterly* 9(4):493–503.

Sainsbury, P. (1955) *Suicide in London: An Ecological Study*, London: Chapman and Hall.

Selvin, H. (1958) 'Durkheim's *Suicide* and Problems of Empirical Research', *American Journal of Sociology* 63(6):607–19.

Simiand, F. (1898) 'L'Année sociologique 1897', *Revue de Métaphysique et de Morale* 6:608–43.

Strauss, J. H. and Strauss, M. A. (1953) 'Suicide, Homicide and Social Structure in Ceylon', *American Journal of Sociology* 58(4):461–9.

Tosti, G. (1898a) 'Suicide in the Light of Recent Studies', *American Journal of Sociology* 3(4):464–78.

(1898b) Review of E. Durkheim, *Suicide*, *Psychological Review* 4:424–6.

(1898c) 'The Delusions of Durkheim's Sociological Objectivism', *American Journal of Sociology* 4(1):171–7.

Tournier, C. (1898) Review of E. Durkheim, *Le Suicide*, *Archives d'Anthropologie Criminelle* 326–35.

Vogt, W. P. (1993) 'L'Influence de la *Division du travail* sur la sociologie américaine', in P. Besnard, M. Borlandi and W. P. Vogt (eds) *Division du travail et lien social. La thèse de Durkheim un siècle après*, Paris: Presses Universitaires de France, pp. 215–30.

Webb, S. D. (1972) 'Crime and the Division of Labor: Testing a Durkheimian Model', *American Journal of Sociology* 78(3):643–56.

Winock, M. (1997) *Le Siècle des intellectuels*, Paris: Seuil.

9

THE RECEPTION OF *SUICIDE* IN RUSSIA

Alexander Gofman

Before approaching the problem of the reception of *Suicide* in Russia, it is interesting to note the nature of Russia's reception in *Suicide*. Durkheim, as Marx before him, did not regard Russia as a subject and recipient for his sociological theories and research. In *Suicide* he notes that Russia 'is only European geographically' (Durkheim 1897a/t.1951a:50).[1] A passing comment, this opinion probably had no great import for him: taken in context, it was probably quite simply intended to explain or justify the fact that suicides in Russia were omitted from his analysis, which in turn, is explained by his lack of the necessary statistics.

The Russian edition of *Suicide* (Durkheim 1897a/t.1912) was the book's first publication outside France. (Durkheim's two other classics – *De la division du travail social* and *Les Règles de la mèthode sociologique* – were also translated for the first time in Russia.) But the appearance of the original French version already aroused quite considerable interest in Russia.

In April 1898 Nikolaï Roussanov,[2] under the pseudonym H. K. (Cyrillic alphabet), published a detailed analysis of Durkheim's *Suicide* in one of his 'Lettres de la France' in the revue *Rousskoïe bogatstvo* (Roussanov 1898). The reviewer emphasizes the advantages of the sociological approach that Durkheim persistently and skilfully utilizes *vis-à-vis* attempts to explain suicide by anthropological, racial, psychological and other causes. On the other hand, Roussanov notes the sociological extremism of some of Durkheim's propositions. While acknowledging the injustice of the general assessment of his previous books by Tarde – which explains the intensity of the polemic with the latter in *Suicide* – the author nevertheless states that Durkheim is not right to deny completely the role of imitation in suicide.

Roussanov rates the Durkheimian typology of suicides as a whole very highly (1898:87ff.). However, he considers the introduction of the 'anomic' type next to the 'egoist' type superfluous, on the grounds that it is a species of the latter. Anomic suicide, in his opinion, is the same as egoist suicide, but committed while 'in an impulsive and unbalanced state of mind' (1898:88).

The author of the review has obviously not interpreted the idea of anomie in Durkheim entirely adequately, which can be seen in the following proposition: 'Thus, what is, in the author's words, a disorganized anomic phenomenon, in fact expresses the permanent tendency which will only disappear under the regulation of social production' (Roussanov 1898:97). But Durkheim himself rightly regarded anomie as the absence of the normative regulation of social production. Therefore, the existence of such regulation, according to him, meant the absence of the anomic condition, and not the means of its elimination, as the critic thinks.

Roussanov acknowledges that the highlighting of the altruistic type of suicide is well founded, but its analysis is not satisfactory. In his view, this is explained by the absence of a solid basis of fact and because 'Durkheim is an abstract sociologist par excellence who starts from certain sometimes successful, sometimes hazardous, abstract propositions; it seems that he does not find descriptive sociology and the facts pleasing' (Roussanov 1898:93). In addition, the critic notes Durkheim's poor knowledge of ethnographical facts. It is strange that in his critique of the Durkheimian theory of the division of labour, written in 1895, he noted that Durkheim's theoretical views were based on a large number of facts, including ethnographical facts.

Demonstrating the inconsistency of the psychological explanation of suicide, Durkheim states that neurasthenia has different effects in different social circumstances. He illustrates this statement by a comparison of French and Russian literature:

> In fact in the writers of both nations one senses an unhealthy fragility of the nervous system, a certain absence of mental and moral equilibrium. But what different social consequences this same condition, at once biological and psychological, produces! While Russian literature is idealistic to excess, while the melancholy which imbues it, emanating from an active compassion for the sadness of mankind, is one of those salutary sadnesses which stir up faith and stimulate action, French literature prides itself on only expressing sentiments of mournful despair and is a reflection of a disturbing state of depression. That is how the same organic condition can serve almost contrary social ends.
>
> (Durkheim 1897a/t.1951a:77, n.30)

On the subject of this excursion into the comparative analysis of two literatures, Roussanov remarks ironically:

> Neurasthenics in general and particularly Russian neurasthenics can certainly be grateful to the author for his protection of their 'absence of mental and moral equilibrium'. But while agreeing with Durkheim that their activity can have a different character, in

> accordance with the state of the society which surrounds them, it would at least be difficult not to see that they are in any case invalids and that, in the words of the proverb, 'one always falls on the side one is leaning towards'; it is just by these abnormal men that the pressure of the social order is most strongly felt, often driving them outside life, outside consciousness and the poetry of the struggle.
>
> (Roussanov 1898:78)

In this same critique Roussanov takes a negative view of the Durkheimian 'realist' interpretation of the *conscience collective*, namely the notion of it as a phenomenon existing outside or above individuals. Lastly, he took a very sceptical view of the Durkheimian recommendation to eliminate anomie and to lower the number of suicides by the development and extension of professional groups or corporations. In his opinion the solution of the problem of suicides lies in the triumph of the conviction which guides all the individual's personal energy towards the achievement of social goals. Then 'each member of the union sees the development and the happiness of his person in the development and happiness of others. But this goal can only be achieved when the individual is made up in a universal way, which excludes the present division of labour' (Roussanov 1898:100).

In May the same year Ostrogorskiï (1898) published an analysis of Durkheim's work containing a minimum of value judgements. He had a high opinion of the book but nonetheless noted the need to analyse the psychological factors of suicide that Durkheim had rejected. Ostrogorskiï emphasized the methodological importance of Durkheim's study, his reliance on facts, on statistical data. This, in his opinion, distinguished the study from many other sociological works, which represented 'solely very ingenious theories that are only rarely supported by brilliant examples' (Roussanov 1898:56).

Ossip Lourié (1898) in his very concise and not very adequate account of *Suicide* has placed its author in the school of sociology that emphasizes collective psychology. He stresses that in his study Durkheim defends the strictly scientific point of view and supports all his observations and conclusions with a large number of statistical data 'drawn from all the civilized countries of Europe and America, except Russia' (Lourié 1898:319–20).

V. A. Bazarov (the pseudonym of Vladimir Roudnev, 1874–1939), philosopher and economist, who was at first a Bolshevik and then ranked as a 'revisionist', published a review of the Russian edition of *Suicide* in which he revised and corrected the translation. He thought very highly of Durkheim's study. However, his attitude towards the Durkheimian project for professional groups was profoundly negative, because in his opinion the state in its classic democratic form was not yet out of date. Nevertheless he agreed with Durkheim and the syndicalists that 'when the end of the present atomism and "anomie" comes, the state should only fulfill functions of general supervision and supreme control; only the professional unions, the syndicates, will be in a position to fulfill the truly creative role in the cause of the material and mental renewal of society' (Bazarov 1912:1150).

Vladimir Iakovenko (1912), a well-known psychiatrist, in his review of the Russian edition of Durkheim's book, noted that some of his propositions were ill-founded and a priori; the depiction of neurasthenia and monomania set out there was already out-of-date. Notwithstanding, in his opinion the book deserved the widest circulation because it transferred the question of the growth in the number of suicides from the 'sterile domain of individual psychology' into the domain 'of social phenomena which they certainly are; the practical measure suggested there entirely coincides with the professional movement which is becoming stronger and stronger' (Iakovrnko 1912:36).

Yet another account of the Russian edition of Durkheim's work (this time anonymous) was published in the revue *Rousskoïe bogatstvo* in 1913. It characterizes Durkheim as one of the most eminent sociologists of the day, whose name was well known to the Russian public. That was why his book did not need special recommendation. The book 'demonstrates the author's great talent as well as his vast scholarship' (Anon. 1913:381). Noting Durkheim's desire to attribute a precise meaning to the idea of 'imitation', which is not present in Tarde, the anonymous critic then goes on to describe exclusively the weaknesses of Durkheim's book, although he acknowledges 'the high qualities' it possesses. In his opinion, the principal shortcoming of Durkheim's sociology in general and of his interpretation of suicide in particular consists of the humiliation 'of individual psychology to the glory of sociology'. He does not deny the important role of the social factor in suicide, but he thinks that Durkheim 'because of his dubious statistical research' has not demonstrated his principal thesis on the social nature of suicide. Contrary to the thesis of the French sociologist, the critic *en passant* presents a hypothesis whereby the number of suicides depends on evolution and the degree of 'men's sense of self-preservation' (Anon. 1913:381).

Mikhaïl Taréev, representing the orthodox Christian point of view, also replied to the Russian edition of *Suicide* with quite a long and detailed analysis. After noting the considerable growth in the number of suicides at that period, he approved of the translation 'of the serious work by the well-known French sociologist'.

In general Taréev's verdict on the moral character of Durkheim's study and his analysis of the moral and social causes of suicide was positive:

> The sociologist's discourse, from the first word to the last, involuntarily becomes a sermon filled with animation. That path, at the end of which there yawns a terrible abyss of voluntary deaths, is recognised as something that must not be. Thus a whole system of

> social life is created and the sociology of suicides merges with moral philosophy. We are persuaded yet again that moral science considered as a *conditio sine qua non* of human life and above all of social life is based on natural necessity.
>
> (Taréev 1912:475)

Nevertheless, the critic certainly does not agree with Durkheim's practical conclusions and recommendations, specifically the idea of corporations and the pessimistic view of the future of religion's role in the prevention of suicides. According to Durkheim, Catholicism (which has 'social strength') leaves no room for free research, therefore it is unacceptable to men of science. Protestantism is impotent in this respect. Durkheim mentions in passing the Greek Catholic Church, but he notes that the low degree of suicides among Greek Catholics cannot be attributed with any degree of certainty to the influence of religion since the civilization of the country in which they live is profoundly different from the civilization of other European countries. As for Orthodoxy, Durkheim does not even mention it – and this the critic interprets as 'the absence of attention to Christian Orthodoxy usually found among western scholars, whereas it is this latter which indicates the only way [out of] this vicious circle. It is in Christian Orthodoxy that we place our hopes in the struggle with the present epidemic of suicides' (Taréev 1912:476).

It is precisely this epidemic in Russia, mentioned in many articles and analyses devoted to Durkheim's book, which has aroused great interest. A large number of intellectuals have seen it as a more serious and more convincing response to the question of the causes of suicide than previous answers, which were often purely literary or journalistic.

Nikolaï Berdiaev also evaluated Durkheim's study from a religious and moral point of view in his short work published in 1931. But his assessment was far more critical than Taréev's. Starting from the thesis that 'only the Christian conscience discloses the truth about suicide and establishes a just attitude towards it', he stated that the sociological point of view, as exemplified by the Durkheimian study, is 'fundamentally false': 'it only sees the external aspect of phenomena' and 'does not penetrate the interior of life' (Berdiaev 1992/t.1931:15). However, it can be supposed that the ideal of corporatist socialism that Berdiaev defended in his social theory must have been formulated under the influence of the Durkheimian idea of the need for the introduction of corporations in contemporary social life. A short book on the same subject by Pitirim Sorokin published in 1913 also shows the influence of the Durkheimian study of suicide.

It is curious that there is a copy of the Russian edition of Durkheim's *Suicide* in the personal library of V. I. Lenin in the Kremlin.[3] But no reaction on Lenin's part to this book or the others is to be found, other than the words he underlined in the book by A. Rey, *Modern Philosophy* (1908) about what 'sociology [as opposed to metaphysics], thanks to the works by Durkheim and his school, worked and acted . . .' (Lenin 1963:511).

The Russian reception of this work by Durkheim, unlike the reception accorded his previous studies (see in particular Gofman 1997), was on the whole almost unanimously favourable, despite some unimportant criticisms. One can suppose that this attitude was influenced by the importance of the problem of suicide in contemporary Russia, as well as by the character and scale of the problems which Durkheim tackles. Since his subject is relatively limited and does not consist, as in the earlier books, of the universal and fundamental problems of the nature of society and sociology, his theses did not touch the deep 'theoretical emotions' which pre-existed in Russian society, and therefore did not arouse much doctrinaire discussion and dissension.

Notes

1 It is strange to compare this opinion with that of the eminent Russian historian V. O. Kliutchevskiï: 'Historically, Russia is certainly not Asia; but geographically it is not completely Europe. It is a transitional country, interspersed between two worlds. Culture has bound it indissolubly to Europe, but nature has marked it with features and influences which always attract it towards Asia and which attract Asia to it' (Kliutchevskiï 1987:65).

2 Nikolaï Roussanov (1859–1939) participated in the populist movement (*narodniks*), and then joined the social-revolutionary party (*essers*). He emigrated for a lengthy period, first under the Tsarist regime, then under the Bolsheviks. He lived in France for many years. He attended Durkheim's courses at Bordeaux University and in 1895 published a lengthy analysis of *De la division du travail social.*

3 Biobliotéka V. I. Lénina v Kremle, Katalogue (Library of V. I. Lenin in the Kremlin, Catalogue), Moscow, 1961.

Bibliography

Anon. (1913) 'Compte rendu de Durkheim, E., *Samooubiïstvo* (*Suicide*)', *Rousskoïe bogatstvo* 3:381–6.

Bazarov, V. (1912) 'Samooubiïstvo kak sotsial iavlenie (Po povodou rousskogo izdania knigui E. Durkheim *Suicide*) [Suicide as a social phenomenon. A propos the Russian edition of the book by E. Durkheim]', *Zaprossy Gizni* 19:1143–52.

Berdiaev, N. (1992) *O samooubiïstve. Psikhologuitcheskiï etiud* [*A propos suicide. Psychological study*], Moscow: Moscow University, 1992. 1st edition Paris, YMCA Press, 1931. French translation, *Le Suicide. Etude psychologique*, translated by E. P. Bellenson, le Cep, 1953.

Durkheim, E. (1897a) *Le Suicide: étude de sociologie.* Paris: Alcan.

— (t.1912) Translated by V. A. Bazarov, *Samooubiïstvo etiud*, preface and bibliography of Russian works on suicide by Dr G. I. Gordon, ed. N. P. Karbasnikov.

Gofman, A. (1997) 'La Réception russe des *Règles* – Durkheim d'un siècle à l'autre. Lectures actuelles des *Règles de la méthode sociologique*', ed. Cuin Ch., Paris: Presses Universitaires de France, pp. 83–101.

Iakovenko, V. (1912) 'Compte rendu de Durkheim, E., *Samooubiïstvo (Suicide)*', *Vestnik Vospitania* 6:23–36.

Kliutchevskiï, V. O. (1987) *Course rousskoï* [*Course in Russian history*], vol. 1, Moscow: Mysl (1st edition, 1904).

Lenin, V. I. (1963) 'Zametchania na knigué A. Reya *Sovremennaïa filossofia*' (Notes on the book by A. Rey, *La Philosophie moderne*, Paris, 1908), in V. I. Lenin, *Polnoïe sobranie sotchinenii* [*Complete Works*], vol. 29, Moscow: Politizdat, pp. 475–525.

Lourié, O. (1898) 'Review of E. Durkheim, *Le Suicide*', *Voprossy filossofii I psikhologuii*, 4(44):319–25.

Ostrogorskiï, A. (1998) 'Samooubiïstvo I ikh ego pritchiny [Suicides and their causes]', Review of E. Durkheim, *Le Suicide. Severnyi Vestnik* 5:23–56.

Roussanov, N. S. (H. K.) (1898) 'Samooubiïstvo i ego pritchiny (Pismo iz Frantsii) [Suicide and Its Causes (A Letter from France)]', Review of E. Durkheim, *Suicide*, *Rousskoie bogatstvo* 4:67–100.

Sorokin, P. (1913) 'Samooubiïstvo kak obchtchestvennoiï iavlenie [Suicide as a Social Phenomenon]', Riga: Naouka I gizn.

Taréev, M. (1912) 'Samooubiïstvo kak sotsialnoïe iavlenie [Suicide as a Social Phenomenon] Compte rendu de Durkheim, E., *Samooubiïstvo*', *Bogoslovskiï Vestnik* 2:451–76.

10

MARRIAGE AND SUICIDE

Testing the Durkheimian theory of marital regulation a century later

Philippe Besnard

Emile Durkheim's study of the effect of marriage on the frequency of suicide may be considered a central – if not *the* central – point of his book. The question is discussed in relation to both egoistic and anomic suicide and provides a unifying principle for the theory's empirical foundation.

For egoistic suicide, Durkheim wanted to show that 'domestic society' – family life – and not 'conjugal society' – the fact of being married – is what protects people from suicide. He therefore tried to isolate the specific effect of marriage in itself by distinguishing between childless couples and couples with children. Lack of data made it impossible for him fully to investigate or prove his hypothesis, but it should be said straightaway that no one has done better since. The census data available to him failed to provide Durkheim with the distribution of couples with and without children by age, while today we lack basic information on persons who have committed suicide.

Durkheim concluded that married men without children were less likely to kill themselves than single men but much more likely to take their own lives than married men with children. Married women without children, on the other hand, were more prone to suicide than single women. This clearly proved that it was not marriage itself that protected people from suicide: 'The immunity of married persons in general is thus due, wholly for one sex and largely for the other, to the influence not of conjugal society but of the family society' (Durkheim 1897a/t.1951a:189).

The question is discussed in greater detail in the theory of conjugal anomie. Commentators have almost uniformly misunderstood this aspect of the book, for Durkheim's demonstration is both brilliant and wrought with difficulties. It must be understood first of all that when he introduced the factor of divorce he was not interested in any direct relation between divorce and suicide but rather in the effect of divorce – the fact that divorce is possible – on the effect of marriage on suicide. The option of divorce has the effect of weakening the marital tie; it thus impinges on suicide by modifying the effect of marriage on suicide. That effect may be measured by the gap between suicide rates for married and single persons, what Durkheim called 'coefficients of preservation'; in this case the preservation of married persons compared with that of single persons.

The weakening of the marriage tie does not have the same effect on men as it does on women because, as just explained, marriage alone, without children, protects men from suicide whereas for women it increases the likelihood of suicide. The institution and spread of divorce reduce these two *contradictory* effects, decreasing the husbands' advantage over single men and childless married women's disadvantage compared to single women.

The difficulty of the demonstration lies in the fact that in studying the effect of divorce on the effect of marriage, and when examining variations in their 'coefficients of preservation', Durkheim could only consider married people as an undifferentiated group – that is, he could not take into account whether or not they had children. But what protects wives from suicide relative to single women is precisely the immunity they enjoy because of the presence of children. The symmetrical effects of marriage on the two genders therefore could not appear directly; rather they were corroborated by the fact that the spread of divorce – a sign that the institution of marriage had weakened – *increased* wives' coefficient of preservation while *decreasing* that of husbands.

This is the empirical basis for the Durkheimian theory of the marital relation, centred around the idea of the 'hostile interests' of the two sexes relative to the institution of marriage: one sex 'needs restraint and the other liberty' (1897a/t.1951a:274). Monogamous marriage is a good thing for the man because it limits the 'horizon' of his desires to a single object. The indetermination of the object of desire – this notion was equivalent for Durkheim to unlimited desire – is inevitably a source of frustration. The effect of marital regulation is thus to contain this 'morbid desire for the infinite' (1897a/t.1951a:271) or anomie. For the woman, however, that same regulation is useless and therefore excessive. Her sexual desires need no such limiting, either because they are 'naturally limited' (1897a/t.1951a:272) or because they are contained 'by mores and public opinion, which are particularly demanding and severe for women on this count' (Durkheim 1909f:279). Durkheim's indecision here – nature or societal pressure – is of little importance to the present argument. The point is that married women suffer from an excess of restraint – or fatalism – and that loosening the marital tie improves their situation.

Once again, this is an improvement relative to the situation of single women, and not an absolute one such as would be indicated by a *lower* rate of suicide among married women where divorce is possible. This is where the reader is most likely to mistake the author's meaning, though it must be admitted that Durkheim himself falls into the same trap in certain passages of the book – and seems to have fallen into it once and for all in a later article on divorce by mutual consent (Durkheim 1906d; Besnard 1973).

Contrary to other points made in the book, Durkheim's theory of marital regulation was not seriously taken up in later suicide research. What quite dropped out of later studies was his empirical starting point, namely the comparison of suicide rates for married persons with and without children. In *Les Causes de suicide*, Maurice Halbwachs (1930:223) noted that science had not advanced 'a single step' on this matter since Durkheim. Halbwachs himself, using disparate and fragile data, sought to prove that 'the more children married men and women have – and married women in particular – the more protected they are against suicide' (1930:236). He was primarily interested in the effect of family and therefore neglected the effect of marriage itself. Further, he made no mention of conjugal anomie.

Recent literature on suicide makes numerous references to the effects of marriage and divorce on suicide, and in almost all cases Durkheim's study is cited or appealed to. But these studies are based on aggregate data and thus on ecological or time-series correlations. Often their conclusions seem to support Durkheim's theory, but the units of analysis are generally so coarse – overall annual suicide and divorce rates, for example – as to make them insufficient tests of that theory. Let us consider some examples of this (somewhat repetitive) work.

Stack (1980) found positive ecological correlations between suicide and divorce in a study of 50 countries (this is one of the crudest studies, with the individual country as unit of analysis), as did Burr *et al.* (1994) in a study of 294 United States metropolitan areas in 1980. Leenars *et al.* (1993) related annual series of suicide rates to divorce and marriage rates in Canada and the US between 1950 and 1985; the results for divorce are clear, but those for marriage are equivocal. In a technically more refined study using monthly data on divorce and suicide in the US from 1964 to 1977, controlling for seasonal variation and rate of unemployment, and introducing a time-lag effect, Wasserman (1984) also found a strong relation between divorce and suicide.

Taking gender difference into account, Lester (1994) calculated correlations between time-series of suicides among men and women and rates of divorce and marriage from 1950 to 1985 in seventeen countries. He found a slightly higher number of negative relations between marriage and suicide for men than women and slightly more significant positive relations between divorce and suicide for men than women. Though the hypotheses and results of this article clearly associate it with Durkheim's work, Lester makes no mention of him.

Chandler and Tsai (1993), in their study of Japanese suicide patterns, are the only researchers to provide a negative ecological correlation between divorce and suicide among women. This same study, based on data from 47 geographic units for 1981, also found a positive relation between divorce and male suicide. We are led back once again to Durkheim's theory: the authors conclude that their results support the hypothesis that marriage is oppressive for Japanese women. Following Iga (1986), they evoke fatalistic suicide.

In a recent article, Kposowa *et al.* (1995) broke with the use of aggregate data and called into question the habitual association between marital status and suicide. Using data from a longitudinal American study of mortality between 1979 and 1985, the authors found that the association between suicide risk and 'single man' and 'widower' statuses does not hold when other variables are controlled for in a logistic regression. Only being divorced or separated has a significant impact. The limitation of this study, which deals with suicide among white men, lies in the very small number of cases: 216 suicides in the sample over a period of five years.

With the exception of Kposowa *et al.*, it is not in suicide literature per se but rather in more general works on causes of death that data on individuals are used to demonstrate the effect of marital status on suicide (see Trovato 1992 for a recent review of the literature). Suicide is shown to be one of the causes of death on which marital status has a distinct effect: married persons are clearly protected in comparison with single persons, widows and widowers, and divorcees of both sexes, but men are more protected than women. The fact that men benefit more from marriage even seems to be attested to for mortality in general (Vallin and Nizard 1977; Mergenhagen *et al.* 1985). The differential effect of marriage by gender is understood to depend on whether or not a given cause of death is psychosocial in nature. That effect is therefore quite pronounced for suicide but non-existent for leukemia (according to Gove 1973 on American data from 1959 to 1961). Some studies (namely Zick and Smith 1991) suggest that divorce and widowhood *as events* increase mortality risk more for men than women. Though some of these works refer to Durkheim's *Suicide*, the interpretations they advance are inspired not by the theory of regulation but that of integration: the explanatory hypothesis most often given is the intensity of the social ties involved. Finally, none of the studies – and this includes those on mortality in general – uses data that distinguish between married persons with children and those without, despite Kobrin and Hendershot's (1977) attempt, which clearly demonstrates the importance of this variable.[1] Nonetheless, they tend to support the Durkheimian idea that marriage is of much greater benefit to the man than the woman, meanwhile substantiating that idea by inviting us to consider suicide as one cause of death among others.

The purpose of this chapter is to determine whether Durkheim's theory of marital regulation can still shed light on variations in suicide rates by marital status – and developments in these variations – in France. The question is highly relevant given that over the last twenty years the institution of marriage has been shaken as never before.

Like Durkheim, we shall primarily be using data on individuals taken from cause-of-death statistics.[2] We shall also be making use of aggregate data – correlations between time-series – with the difference that here they concern developments in suicide rates over time within certain categories – age and gender groups, marital status groups – rather than the population at large. Furthermore, instead of taking such correlations as proof in and of themselves, we shall be comparing them to each other, thus attributing to them only relative value.

Before proceeding to the core of the demonstration, I shall approach the question from two slightly oblique perspectives: first, a comparison of the effects of marital status on suicide then and now, a century after Durkheim's work; second, an attempt to measure the possible effects of a change in marital status – a question Durkheim rarely raised.

Marital status and suicide a century later

Let us first consider variations in suicide in France by marital status exactly one century later by comparing the years 1889–91 with 1989–91. Durkheim chose the years he did because they were the last for which files on individual suicide cases were kept in the department of legal statistics.[3] From these files he compiled his well-known table of suicide rates for 'each age and civil status group' (single, married and widowed) of both sexes.

For the three years Durkheim studied, the average annual suicide rate was around 22 per 100,000; it was 34.6 for men and 9.7 for women. A century later that rate is about the same – 21 – with a slight closing of the gap between the sexes: 29.9 for men, 11.5 for women.

What conclusions can be drawn by comparing Durkheim's table with an identical one – using the same age groups – for the years 1989–91? (We have eliminated the 15–19 age group for married persons simply because there were no suicides in it. As we know, including this group led Durkheim to make risky conjectures about suicide among extremely young husbands – the rate was calculated on the basis of a mere four cases).

We cannot help being struck first of all by how stable numbers have remained. That stability is especially surprising given that the two sets of statistics are qualitatively different: for Durkheim they were legal statistics, while for this study they are health statistics (cause of death). Particularly remarkable is the consistency in rates for women from one century to the next.

For men, on the other hand, we see significant changes. Unmarried men between 40 and 79 and married men between 50 and 79 do not kill themselves nearly as often as they did a century ago. On the other hand, young (and very old) widowers succumb more readily to despair.

We see that for suicide among men, age is not as discriminating now as it was at the end of the last century. The uniformity of the age of suicide is a strong trend found in many countries (see Chauvel 1997). Remaining with the present comparison, the most significant fact seems to be the decrease in suicide among older men (with the exception of those over 80), not any increase among young men.

This last point, however, should be qualified. It brings us to inevitable methodological precautions. We are comparing data from two different sources: the legal statistics that Durkheim used included some non-fatal attempts, which are obviously not counted in cause-of-death statistics. In fact, suicide attempts are more frequent among young people (this has long been attested). The figures for 1889–91, therefore, slightly over-evaluate suicide among young people. This in turn means there has probably been a slight increase in suicide among young people from last century to this. Such an increase is indeed attested if we take cause-of-death statistics for the 1950s as the point of comparison.

Let us remain with questions of method. Our comparison is in terms of age groups. We therefore do not have to calculate comparative rates with age-group structure constant – a precaution usually taken when comparing overall suicide rates over time or space. That procedure is implicitly based on a particular conception of the act: suicide as a kind of disease is more likely to appear in an older population than a younger one. But this does not take into account the fact that being 50 in 1890 had quite different social and physical significance than it had in 1990.

Another different way of conceiving the increase in suicide with age is to consider suicide not as a disease linked to aging but rather the deliberate sacrifice of a certain amount of the time one has to live – a greater sacrifice for young people than old and therefore one more rarely made by them. We may then ask whether it is legitimate to compare the same age groups a whole century apart. Should we not take into account the effect of the remarkable increase in life expectancy over that time on the calculation made by someone contemplating suicide? If this interpretation of suicide is sound, then our comparison over time should reveal a decrease in suicide for all ages except the most advanced, a displacement, as it were, of suicide rates within the age structure. In fact, the figures neither disprove nor corroborate this hypothesis. It is true that for men, the age group of those 80 and over now contains many more suicides than a century earlier. It is also true that for single men, as for married men and widowers, the increase in suicide in the upper age groups appears later. Among married men we find a kind of plateau between the ages of 40 to 80. But there is no consistent displacement. The already mentioned case of young widowers does not fit into this framework, much less the rates of suicide among women.

Table 10.1 reveals a major difference between recent data and Durkheim's: persons of both sexes in the 'widowed' category are now the most likely to commit suicide. In Durkheim's time, widowers killed themselves much less often than single men of the same age, and widows only began losing their

Table 10.1 Suicides by sex, age, and marital status a century apart: 1889–91 and 1989–91 (per 100,000)

	Men					
	Single		*Married*		*Widowed*	
	1889–91	*1989–91*	*1889–91*	*1989–91*	*1889–91*	*1989–91*
15–19 yrs	11.3	7.7				
20–24 yrs	23.7	23.1	9.7	9.3		
25–29 yrs	39.4	38.0	12.2	13.2		
30–39 yrs	62.7	57.5	22.6	25.1	56.0	150.2
40–49 yrs	97.5	69.1	34.0	30.1	72.1	104.5
50–59 yrs	143.4	68.6	52.0	31.1	97.9	87.0
60–69 yrs	176.8	82.4	63.5	33.9	116.6	105.1
70–79 yrs	198.3	90.9	70.4	51.8	128.8	141.3
> 80 yrs	157.1	144.8	77.0	97.2	115.4	212.8
	Women					
	Single		*Married*		*Widowed*	
	1889–91	*1989–91*	*1889–91*	*1989–91*	*1889–91*	*1989–91*
15–19 yrs	7.9	2.8				
20–24 yrs	10.6	6.6	5.3	1.7		
25–29 yrs	15.1	12.7	6.8	4.0		
30–39 yrs	12.6	20.7	8.2	7.3	20.5	21.5
40–49 yrs	17.1	24.7	10.6	12.2	16.8	25.7
50–59 yrs	20.4	23.6	15.1	15.6	19.9	27.6
60–69 yrs	18.9	20.8	15.8	15.3	25.7	23.7
70–79 yrs	20.6	18.2	20.9	19.2	24.8	27.8
> 80 yrs	17.6	17.8	11.0	22.5	24.0	30.0

protection advantage at age 60. The more spectacular reversal concerns the male sex: the condition of widowhood is not borne as well today as in Durkheim's time and it is especially difficult for men. In other words, widowhood disadvantages men more than women to a greater degree than in Durkheim's time. This difference between the sexes, already perceptible in the last century, has become colossal today. We should note in passing that this once again gives the lie (should there still be any need to do so) to the law or 'theorem' Durkheim formulated: 'In an identical society, the tendency to suicide in the state of widowhood is for each sex a function of the suicidal tendency of the same sex in the state of marriage' (1897a/t.1951a:194), or 'whichever the favoured sex, widowhood regularly corresponds to marriage' (1897a/t.1951a:195). Durkheim's whole purpose – in a demonstration that was adulterated from the start because based on extremely dubious calculations (Besnard 1973:54) – was to explain the fact that with age constant, widowers committed suicide less often than single men and thus seemed to maintain something of their former status as husbands. This fact could be used to support the hypothesis of selection through marriage, a hypothesis Durkheim was not comfortable with. With today's figures he would not have had to get himself into such a crooked demonstrative enterprise – one that Halbwachs (1930) pursued just as doggedly.

Changes in status

Thus far we have discussed widowhood and marriage as ongoing states. What can be said of their impact as events, as passages from one state to another? Durkheim only rarely alluded to this question, namely in the matter of the 'domestic anomie' that widowhood gives rise to. And we are no better equipped than he to study it because our statistics do not provide us with the dates of these 'events'.

The clearest change to have taken place from one century to the next is in the state of widowhood, for it is now young widowers who are most likely to kill themselves. To isolate the effect of widowhood as event – that is, the death of one's spouse – as against widowhood as condition, we can focus on the youngest age groups which, moreover, span five rather than ten years. We may suppose that most of these suicides, following fairly close on the partner's death, are a consequence of that death. But such suicide is rare; the population concerned is small: from 1989 to 1991 there were only 4 suicides for each sex in the 25–29 age group. To have higher numbers, we have had to lengthen the period. Over the 13 years from 1981 to 1993, there were 16 cases of suicide among young widows 25–29 years old, which comes to an average rate of 16.3 for 100,000, as opposed to 29 suicides among young widowers in the same age group, or an average rate of 148.9 for 100,000 (see Table 10.2).[4] The gap between the rates for men and women in this age group is even greater than that for the 30–39 age group. It does diminish (while remaining quite wide) for ages 40 to 69.[5]

These figures lead us to conclude that the difference between the sexes is even sharper for widowhood as event than state. Women adjust to the death of their spouses better than men in both the short and long term. The accentuation of this phenomenon may be taken as one indicator among others of the persistent and even increased validity of Durkheim's thesis: marriage benefits the man more than the woman.[6]

What of the effect of divorce? Divorced men committed suicide frequently in the last century – more often than widowers, affirmed Durkheim. This is no longer the case (and has not been since the 1950s): divorced men have rates much closer to those of single men than of widowers.

As we did for widowhood, we can try to evaluate the impact of the event of divorce by looking at the youngest divorcees. Over the same 13 years the

Table 10.2 Suicide rates by sex, age, and marital status for 1981–93 (per 100,000)

	Men			
	Single	*Married*	*Widowed*	*Divorced*
15–19 yrs	7.8	8.5		
20–24 yrs	24.9	10.5	99.4	53.4
25–29 yrs	43.4	15.5	148.9	55.8
30–39 yrs	63.6	25.0	159.6	84.0
40–49 yrs	72.8	31.5	115.1	94.0
50–59 yrs	79.1	34.4	108.8	84.2
60–69 yrs	86.7	36.7	111.6	77.9
70–79 yrs	97.9	57.2	157.1	105.4
> 80 yrs	129.7	96.0	219.1	201.8
	Women			
	Single	*Married*	*Widowed*	*Divorced*
15–19 yrs	2.8			
20–24 yrs	7.7	2.6	10.9	
25–29 yrs	15.7	4.7	16.3	14.1
30–39 yrs	22.6	8.1	26.3	21.7
40–49 yrs	26.2	12.6	25.7	29.8
50–59 yrs	24.0	15.8	28.3	28.6
60–69 yrs	22.8	16.4	27.1	24.7
70–79 yrs	18.8	20.0	30.4	26.5
> 80 yrs	17.6	23.0	31.3	36.0

rate of suicide among divorced men aged 20–24 was 53.4 (n = 25); it was 55.8 for ages 25–29 (n = 286). The rates increase up to age 50, then regress from 50 to 70 (Table 10.2). As for widowers, the variations curve by age of suicide for divorced men displays a bimodal tendency. If we consider the differences between divorce and other marital statuses – a way of neutralizing the general effect of age in order to bring out the specific effect of divorce – we see that the ratio of the rate for divorced men:married men, while very high in the youngest age group, decreases regularly with age (see Table 10.3). The divorced men:single men ratio is also highest among 20- to 24-year-olds; this difference is reduced – in fact the positions are reversed – for men in their sixties and only reappears at age 80 and over. These observations strongly suggest that divorce as event does increase the likelihood of suicide among men.

And for women? The change with age of the divorced:married ratio closely resembles that for men. The aggravating effect of divorce is weaker for women than men, but this difference between the sexes does not vary with age. This result suggests once again that divorce as change in status does have an aggravating effect. If we look at the divorced women:single women

Table 10.3 Ratios of suicide among divorced persons to suicide among married persons and suicide among divorced persons to suicide among single persons, 1981–93

	Men		*Women*	
	Divorced:Married	*Divorced:Single*	*Divorced:Married*	*Divorced:Single*
20–24 yrs	5.1	2.2	4.2	1.6
25–29 yrs	3.6	1.3	3.0	0.9
30–39 yrs	3.4	1.3	2.7	1.0
40–49 yrs	3.0	1.3	2.4	1.1
50–59 yrs	2.4	1.1	1.8	1.2
60–69 yrs	2.1	0.9	1.5	1.1
70–79 yrs	1.8	1.1	1.3	1.4
> 80 yrs	2.1	1.6	1.6	2.1

ratios we see that divorced women from 25 to 70 hardly kill themselves more than single women in the same age span. The only perceptible worsening is among the very young (20–24) – where in any case the total number of cases is low (22) – and the old, aged 70 and over. Durkheim would say that domestic integration – the presence of children – had come to compensate for the negative effect of divorce. This factor probably goes a long way towards explaining why divorce aggravates men's situation more than women's, for women are much more likely to have custody of their children. We shall encounter this difficulty – of determining the respective importances of conjugal deregulation and familial integration – again further on.

We cannot say anything about the effect of marriage as event. As mentioned, Durkheim made much of the suicide of very young husbands even though his rates were calculated on the basis of very few cases (4, one of which was in the Department of the Seine, if we put together what Durkheim says on p. 178 of *Suicide* with the tables he presents on pp. 196 and 397). Moreover, he interpreted this overly high degree of suicide among very young husbands less in terms of marriage as event than marriage as state, seeing it as the result of an excessive regulation of sexual desire. Over our 13 years we have no more than 4 cases of suicide among husbands under 20 years of age. If we dared do the calculation, this would come to a rate of 8.5 – slightly above the rate for single men under 20 but below that for young married men 20–24. Nothing may be adduced here to support Durkheim's conjecture (for married women under 20, there were 11 suicides – a rate of 2.2).

Effects of the shaking of the marriage institution

As we know, the institution of marriage underwent significant changes in the last quarter of the twentieth century; never have there been such great

Table 10.4 Time-series correlations between four marital indicators, 1968–93

	Men			*Women*		
	Marrying	*Divorce*	*Age at marriage*	*Marrying*	*Divorce*	*Age at marriage*
Marrying	–			–		
Divorce	–0.99	–	–	–0.98	–	
Age at marriage	–0.89	0.92	–	–0.88	0.91	–
Births outside marriage	–0.88	0.92	1.00	–0.88	0.92	1.00

changes over such a short space of time. Between 1973 and 1975, several things began to happen at once in France: the age at which people got married for the first time went up (the reversal of a century-long trend) and the dispersion of first-marriage ages increased; the first-marrying index began a spectacular decrease while the growth rate of divorce accelerated; finally, the number of births outside marriage – until recently such births were called 'illegitimate' – and of 'marriages' without a licence ('living together') began to go up.[7] These changes provide interesting ground on which to test the relevance of Durkheim's theory, centred as it was around the normative definition of conjugal society.

A first test, somewhat coarse, relates developments that have occurred since 1968 (in the various indicators that marriage as an institution is weakening) with developments in suicide rates for the different categories of marital status at different ages. The marital indicators we have chosen are as follows: average age upon first marriage by gender; percentage of births outside marriage (the respective changes in these two indicators are ever so closely linked: r = +1.00!); the first-marrying index; and divorce. For this last indicator there is no unique series for the whole of the period; instead, we have two series with one year in common, 1979, from which we have constructed a homogeneous series, aligning the initial series with the more recent one by applying the difference observed in 1979 calculated as a ratio. This series stands in strong (negative) correlation to the one for first marrying: –0.99 for men and –0.98 for women.

We should probably not attribute too much importance to the fact that these correlation coefficients are so high. Such coefficients for relations between time series are not surprising in cases where variations in phenomena over time follow the same, univocal tendency. Still, our four indicators do fall into two singularly homogeneous groups: age upon first marriage and proportion of births outside marriage can practically be substituted for each other, as can divorce and the intensity of first marrying (see Table 10.4). And the correlations between these two pairs are also quite high.

We are of course concerned here with correlations between developments in these demographic indicators and in suicide rates for persons married

Table 10.5 Time-series correlations between four marital indicators and suicide rates of single and married persons by sex and age, 1968–93

	Men							
	20–29		*30–39*		*40–49*		*50–59*	
	Single	*Married*	*Single*	*Married*	*Single*	*Married*	*Single*	*Married*
First marrying	−0.71	−0.83	−0.80	−0.97	−0.44	−0.82	0.28	0.14
Divorce	0.67	0.79	0.76	0.97	0.39	0.82	−0.35	−0.17
Age at marriage	0.36	0.52	0.48	0.84	0.23	0.78	−0.56	−0.33
Births outside marriage	0.35	0.51	0.46	0.84	0.18	0.76	−0.57	−0.34
	Women							
	20–29		*30–39*		*40–49*		*50–59*	
	Single	*Married*	*Single*	*Married*	*Single*	*Married*	*Single*	*Married*
First marrying	0.20	−0.20	−0.52	−0.67	−0.75	−0.89	−0.57	−0.80
Divorce	−0.24	0.12	0.51	0.62	0.74	0.88	0.54	0.79
Age at marriage	−0.56	−0.13	0.16	0.34	0.59	0.73	0.56	0.64
Births outside marriage	−0.56	−0.14	0.17	0.34	0.59	0.74	0.54	0.65

at different ages (Table 10.5). As explained, I am using these correlations relatively and comparatively, asking whether the strongest among them are indeed those that may be deduced from Durkheim's theory. To extend the field of comparison (and introduce a control), I have included single persons in Table 10.5, while eliminating the upper age groups, whose components are less likely to have been affected by the collapse of matrimonial norms (as a result, such correlations are distinctly weaker).

A first glance at Table 10.5 reveals that the category in which the correlations between developments in suicide and developments in indicators of the de-institutionalization of marriage are strongest is married men aged 30–39.

More generally, it is the first-marrying index, closely followed, of course, by divorce, that varies best with suicide rates for married persons. As just mentioned, the strongest correlations are obtained for married men between 30 and 39: −0.97 and 0.97. This relation is illustrated in Figure 10.1, where I have used first-marrying figures for men – on an inverted scale – rather than the divorce indicator (the series for divorce might seem suspect because reconstructed).

The parallel between the overall *decrease* in marrying (the scale has been inverted) and the increase in suicide among married men aged 30–39 is

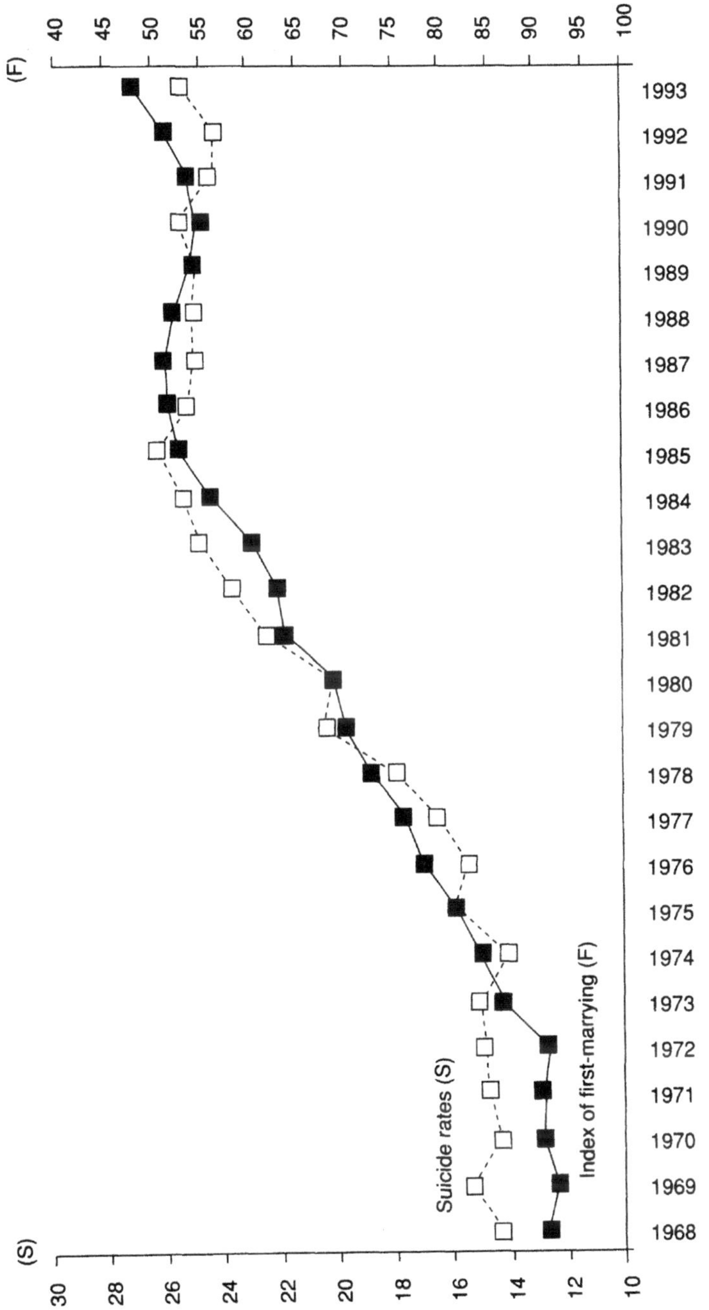

Figure 10.1 Suicide rates for married men aged 30–39 and first-marrying index among men (inverted scale), 1968–93

quite striking. And we also observe a strong parallel for married men aged 20 to 29 ($r = -0.83$). But we must not be misled here. First, we find a less distinct but nonetheless strong relation between the marrying index and rates of suicide among *single* men of the same ages (–0.80 and –0.71 respectively). Second – and this argument is tied to the first – such parallels might only be the effect of a cause common to both developments, one to be sought in the particular economic context (Chauvel 1997). It makes sense that this context should affect the frequency of both suicide and marriage.

In fact, if we use the same economic-context indicator as Chauvel – namely unemployment among young people aged 15 to 24 – we find that developments in this indicator are closely tied to those in suicide. The correlation between the time series for unemployment among young people and the time series for suicide among married men aged 30–39 is 0.95. And we find correlations that are just as high between unemployment and our best marital indicators, first-marrying and divorce.

This last result is, moreover, intriguing: the positive relation between economic context and divorce is less immediately intelligible than the negative relation between economic context and first-marrying. And we have other reasons to doubt that these parallel developments are due solely to the economic context. These become clear if we look once again at Table 10.5.

First of all, the marital indicators are in all cases better linked to suicide among married persons than among singles. This fact, which might seem insignificant, is nonetheless reassuring in that it suggests (1), that the correlations between time series are meaningful, and (2), that they cannot be understood solely as the effect of the economic context. Moreover, for the economic-context indicator (unemployment among the young) we do not find the same difference between singles and marrieds, though that indicator is a bit more closely tied to suicide among young marrieds than among singles.

Second, the correlations between matrimonial indicators and suicide are very strong for married men under 40, the most likely to have been affected by the overall weakening of marriage, whereas those correlations are weak or nonexistent for married women of the same age. This result – suicide rates for husbands are more sensitive to the weakening of the conjugal tie than suicide rates for wives – conforms well to the Durkheimian theory.

Let us look directly now at developments in (1) suicide rates for the different age groups and marital statuses, and (2) the preservation coefficients so dear to Durkheim; that is, ratios of suicide rates for single men to suicide rates for married men. To get an overall view of these developments (and have a sufficient number of cases), we have divided the 26 years for which we have statistics – 1968–93 – into five periods, the first spanning six years, the others five (Table 10.6).

The first period – 1968–73 – provides a useful point of comparison for judging the effect of later changes. Coming just before the shock to matrimonial indicators, it marks the triumph of the institution of marriage, at

Table 10.6 Marital indicators by time period, 1968–93

	1968–73	*1974–8*	*1979–83*	*1984–8*	*1989–93*
% births outside marriage	7.1	8.7	12.9	21.9	31.6
Average age at marriage: women	22.4	22.6	23.2	24.4	25.8
Average age at marriage: men	24.5	24.7	25.3	26.5	27.8
First-marrying: women	91.6	82.4	67.1	54.1	53.9
First-marrying: men	91.0	79.0	65.5	53.0	52.6
Divorce	11.6	16.9	24.3	30.5	33.0

least if we consider the population as a whole. It is the culminating moment of the centuries-old trend of a decrease in the age at which people get married for the first time. The tie between marriage and procreation was as strong as ever: 1972 was a record year for premarital conception, and in more than two cases out of three, it was followed by marriage before the child was born.

Comparing the last two periods, we observe a slowdown in the increase of divorce and a quasi-stabilization of first marrying. In fact, the divorce index went down in 1987, then began progressing again in 1988, but much more slowly than it had from 1977 to 1985. First-marrying went up from 1988 to 1990; only in 1993 did that indicator go below the 1987 level. On the other hand, marriage age and the proportion of births outside marriage pursued their regular parallel increase.

To evaluate variations in the frequency of suicide in each category in relation to the general development of the phenomenon, we have indicated in Table 10.7 the overall suicide rate for each sex for the five periods.

Between the first and second periods, the overall rate of male suicide went up only slightly (+0.5%), but the change varied with age. For instance, the suicide rate for marrieds remained stable and even decreased over age 40, but it went up significantly below that age. It seems logical that the youngest marrieds would be the first to feel the effect of the shakeup of marriage as an institution. However, this interpretation runs up against the fact that the progression among young singles was even sharper. There again, between the first and second periods, suicide in general stagnated or regressed over age 40, while greatly increasing among persons under 40.

Generally, among singles the highest suicide rates were reached by older rather than younger people. This is true for both sexes. But it was not the case for married persons. For almost all age categories, married persons' suicide rates reached their peak in the fourth period – 1984–8 – together with the overall suicide rate. Once we have broken down the age groups according to marital status, therefore, we don't see anything like a generation effect.[8] This potential generation effect seems nullified by marriage.

Table 10.7 Suicide rates for single and married persons by sex and age, 1968–93 (per 100,000)

	Men			
	1968–73		*1974–8*	
	Single	*Married*	*Single*	*Married*
20–24 yrs	16.3	6.1	23.5	7.9
25–29 yrs	35.1	9.0	42.2	11.7
30–39 yrs	45.0	14.8	53.4	16.1
40–49 yrs	67.3	26.0	67.0	24.8
50–59 yrs	83.9	35.5	78.6	32.2
60–69 yrs	96.5	41.0	73.9	34.4
70–79 yrs	84.1	49.4	88.5	49.2
> 80 yrs	109.5	65.8	83.8	67.4
Men in general	22.8		23.3	
	Women			
	1968–73		*1974–8*	
	Single	*Married*	*Single*	*Married*
20–24 yrs	8.7	2.7	10.3	3.2
25–29 yrs	16.3	4.3	19.3	4.6
30–39 yrs	14.5	6.2	23.6	7.0
40–49 yrs	16.5	8.8	17.6	8.7
50–59 yrs	20.6	13.3	19.7	13.6
60–69 yrs	16.8	15.3	17.3	14.2
70–79 yrs	16.1	15.9	17.2	17.0
> 80 yrs	19.1	19.3	15.0	19.4
Women in general	8.8		12.6	

Following Durkheim, we are mainly interested in the impact of changes in matrimonial norms on the effect of marriage on suicide. And here changes in the ratio of suicide rates for singles to suicide rates for marrieds constitutes the decisive test (see Table 10.8). If Durkheim's theory of conjugal regulation is at all founded, the fact that the marriage institution has been so radically called into question should have diminished the protection men obtain from the state of marriage; on the other hand, it should have improved wives' situation relative to single women's.

Among women under 50, the difference between wives and singles first tended to increase, in conformity with the Durkheimian theory; that increase was particularly strong among wives aged 30–39. But starting in the third or fourth period that trend was reversed. Wives seem to have benefited

Men					
1979–83		*1984–8*		*1989–93*	
Single	*Married*	*Single*	*Married*	*Single*	*Married*
27.3	11.2	24.9	10.4	23.8	9.4
52.3	15.8	46.3	16.7	38.4	13.2
68.9	22.5	67.0	25.6	59.2	25.1
75.4	29.4	76.2	32.7	70.2	31.2
85.3	35.6	85.7	36.0	68.0	31.3
87.7	38.9	96.4	39.0	80.2	33.1
95.5	59.3	102.3	61.3	90.1	49.8
127.6	87.4	129.3	97.9	130.0	95.0
29.2		32.0		30.3	
Women					
1979–83		*1984–8*		*1989–93*	
Single	*Married*	*Single*	*Married*	*Single*	*Married*
10.4	3.3	7.6	2.6	6.8	2.0
21.4	5.2	17.8	4.9	12.3	4.0
25.4	8.4	25.1	8.6	19.6	7.5
25.4	11.4	28.9	13.6	25.0	12.3
21.3	15.1	24.4	16.5	24.8	15.3
22.8	17.1	25.3	17.8	19.8	14.8
18.6	20.3	20.0	21.0	17.0	17.8
18.0	22.4	17.4	23.7	17.0	21.8
11.4		12.4		11.3	

very quickly from the loosening of the marriage tie, but that effect seems to have lasted only a short time. Why?

This reversal in trend makes sense if we relate it to the very strong growth over this period of 'living together', what I have called marriage without a licence. In fact, the 'singles' category came to include more and more couples.[9] This in itself does not directly challenge the Durkheimian theory, which is, as we have said, focused on the *institution* of marriage. What does pose a problem are the children born to these non-married couples (and secondarily, children in single-parent families, whose numbers also increased over this period but not at all as much as those of children born to unofficial couples).[10] The extremely sharp progression in births out of marriage during the 1980s could only have helped reduce – as early as the third

Table 10.8 Ratios of suicide rates for singles to suicide rates for marrieds since 1968

	Men				
	1968–73	*1974–8*	*1979–83*	*1984–8*	*1989–93*
20–24 yrs	2.66	2.98	2.44	2.39	2.53
25–29 yrs	3.89	3.62	3.30	2.76	2.90
30–39 yrs	3.04	3.32	3.06	2.62	2.36
40–49 yrs	2.59	2.70	2.56	2.33	2.25
50–59 yrs	2.37	2.44	2.40	2.38	2.17
60–69 yrs	2.36	2.15	2.25	2.47	2.42
70–79 yrs	1.70	1.80	1.61	1.67	1.81
> 80 yrs	1.66	1.24	1.46	1.32	1.37
	Women				
	1968–73	*1974–8*	*1979–83*	*1984–8*	*1989–93*
20–24 yrs	3.20	3.22	3.18	2.92	3.33
25–29 yrs	3.79	4.17	4.14	3.65	3.04
30–39 yrs	2.33	3.38	3.01	2.92	2.61
40–49 yrs	1.88	2.03	2.23	2.13	2.03
50–59 yrs	1.56	1.45	1.42	1.48	1.62
60–69 yrs	1.10	1.22	1.33	1.42	1.34
70–79 yrs	1.01	1.02	0.92	0.95	0.96
> 80 yrs	0.99	0.77	0.80	0.73	0.78

period and especially during the last two periods – the difference between legal couples and singles.

The combination of Durkheimian theories of marital regulation and familial integration can, therefore, account for the developments over this period in the ratio of suicide rates for singles to suicide rates for wives. We may hypothesize that at first, the weakening in matrimonial norms resulted in an improvement for wives relative to single women; this explains the increase in their advantage over single women from the first to the second periods. Starting in the middle 1980s, however, the increase in the volume of births out of marriage and thus in the number of *officially single* mothers became such that the gap between marrieds and singles was reduced. We shouldn't forget that in Durkheim's theory wives' immunity was entirely due to their status as mothers. The fact that the gap does not develop one way or the other in the third period is due to its intermediary position between these two trends, the effects of which work against each other.

It may be objected that the theory does not apply to persons over 50, for whom we observe a relative stability in preservation coefficients over time. But the weakening of the marriage tie, like the presence of children, is hardly relevant for people of such ages. We could, however, interpret the increase in the advantage of married women aged 50–59 in the last period as resulting from the recent increase in France in the length of time parents and children live together, combined with the rise in the age at which women become mothers.

Things are less clear for men, because the two trends are understood to point in the same direction: the weakening of marriage as an institution should have the same effect as the increase in the number of fathers among the 'singles' – namely a reduction in the difference between marrieds and singles. It is therefore difficult to distinguish the respective impacts of these two factors.

Table 10.7 clearly reveals a decrease in the immunity due to marriage for men aged 25–39. But this only appears at the end of the 1970s. For most of the age groups, the gap between married and single men begins to grow (before narrowing, as for women but less so). And this is not at all consistent with Durkheim's hypothesis, though it is true that for certain indicators – age upon marriage and births outside marriage – the de-institutionalization of marriage had only just begun in 1974–8 (see Table 10.6). We also observe that among young people this gap tends to widen again in the last period, as if a time of rapid change had been followed by a certain degree of normative stabilization.

The only thing we can cite on this point in support of the Durkheimian theory of regulation is that the decrease in immunity due to marriage for men aged 20–49 between the third and fourth periods is probably more a matter of conjugal anomie than familial integration, since the increase in births outside marriage remains fairly slight whereas divorce increased the most then, and the male marrying rate decreased the most (see Table 10.6). Furthermore, as Durkheim (following other nineteenth-century moral statisticians) reminds us, the presence of children protects mothers much more than fathers. This factor may thus have less impact on men than on women, which would help explain the tendency towards a narrowing of the gap between husbands and singles that may be observed starting at the end of the 1970s among men aged 30 to 60.

While we are hardly troubled by the non-effect of the shakeup of the marriage institution on older couples, the relative constancy over time of the immunity marriage gives to young people aged 20–24 is surprising. Here we must take into account the rise in the age at which people first marry. For men that age was 24.5 years in the first period; 27.8 in the last. Young marrieds became a small minority group. In 1972 there were 728,000 married men between 20 and 24 – 33% of the age group – while by 1993 that number had gone down to 126,000: a mere 5.7% of the age group. In 1972, the majority of women in that age group – 1,153,000 women or 54.3% – were wives, as against 44.9% single women; by 1993 that number had gone down to 322,600, or a mere 15% of the same age group.[11]

Young people, who at the beginning of the 1970s were following the norm (the statistical norm, at least) by getting married, now go against that norm when they marry. It is probable that the psychological and social profile of young marrieds changed significantly over the period under consideration. We can hypothesize, for example, that those who married young in the 1990s are more traditionalist as regards the marriage institution than those who got married at the same age twenty years earlier.[12]

Analysis of recent data on suicide by marital condition in France gives fragmentary but convergent results that tend to confirm the central thesis of Durkheim's theory of marital regulation: marriage as an institution benefits men more than women.[13]

Correlations between time series for the years 1968–93 suggest that the de-institutionalization of marriage has essentially affected suicide rates among young married men, whereas it has not affected rates for married women. This is consistent with Durkheim's theory.

Data on individuals reveal that widowhood and divorce, whether as events or conditions, increase the risk of suicide more for men than women. Familial integration – the presence of children – can play a role in this difference, because many more divorced women than men live with children. But this factor cannot suffice to account for the differential effect of widowhood by gender. It is true that widows live more often than widowers with their own or other children, but this difference is not at all proportional to the enormous difference between the sexes in the effect of widowhood on suicide. The loss of one's spouse (event) or the spouse's absence (state) makes men fragile much more than women. If we add that this difference has strongly increased over the century, we can find support here for the Durkheimian thesis that the interests of the respective sexes within the marriage institution are antagonistic to each other.

As for the specific effect of marriage and of the recent crisis in this institution, we have seen that it is not easy to determine what is due to conjugal deregulation and what to domestic integration, simply because the data we have do not enable us to classify individual cases of suicide according to whether the person did or did not have children. In the last century, this problem pertained only to married persons; now it has become just as relevant for singles. I have nevertheless proposed an interpretation of developments in the effect of marriage on suicide – the gap between suicide rates for marrieds and singles – over a quarter of a century that takes into account both the weakening of marriage and the fact that a growing number of officially single persons are parents. It is the combination of these two factors – given that they have opposite effects – that accounts for developments in the ratio of suicide among married women to suicide among single women. We have seen that for men, on whom these factors have the same effect, it is more difficult to untangle them and thus to arrive at any full confirmation of the Durkheimian thesis according to which the weakening of the marriage tie diminishes the advantage conferred by marriage on the male sex.

Silent on the parental status of individuals who have committed suicide, cause-of-death statistics likewise do not tell us whether those persons were or were not a partner in an unmarried couple. This second information gap is singularly inconvenient today, for it prevents us from determining whether the legal tie of marriage really has an effect of its own, as the Durkheimian theory assumes. In sum, because the procedures by which deaths are recorded have not been adapted to conjugal and familial change, the deinstitutionalization of marriage, whose 'morbid' effects Durkheim feared, has also made it impossible for us to fully verify his theory a century later.

Notes

First published in *Revue française de sociologie* (1997) 38:735–8. Translated from French by Amy Jacobs.

1 Between 1966 and 1968 in the United States a questionnaire was distributed to the families of 20,000 persons who had died at age 35 or over requesting information about the deceased's marital and parental status. Despite the technical difficulties involved, the results are suggestive. In the 35–44 age group, the mortality figure for married women without children – 378 – was fairly close to that for 'unmarried women', a category that included single women, widows and divorcees – 408 – whereas for married women with children it was only 160. For men in the same age group the respective figures were 557, 1008 and 268.

2 INSERM has provided us with figures on suicides per age group and marital status category for the years 1968–93. The rates were calculated by the Observatoire Sociologique du Changement from Daguet's data (1995). My thanks to Mireille Clémençon for her assistance in the calculations and in collecting and analysing the literature, and to Louis Chauvel for communicating data from INSEE's employment studies, provided by LASMAS-IDL.

3 The department was headed by Gabriel Tarde during the period in question. Tarde gave Marcel Mauss access to the files, thus providing ammunition to those who would later use it against him. Durkheim had charged Mauss to report on the files for him.

4 By further lengthening the period we would have arrived at still more demonstrative figures: between 1976 and 1980 there were 12 registered suicides of widows aged 25–29, 26 among widowers of the same age, and even 9 suicides of widowers under 25. But obviously if we lengthen the period too much we can no longer clearly discern developments over time. On this count, 13 years is already quite long.

5 It is true that suicide rates go up again for the most advanced ages. But this increase is probably only a reflection of the lesser general sensitivity of women's suicide to the effect of aging.

6 It might be objected here that there are fewer and fewer young widowers; early loss of one's wife may be considered that much more painful because that much more rare. In fact, in 1993 there were 8.4 times fewer widowers in the 25- to

39-year-old population than in 1901 (calculation follows Daguet 1995). However, while there were five times fewer widows in the same age span in 1993 than in 1901, that decrease did not affect their suicide rates.

7 The figures used are taken from several publications, namely Daguet (1995), Sardon (1996) and Monnier and Guibert-Lantoine (1996).

8 It is true that using age spans of ten years (Durkheim's choice) does not facilitate bringing out this effect. On the relation between generation and suicide see Surault (1995) and Chauvel (1997).

9 In 1993, 22% of women aged 20–24 and 21% of women aged 25–29 were single and living with single men in independent couples; the corresponding figures for 1982 were 7% and 4%. For men, the figures moved from 5.8% of men 20–24 and 5.6% of men 24–29 in 1982 to 14.2% and 25.1% in 1993 (source: INSEE's 'Enquêtes sur l'emploi').

10 From 1982 to 1993 the percentage of single women aged 25–29 living with one or more children (regardless of whether they were also living with a man) went from 2.6 to 11.2. For men the corresponding figures are 2.2% and 9.3% (source: INSEE's 'Enquêtes sur l'emploi').

11 Source: Daguet (1995).

12 A possible indication of this: in the context of a strong rise in the average age of maternity (or paternity), the percentage of fathers among married men aged 20–24 remained stable from 1982 to 1993 – 50% – whereas it fell sharply over those years in the 25–29 age group, going from 65.5% to 53% (source: INSEE's 'Enquêtes sur l'emploi').

13 I have not discussed the most delicate question here, and it remains an open one: what explains the permanence of this opposition? Does it mean that the respective positions of the two sexes in the couple have not substantively changed in the course of a century, and that married women, as opposed to men, still have a 'need for freedom'?

Bibliography

Besnard, P. (1973) 'Durkheim et les femmes ou le *Suicide* inachevé', *Revue Française de Sociologie* 14(1):27–61.

(1987) *L'Anomie*, Paris: Presses Universitaires de France.

Burr, J. F., McCall, P. L. and Powell-Griner, E. (1994) 'Catholic Religion and Suicide: The Mediating Effect of Divorce', *Social Science Quarterly* 75(2):300–18.

Chandler, C. R. and Tsai, Y. M. (1993) 'Suicide in Japan and in the West: Evidence for Durkheim's Theory', *International Journal of Comparative Sociology* 34(3–4):244–59.

Chauvel, L. (1997) 'Ralentissement économique et suicide', *Revue de l'OFCE* 60: 100–4.

Daguet, F. (1995) *Un siècle de démographie française. Structure et évolution de la population de 1901–1993*, *Insee Résultats* 434–5, Paris: Insee.

Durkheim, E. (1897a) *Le Suicide: étude de sociologie*, Paris, Alcan.

—(t.1951a) by J. A. Spaulding and G. Simpson, *Suicide: A Study in Sociology*, edited with an introduction by G. Simpson, Glencoe, IL: Free Press (London: Routledge and Kegan Paul, 1952).

(1906d) 'Le Divorce par consentement mutuel', *Revue Bleue* 44(5):534–49.

(1909f) 'Intervention dans un débat sur "Mariage et divorce"', *Libres entretiens* (Union pour la vérité), 5th series: 258–93.

Gove, W. R. (1973) 'Sex, Marital Status, and Mortality', *American Journal of Sociology* 79(1):45–67.

Halbwachs, M. (1930) *Les Causes du suicide*, Paris: Alcan.

Kobrin, F. E. and Hendershot, G. E. (1977) 'Do Family Ties Reduce Mortality? Evidence from the United States, 1966–1968', *Journal of Marriage and the Family* 39(4):737–45.

Kposowa, A. J., Breault, K. D. and Singh, G. K. (1995) 'White Male Suicide in the United States: A Multivariate Individual-level Analysis', *Social Forces* 74(1):315–23.

Leenaars, A. A., Yang, B. and Lester, B. (1993) 'The Effects of Domestic and Economic Stress on Suicide Rates in Canada and the United States', *Journal of Clinical Psychology* 49(6):918–21.

Lester, D. (1994) 'The Protective Effect of Marriage for Suicide in Men and Women', *Italian Journal of Suicidology* 4(2):83–5.

Iga, M. (1986) *The Thorn in the Chrysanthemum: Suicide and Economic Success in Modern Japan*, Berkeley: University of California Press.

Mergenhagen, P. M., Lee, B. A. and Gove, W. R. (1985) 'Till Death Do Us Part: Recent Changes in the Relationship between Marital Status and Mortality', *Sociology and Social Research* 70(1):53–6.

Monnier, A. and Guibert-Lantoine, C. (1996) 'La Conjoncture démographique: l'Europe et les pays développés d'outre-mer', *Population* 51(4–5):1005–30.

Sardon, J.-P. (1996) 'L'Evolution du divorce en France', *Population* 51(3):717–50.

Stack, S. (1980) 'The Effects of Marital Dissolution on Suicide', *Journal of Marriage and the Family* 42(1):83–92.

Surault, P. (1995) 'Variation sur les variations du suicide en France', *Population* (4–5):983–1012.

Trovato, F. (1992) 'Mortality Differentials in Canada by Marital Status', *Canadian Studies in Population* 19(2):111–43.

Vallin, J. and Nizard, A. (1977) 'La Mortalité par état matrimonial. Mariage sélection ou mariage protection', *Population* 32:95–123.

Wasserman, I. M. (1984) 'A Longitudinal Analysis of the Linkage between Suicide, Unemployment, and Marital Dissolution', *Journal of Marriage and the Family* 46(4):853–9.

Zick, C. and Smith, K. Z. (1991) 'Marital Transitions, Poverty, and Gender Differences in Mortality', *Journal of Marriage and the Family* 53(2):327–36.

11

SOCIAL INTEGRATION AND MARITAL STATUS

A multi-variate individual-level study of 30,157 suicides

K. D. Breault and Augustine J. Kposowa

Introduction

The rationale for this research is that in sociology few studies have rigorously looked at individual-level suicide data. More common are aggregate analyses with units of analysis such as countries, states, counties, cities, etc. (e.g. Stack 1982, 1985; Wasserman 1983, 1984; Breault 1986; Girard 1988; Pescosolido and Georgiana 1989; Lester 1993). Moreover, one of the enduring themes of this literature concerns methodology, much of which is related to the 'ecological fallacy' (e.g. Moksony 1994; Pescosolido 1994). In one recent paper, Breault (1994) presents data to suggest that aggregate level findings at the national level, which are generally supportive of Durkheim's theory, are ambiguous because results at lower levels of aggregation are substantially different. In the same paper, Breault suggests that the lower level results are inadequate for other methodological reasons, i.e. small sample size and limitations on the number of variables.

At the same time, suicide studies in psychology, research psychiatry and medicine at the individual level are not unproblematical. Sample sizes are often small and controls for socio-economic status (SES) variables are conspicuously lacking (e.g. Teicher and Jacobs 1966; Humphrey 1977; Robins *et al.* 1977; Goldney 1981; Shafi *et al.* 1985). In addition, there exist no large sample multivariate individual-level studies of female or minority suicide.

In sociology, individual-level studies of note are Gibbs (1969), Gove (1972, 1973), Rico-Velasco and Mynko (1973), Kobrin and Hendershot (1977), Stack (1990), Stack and Wasserman (1993), Kposowa *et al.* (1995), van Poppel and Day (1996), and Thorlindsson and Bjarnason (1998). In a descriptive study, based on suicides for 1959–61, Gibbs calculates suicide rates for whites by age and marital status with the finding, among others, that married people have lower suicide rates than those of other marital status categories. Following Gibbs, Gove (1973) analysed age-specific mortality rates for selected causes by sex and marital status for whites aged 25–64 for the period 1951–61, with the finding that the married have lower overall mortality rates than singles, widows and the divorced. Using data from the Public Health Service and Durkheim's 'coefficient of preservation', Gove (1972) found the same marital status pattern for suicide. In addition, the latter study found greater mortality disparity among men compared to women between the married and the other three statuses. In a study of 907 cases of suicide during an eleven-year period, 1960–70, in Franklin County, Ohio, Rico-Velasco and Mynko (1973) found that married people did not have lower suicide rates than singles, even though the married rates were lower than those of widows and the divorced. Kobrin and Hendershot (1977), in research based on the National Mortality Survey involving 20,000 deaths from all causes, found that overall mortality was lower for married persons compared to the non-married. Based on 1979 suicide data for white males and females, Stack (1990) updates the suicide rate calculations of Gibbs (1969) with essentially the same results: marriage is more protective against suicide than other marital statuses. With a national sample of 10,906 deaths from all causes, Stack and Wasserman (1993) found that, compared to married persons, the non-married have a significantly higher risk of suicide. In the work by Kposowa *et al.* (1995), based on the 1979–85 *National Longitudinal Study*, the suicides of 216 white males were analysed, with mixed results for Durkheim's social integration thesis and marital status. While divorced white men had significantly higher suicide risks compared to married men, single and widowed men were not at greater risk. We began the present study by suspecting that the failure of Kposowa *et al.* to find the expected Durkheimian effects for single and widowed white men was due to their small sample. In a study using individual data from the Netherlands to assess Catholic–Protestant differences in suicide rates, van Poppel and Day (1996) find no support for Durkheim's theory. In a study by Thorlindsson and Bjarnason (1998) on youth suicidality, in which Durkheim's concepts of integration and regulation are operationalized on the individual level, support is generally found for Durkheim. Unfortunately, this last study lacked the control variables that are usually included in similar studies.

The present study, based on data from the *Mortality Detail File* (National Center for Health Statistics 1994), extends the interest in the study of individual-level data by analysing the largest sample of suicides to date, 30,157 suicides in the year 1992, and covers males, females, whites, African Americans, Hispanics, Asian Americans and Native Americans.

Theoretically, the underpinnings of the study are quite familiar. Briefly, Durkheim argues that marriage and other social attachments offer protection from suicide. Specifically, married persons are said to have lower suicide rates than the widowed, divorced and single; the widowed have lower suicide rates than the divorced and single; and the divorced have lower suicide rates than singles.

At this point in our discipline's history, and given the long list of individual studies cited above, it is, perhaps, unnecessary to justify analysis at the individual level. Certainly, many areas in sociology routinely use such data. Yet Durkheim was, with important exceptions, generally opposed to individual-level analysis, and it is not inappropriate briefly to discuss the issue in the context of testing his theory (and see the discussion in the recent individual-level studies of suicide by van Poppel and Day 1996 and Thorlindsson and Bjarnason 1998). We would like to make two brief points on this issue and refer readers to our extended discussion on the matter (Breault 1994, 1997; Kposowa *et al.* 1995). First, Durkheim's fundamental interest in *Suicide* is to carve out a place for sociology in the social science landscape. In part, his almost exclusive focus on aggregates and his opposition to individual-level study is a strategic attempt to advocate an unique character for sociology and sociological explanation in a competitive explanatory environment. But above all, Durkheim is interested in developing a scientific sociology that could compete with the other social sciences on the basis of truth-value. What mattered most for Durkheim was that sociology be empirically grounded, that our theories satisfy scientific scrutiny. Second, because the adequacy of aggregate-level study empirically to adjudicate his theory has been seriously questioned, Durkheim would today be forced to choose between his exclusionary methodology and the possibility that at the individual level his theory might be supported. It is our belief that if he were with us today he would choose the latter course over an empirically outmoded methodological dogma. Durkheim's error, repeated by many sociologists since, was in seeing sociology as a distinct methodology rather than a set of theoretical notions inspired by group and social interaction that could benefit from a variety of methodological approaches.

Moreover, while Durkheim was generally opposed to individual-level analysis (but see his individual-level arguments in *Suicide*, Book Two, Chapter 3 on age, sex, and marital status, especially his attempt to separate conjugal and familial effects) he was not as dismissive of individual-level explanations as is usually thought – at least not for overarching sociologistic reasons. For example, in his discussion of alcoholism, Durkheim repudiates the link between it and suicide, but not because it is an individual-level or psychological cause. Rather, Durkheim's rejection of alcoholism is empirically based. He shows that there is no correlation between suicide rates, alcohol consumption and alcohol-related illnesses. (Note that Pope 1976 showed that Durkheim had misread his data – suicide and alcohol were related.) Similarly, with regard to mental illness, Durkheim rejects the idea after consulting the empirical data then available to him. Thus, Durkheim's overriding interest in sociology as an empirically grounded, quantitative science would seem to buttress the view that today he would prefer his theory to be tested at the individual level rather than letting it be held hostage to (his own) sociologistic or philosophical arguments that may now preclude his theory from empirical falsifiability.

We would like to make it clear that we are not adopting the position opposite to that of Durkheim. We do not reject aggregate-level analyses for reasons of philosophy or methodological individualism, and in general we are open to any methodology, including aggregate study, that has the potential for revealing truth. Our view is considerably narrower. There is now reason to believe (as indicated above) that by itself the aggregate level is not adequate to test Durkheim's theory of social integration. Therefore, the choice we face is a simple one: do individual-level study (perhaps in combination with aggregate study) or give up the hope of testing Durkheim's theory. For us, the latter option is both irresponsible and unreasonable. In addition, as we argue at the conclusion of this chapter, failing to consider important variables that can only be studied at the individual level, such as those that have been generated by the medical and psychological literature, is a general prescription for bad science.

Finally, in the area of theory, it is not unreasonable to suggest that one hundred years after *Le Suicide* we venture beyond Durkheim. As Gibbs (1994), one of the principal authors of status integration theory, correctly points out, sociologists have been all too reluctant to 'transform Durkheim's theory or seriously consider alternatives (even those clearly inspired by Durkheim's work)'. But going beyond Durkheim and constructing new theory, as Durkheim himself would argue, means having the relevant empirical observations in the first place. As we demonstrate in this chapter, because of small samples and the failure to explore sex and race/ethnic categories other than that of whites, much of the empirical work has not been done. Thus this chapter is both a test of Durkheim's theory and an empirical starting point for new sociological theory of suicide.

Methods

Data

The data used in this study were derived from the national *Mortality Detail File* for 1992 (NCHS 1994). The *Mortality Detail File* contains mortality statistics based on information from death certificate records of all deaths occurring in the United States in 1992. The information is either received on computer tapes coded by the states and provided to the National Center for Health Statistics (NCHS) through the Vital Statistics Cooperative programme, or is coded by the NCHS from copies of the original certificates received from the registration areas. NCHS receives data for the *Mortality Detail File* from the registrations offices of all states, the District of Columbia, and New York City. Data on Hispanic origin were obtained from the District of Columbia and all states with the exception of New Hampshire and Oklahoma, which were excluded because their death certificates did not include an item to identify Hispanic or ethnic origin.

Mortality data for the United States are limited to deaths occurring within the United States to residents and non-residents. Deaths of non-residents of the United States were excluded from all tabulations, and deaths occurring to US citizens outside the United States are not included in the *Mortality Detail File* (NCHS 1994).

For the purposes of this analysis, we considered suicide deaths among males, females, whites, African Americans, Hispanics, Asian Americans (including Pacific Islanders) and Native Americans. The results presented are based on virtually all those who died of suicide in 1992. Cases under 15 years of age were not analysed because of empty cell problems.

In 1992, a total of 2,179,187 deaths took place in the United States. Of this number, 3,574 were to foreign residents. When these are removed, the *Mortality Detail File* for 1992 has a total of 2,175,613 deaths. Of the 30,157 due to suicide, 24,216 were male, 5,941 female, 27,329 white, 2,107 black, 2,351 Hispanic, 537 Asian American and 224 Native American. Note that the race/ethnic subgroups total more than the full sample mainly because of overlapping identifications involving Hispanics.

Note that the reliability of official suicide data has been debated in the literature. The view we take is that the limitations of the data are not systematic and that, as Pescosolido and Mendelsohn (1986) have shown, countervailing forces work to produce highly reliable data. At this point there is no evidence to suggest that scientific research on such data, especially in the present case where a great many suicides are analysed, is seriously biased. The interested reader should turn to a book edited by Lester (1994) that discusses the matter in some detail. See especially the chapter by Jack Gibbs (1994).

Variables and measures

Following a common practice borrowed from epidemiology, the dependent variable in the study was the odds of death by suicide versus deaths from other causes. Of course, due to the nature of the data, there is no population 'at risk' (group) for comparison, since all individuals analysed are in fact dead. That is, the data do not permit a comparison of victims versus non-victims (those still alive), so the 'non-victims' in the analysis are those who died of other (natural) causes. Deaths resulting from suicide were defined according to the Ninth Revision of the International Classification of Diseases (ICD-9), with the underlying cause codes E950–E959 (Health Care Financing Administration 1998). Suicide cases were coded 1. Due to the large number of deaths from all causes (2.8 million) and computational considerations, random probability samples (between 5% and 50%, depending on the number of suicides per analysis/subgroup) were taken of persons who died of natural causes (other than homicide, motor vehicle accidents and non-motor vehicle accidents, e.g. falls), the conventional standard. Different sample cut-off points were considered for each run but with negligible effects on the estimates (although computational time increased substantially with sample increases). The natural deaths were coded 0.

The risk (odds) of suicide (versus deaths from other causes) was estimated as a function of marital status, and control variables, sex, race/ethnicity, education, immigration status, community size, region of country, occupation (nine categories including unemployment) and age – variables typically used in the suicide literature. In order to save space here, the analyses for the occupational categories were eliminated. (Contact the authors for more information.) Marital status was measured by a set of dummy variables, one each for single, divorced/separated and widowed. Those married at the time of death constituted the reference category. Following common practice, reference categories were chosen on the basis of the prior literature.

Age at death was captured by defining it in terms of a series of dummy vectors, one each for age groups 15–24, 25–34, 35–44, and 45–64. Individuals aged 65 or more were treated as the reference category. Race/ethnicity comprised whites, African Americans, Hispanics, Asian Americans and Native Americans. In the full sample, when all race and ethnic groups were considered, African Americans were treated as the reference category. Education was defined as a series of dummy vectors: some graduate education or a graduate or professional degree, less than a high school education, a high school education and some college. The omitted group was those with some graduate education or had graduate or professional degrees. For immigration status, foreign and non-foreign born, persons born in other countries were the reference group. For sex, females were the omitted group. With regard to region of the country, we used the census classification, instead of the usual South/non-South division, i.e. Northeast, West, Midwest and South. The Northeast was the reference group. Five city sizes were employed: cities with populations under 100,000, over 1 million, 500,000–1,000,000, 250,000–499,999 and 100,000–249,999. The reference group was cities with populations under 100,000. Nine occupational categories were available: professional, managerial or specialty occupations, sales, service, farm, craft, labourer, military, homemaker and unemployed. The omitted group comprised those in professional, managerial or specialty occupations.

One variable we would have liked to include in the study is income or poverty. Unfortunately, death certificates and the *Mortality Detail File* lack such information. Instead, good proxy variables were available, namely education and occupation (unemployment, etc.).

Note, again, that in this methodology death from suicide is being compared to death from natural causes. Because natural mortality and certain of the co-variates are related to age, e.g. widow marital status, all of the coefficients are adjusted for the potentially confounding effects of age, as they are for the other co-variates.

The statistical model

Since the dependent variable is categorical (binary), maximum likelihood estimation (MLE) in multivariate logistic regression was employed (SAS, version 6.11). Estimated odds ratios (ORs) were obtained by exponentiating the logistic coefficients (parameter estimates). An OR associated with a given co-variate measures the increase in the odds for a 1-unit change in the risk factor. The more an OR deviates from one in a plus or minus direction, the more the co-variate affects the odds of the dependent variable. If the OR is 1.0, it is an indication that the co-variate in question lacks 'substantive' significance. An OR greater than 1 indicates that the odds of suicide are higher for the co-variate compared to the reference group. An OR less than 1 has the opposite interpretation. A 95% confidence interval (CI) was computed for each odds ratio (many of these were eliminated for reasons of space – see authors).

ORs can be turned into easily interpretable percentages by use of the formula: 100(OR–1). For example, the OR for single status on Table 11.1 (below) is 0.766. Thus, 100(0.766–1) = –23.4, or singles are 23.4% less likely to commit suicide compared to the married reference group. An extended discussion of the statistical model follows.

Results

Full sample

Table 11.1 presents results for the entire sample of 30,157 suicides. As indicated, the divorced/separated have a significantly elevated risk of suicide, or approximately 68% greater than the married. Contrary to Durkheim, the widowed do not have a higher risk for suicide and, as mentioned above, singles are significantly less likely to be suicide victims.

The odds ratios for age are impressive and remain so for every group with the exception of Native American females (not shown in the table). The beginning of this decade represented accelerated growth in the suicides of young people relative to older people and a reduction in the suicides of the elderly, a pattern that has only recently begun to change. It is nonetheless remarkable that the patterned effect holds for almost all of the groups investigated.

The results for race/ethnicity and sex, excluded from the other group-specific tables, tell a familiar story. Whites are much more likely to be suicide victims compared to blacks (276.2%), followed by Asian Americans

Table 11.1 Risk of suicide by marital status and other co-variates – full sample, 1992

Co-variate	*b*	*Odds* *Ratio*	*95% CI* *Lower*	*Upper*
Marital status				
Married		1.000		
Single	−0.253	0.776	0.733	0.822
Widowed	0.020*	1.020	0.969	1.074
Divorced	0.517	1.678	1.597	1.763
Race				
African American		1.000		
White	1.325	3.762	3.519	4.023
Native American	0.777	2.176	1.697	2.790
Asian American	1.131	3.099	2.620	3.667
Hispanic origin				
Hispanic		1.000		
Non-Hispanic	0.499	1.649	1.503	1.809
Sex				
Female		1.000		
Male	1.048	2.852	2.736	2.973
Education				
Graduate/prof. degree		1.000		
Less than high school	−0.232	0.793	0.754	0.834
High school graduate	0.012*	1.012	0.966	1.060
Some college	0.092	1.096	1.033	1.163
Age				
65 years or more		1.000		
15–24 years	5.364	213.647	189.000	241.509
25–34 years	4.003	54.768	50.917	58.910
35–44 years	3.065	21.426	20.223	22.701
45–64 years	1.516	4.554	4.365	4.752
Immigration status				
Foreign born		1.000		
Native born	−0.173	0.841	0.785	0.901
City size of residence				
Fewer than 100,000		1.000		
Over 1 million	−0.221	0.802	0.743	0.865
500,000–1,000,000	−0.110	0.896	0.826	0.972
250,000–499,999	−0.014*	0.989	0.920	1.062
100,000–249,999	−0.066	0.936	0.878	0.998
Region of country				
Northeast		1.000		
West	0.641	1.898	1.795	2.008
Midwest	0.319	1.376	1.302	1.455
South	0.492	1.636	1.554	1.722

Intercept	−5.071	Total suicides	30,157
Model chi-square	51575.805	Number of observations	129,604
Degrees of freedom	32		

Note: coefficients are age adjusted. All coefficients are significant at the 0.05 level with the exception of those indicated by *.

(209.9%) and Native Americans (117.6%). Similarly, Hispanics have a significantly higher suicide rate than non-Hispanics. Males are 185.2% more likely to commit suicide than females.

Among other findings, large city size (over 100,000) is not positively related to suicide risk, the unemployed do not have a significantly high suicide rate, and those with less than high school education enjoy significant protection from suicide (20.7% less than those with graduate/professional degrees). In addition, the only significant occupational category is that of craft workers who have higher suicide risk (15.7% compared to the professional/managerial category–analysis not shown).

White males

Table 11.2 presents the results for whites. Recall that Kposowa *et al.* (1995) found that divorced white men had significantly higher risk for suicide but that, contrary to Durkheim, neither singles nor widowers were significant. With a much bigger sample, this study replicates the previous findings for the divorced (70.8%) but shows that the widowed have significantly elevated risk compared to the married (36.4%), and singles are significantly *less* likely to be suicide victims (14.7%). That white men enjoy greater suicide protection when they are single may indicate that they have greater social ties prior to marriage. This is an unexpected finding. It flies in the face of the received wisdom that males enjoy more social integration benefits while married. That is true when males are compared to females (males derive more protection from marriage than females, e.g. Gove and Tudor 1973, Helsing *et al.* 1981, and see Ross *et al.* 1990 for literature review), but we find that the most advantageous marital status for white men is being single (and see African American and Hispanic males in Tables 11.3 and 11.4).

Note that the present findings contradict work by Gibbs (1969) and Stack (1990), who found that married white males enjoy the greatest protection. In the present study we are investigating the individual-level causes of suicide by controlling for relevant co-variates in a comparison of suicide with natural causes of death. In the studies by Gibbs and Stack, suicide rates by category are descriptively created (followed by various theoretical interpretations), i.e. the number of suicides in a particular category (e.g. divorced white males) is divided by the number of living people in that category. In other words, Gibbs and Stack create crude rates without investigating possible confounding factors (other than sex, marital status and age), while the present study constructs odds of suicide based on all the co-variates used. It would be possible, if much more difficult, to follow the methodology of Gibbs and Stack and create suicide rates by including all the categories in our study, i.e. sex, race and ethnicity, marital status, age, education, immigration status, city size, region and occupation. Putatively, if this were done, there would either be no discrepancies or what differences there might be

Table 11.2 Risk of suicide by marital status and other co-variates – whites

Co-variate	Males *b*	Males *OR*	Females *b*	Females *OR*
Marital status				
Married		1.000		1.000
Single	–0.159	0.853	–0.007	0.993
Widowed	0.311	1.364	–0.210	0.811
Divorced	0.535	1.708	0.597	1.816
Education				
Graduate/prof. degree		1.000		1.000
Less than high school	–0.169	0.844	–0.634	0.531
High school graduate	0.012*	1.013	–0.180	0.835
Some college	0.005*	1.005	0.090	1.094
Age				
65 years and over		1.000		1.000
15–24 years	5.051	156.241	5.029	152.760
25–34 years	3.797	44.603	4.321	75.280
35–44 years	2.824	16.847	3.570	35.515
45–64 years	1.342	3.827	2.099	8.162
Immigration status				
Foreign born		1.000		1.000
Born in the USA	0.021*	1.021	–0.055*	0.947
City size of residence				
Fewer than 100,000		1.000		1.000
Over 1 million	–0.409	0.665	–0.062*	0.940
500,000–1 million	–0.256	0.774	0.257	1.293
250,000–499,999	–0.065*	0.937	0.058*	1.060
100,000–249,999	–0.164	0.848	0.015*	1.015
Region of country				
Northeast		1.000		1.000
West	0.564	1.758	0.771	2.162
Midwest	0.245	1.278	0.352	1.422
South	0.439	1.552	0.556	1.676
Intercept	–2.266		–3.746	
Model chi-square	24825.268		21511.389	
Degrees of freedom	26		26	
Number of white suicides	21,921		5,408	
Number of observations	65,026		49,055	

Note: coefficients are age adjusted. All coefficients are significant at the 0.05 level with the exception of those indicated by *.

would be based on the different time periods used (this study uses data from 1992, compared to 1979 in Stack, and 1959–61 in Gibbs). Note, finally, that in the Stack paper, and perhaps in that by Gibbs, separated persons are placed in the married category owing to limitations of the data. The present data allow for the inclusion of the separated with the divorced.

Not surprisingly, given the large proportion of white males in the sample (greater than 70%), the findings for the other co-variates closely match that of the full sample. Notably, white males who are unemployed do not have significantly high suicide risk, a finding that contradicts some small sample studies (analysis not shown).

White females

Among white females (Table 11.2), the divorced have increased risk (81.6%), but the results for the other marital statuses are almost the opposite of those of white men. White women are significantly less likely to commit suicide when they are widows (by 18.9%) and single status is unrelated to suicide risk. Thus, for white men, being single protects against suicide, while widow status protects white women. Conversely, widow status for white men is a suicide risk, and single status for white women is unrelated to suicide.

The suicide protection for white widow females (one that is stronger than that of marriage) could be the result of social ties following the deaths of their husbands. The typical older white female is more likely to become part of a social network compared to older white males who are widowed (e.g. Gerstel 1988). Thus the death of a spouse might increase the social integration of white women but decrease that for white men.

An alternative hypothesis to that of Durkheim's social integration theory, one involving differential sex socialization, is suggested by the disparate results for males and females. Accordingly, males (compared to females) are less likely to injure or kill themselves and more likely to hurt others – the male socially learned propensity for violence is aimed outward, the female inward. Note that while more males commit suicide than females, many more females attempt suicide and fail for reasons mainly having to do with the method of suicide (Lester 1993). Single males may enjoy the most protection from suicide because marital status is the least 'feminized' in our culture. Marriage is less protective for men because marriage feminizes men.

While divorce may be a suicide risk for both males and females for reasons of weakening social integration, alternative social factors may play a significant part. For example, divorce often entails the loss of an accustomed social role involving status, prestige, legitimacy and, for some, rejection by the married peer group.

Widow status may be risky for men and not for women because of a social integration explanation not suggested by Durkheim. That is, because of different mortality rates (from natural causes) there are fewer older males than females, and therefore widowers are less likely to obtain social support from a peer group.

With regard to the findings for the other co-variates, one interesting result is that unemployed white women are at increased risk of suicide (22.4%), while homemakers are not (analysis not shown). These results suggest that unemployment for white women who must work is a suicide risk while women who stay at home are not at increased risk. For white men, unemployment is not a suicide risk, suggesting that perhaps many of them have significant social ties to weather the temporary hardship, i.e. spouses, and alternative sources of income (spousal income). Many working women who are unemployed are not married and lack both the additional source of income and the social ties marriage provides.

Black males

The results for black males (Table 11.3) are more surprising and run contrary to Durkheim's expectations. Like white males who are single, black single males are less likely to be suicide victims, but the effect is far stronger for single black males (by 51% compared to by 14.7%). Unlike white males, neither widows nor divorced/separated black males have significant suicide risks. Several factors may help to explain these findings. First, based on homicide research in which single black men were found to have high homicide rates (e.g. Kposowa *et al.* 1994), it is conceivable that many single black males would have killed themselves had they not been victims of homicide. Second, widowed black men may have significantly more social ties, especially family involvement, than widowed white men (e.g. Chatters *et al.* 1985). We do not have a simple explanation for the divorce findings (see below), but they are especially interesting in light of those for black females and Hispanics.

Among the other co-variates, black males born in the US (32.9%) and those living in large cities (greater than 500,000) have significantly lower suicide risk (by 26.1–26.4%). Note that none of the occupational categories is positively significant for black males, including the unemployed, and black males in service and craft occupations are protected from suicide (analysis not shown).

Black females

For black females (Table 11.3), divorced/separated was the only marital status category significantly related to suicide (up by 54.5%). Single and widow status, while negatively related, did not reach the level of significance. Thus for black females, and quite contrary to Durkheim, marriage, single and widow status carry the same relative risk of suicide. Interestingly, black females born in the US were significantly less likely to be suicide

Table 11.3 Risk of suicide by marital status and other co-variates – blacks

	Males		*Females*	
Co-variate	*b*	*OR*	*b*	*OR*
Marital status				
Married		1.000		1.000
Single	–0.714	0.490	–0.183*	0.833
Widowed	0.098*	1.103	–0.251*	0.778
Divorced	0.126*	1.134	0.435	1.545
Education				
Graduate/prof. degree		1.000		1.000
Less than high school	–0.100*	0.905	–0.234*	0.791
High school graduate	0.157*	1.170	–0.099*	0.906
Some college	0.247*	1.280	–0.003*	0.997
Age				
65 years and over		1.000		1.000
15–24 years	6.116	453.184	5.111	165.858
25–34 years	4.247	69.901	4.209	67.318
35–44 years	2.815	16.695	3.191	24.313
45–64 years	1.199	3.317	1.744	5.721
Immigration status				
Foreign born		1.000		1.000
Born in the USA	–0.398	0.671	–0.669	0.512
City size of residence				
Fewer than 100,000		1.000		1.000
Over 1 million	–0.303	0.739	–0.062*	1.065
500,000–1 million	–0.306	0.736	0.011*	1.011
250,000–499,999	–0.069*	0.932	0.160*	1.174
100,000–249,999	–0.172*	0.842	–0.019*	0.896
Region of country				
Northeast		1.000		1.000
West	0.191*	1.210	0.863	2.370
Midwest	0.206*	1.228	0.614	1.849
South	0.099*	1.104	0.255*	1.291
Intercept	–2.347		–6.509	
Model chi-square	3143.515		932.486	
Degrees of freedom	25		25	
Number of black suicides	1,774		333	
Number of observations	5,957		55,497	

Note: coefficients are age adjusted. All coefficients are significant at the 0.05 level with the exception of those indicated by *.

victims compared to those foreign born (by 48.8%). In addition, black females in the South fail to have an increased risk of suicide, unlike those in the West and Midwest who have significantly high rates compared to those in the Northeast. Indeed, black females in the West are a surprising 137% more likely to commit suicide than those in the Northeast. Note that unlike white females, the unemployed occupational category is not significant for black females (analysis not shown). That may be because black or other minority females (see below) more often experience unemployment and are better able to make the adjustment and/or have sufficient social attachments to tide them over.

Hispanic males

The marital status results for Hispanic males (Table 11.4) mirror those for black males. This is interesting because of all the subgroups studied in this research, an argument can be made that Hispanic and African Americans have the most in common. Note, however, that the similarity only applies to males. Like white and black males, Hispanic males who are single enjoy significant suicide protection (41.9%). As with black males, widowed or divorced Hispanic males do not have significant suicide risks. The explanation for the widowed results may be similar to that for blacks, but note that the results for the divorced/separated similarly show disparate results for Hispanic males and females (see below).

Why divorced African American and Hispanic females show increased suicide risk while males do not runs counter to Durkheim's *Suicide* predictions and, without further study, is a matter of speculation. One possibility is that males of minorities are less affected by the social stigma that is typically attached to divorce. Note that some minorities have much higher divorce/separation than whites (Norton and Moorman 1987), and that, compared to whites, blacks have fewer adjustment problems following divorce (Gove and Shin 1989). Another possibility is that because of unemployment, incarceration, residential segregation and reduced marriageability (Wilson 1987), minority males may more easily be able to return to the peer groups with which they associated when they were singles, or join new groups of same age singles, and thereby benefit from the social ties and social integration such groups putatively provide. By contrast, majority males may find themselves divorced not only from their spouses but their prior singles peer group. This is because there are fewer single white males and finding a singles peer group following divorce may not be easy. Note that many minority women do not have integrative opportunities that are similar to those of minority males because of obligations to young children. In addition, the economic consequences of divorce for some minority group women may be relatively greater than is the case for white women (e.g. Duncan and Hoffman 1985).

Table 11.4 Risk of suicide by marital status and other co-variates – Hispanics

	Males		*Females*	
Co-variate	*b*	*OR*	*b*	*OR*
Marital status				
Married		1.000		1.000
Single	−0.544	0.581	−0.245	0.783
Widowed	−0.053*	0.948	−0.517	0.596
Divorced	0.149*	1.162	0.213	1.238
Education				
Graduate/prof. degree		1.000		1.000
Less than high school	−0.138*	0.871	−0.392	0.676
High school graduate	0.004*	1.004	−0.106*	0.899
Some college	0.189*	0.827	−0.013*	1.013
Age				
65 years and over		1.000		1.000
15–24 years	5.359	212.593	4.619	101.441
25–34 years	3.736	41.951	3.327	27.861
35–44 years	2.788	16.261	2.517	12.386
45–64 years	1.578	4.846	1.388	4.009
Immigration status				
Foreign born		1.000		1.000
Born in the USA	−0.121	0.886	−0.189	0.828
City size of residence				
Fewer than 100,000		1.000		1.000
Over 1 million	−0.411	0.663	−0.119*	0.888
500,000–1 million	−0.354	0.702	−0.327*	0.721
250,000–499,999	−0.042*	0.959	−0.029*	0.971
100,000–249,999	−0.104*	0.902	0.009*	1.009
Region of country				
Northeast		1.000		1.000
West	0.672	1.959	0.530	1.700
Midwest	0.582	1.791	0.538	1.712
South	0.784	2.190	0.732	2.080
Intercept	−5.191		−4.615	
Model chi-square	3153.129		1711.307	
Degrees of freedom	26		26	
Number of Hispanics suicides	1,496		855	
Number of observations	26,160		23,631	

Note: coefficients are age adjusted. All coefficients are significant at the 0.05 level with the exception of those indicated by *.

With respect to the other variables, male Hispanics who are born in the US (11.4%) and those who live in cities with more than 500,000 population (29.8–33.7%) are significantly less likely to be suicides. In addition, craft (32.5%) and labourer (27.9%) occupations are associated with increased risk of suicide for Hispanics (analysis not shown).

Hispanic females

Hispanic females who are divorced are at higher risk for suicide (23.8%) but, contrary to Durkheim, single (21.7%) and widow (40.4%) Hispanic females are significantly less likely to fall victim to suicide (Table 11.4). Hispanic females with less than high school education are significantly less likely (32.4%) to be suicides compared to those with graduate/professional degrees. In addition, Hispanic females who are born in the US (17.2%) and homemakers (72%, analysis not shown) are significantly less likely to commit suicide. Note that city size is unrelated to suicide risk and that every regional category is significantly different from the Northeast in the positive direction, the South leading with an OR = 2.08 or 108% greater risk. Finally, consider the non-significant results for farm workers for both Hispanic males and females (analysis not shown). Because deaths from non-residents are excluded, most migrant Hispanic workers are not represented in the data. In any case, anecdotal evidence would not lead us to believe migrant workers have high suicide rates.

Asian American males

Asian American males (Table 11.5) who are single do not share in the suicide protection of white, black and Hispanic single males, yet, contrary to Durkheim, they do not have increased suicide risk. However, the divorced (67.1%) have elevated risk and the widowed have an unusually high risk (162.5%). The latter result may indicate that for Asian American males, marriage is both an extremely important social role and source of social integration or both.

Among the remaining co-variates, Asian American males who are farm workers (310.7%), and those who live in the West (62.6%) and South (98.9%) have increased risk of suicide. We have no explanation for the high suicide risk for either farm workers (analysis not shown) or those living in the South, or why cities with populations between 500,000–1,000,000 offer Asian American males protection from suicide (44.2%).

Asian American females

For Asian American females (Table 11.5), of the marital status categories only divorced has an increased risk of suicide, but it is nevertheless strikingly

Table 11.5 Risks of suicide by marital status and other co-variates – Asian/Americans

	Males		*Females*	
Co-variate	*b*	*OR*	*b*	*OR*
Marital status				
Married		1.000		1.000
Single	0.226*	1.253	0.143*	1.154
Widowed	0.965	2.625	−0.179*	0.836
Divorced	0.514	1.671	0.746	2.108
Education				
Graduate/prof.degree		1.000		1.000
Less than high school	−0.252*	0.777	−0.425*	0.654
High school graduate	−0.155*	0.856	−0.107*	0.898
Some college	−0.208*	0.812	−0.306*	0.737
Age				
65 years and over		1.000		1.000
15–24 years	5.427	227.467	5.140	170.721
25–34 years	4.220	68.032	3.808	45.057
35–44 years	3.203	24.616	2.945	19.014
45–64 years	1.632	5.116	1.525	4.596
Immigration status				
Foreign born		1.000		1.000
Born in the USA	−0.126*	0.882	−0.433	0.649
City size of residence				
Fewer than 100,000		1.000		1.000
Over 1 million	−0.292*	0.746	0.101*	1.106
500,000–1 million	−0.584	0.558	0.393*	1.482
250,000–499,999	−0.172*	0.843	0.026*	1.026
100,000–249,999	−0.166*	0.847	0.452*	1.572
Region of country				
Northeast		1.000		1.000
West	0.486	1.626	−0.325*	0.723
Midwest	0.445	1.560	−0.633*	0.531
South	0.687	1.989	−0.348*	0.706
Intercept	−5.215		−4.236	
Model chi-square	913.340		539.307	
Degrees of freedom	25		23	
Number of Asian Americans suicides	337		200	
Number of observations	6,085		6,043	

Note: coefficients are age adjusted. All coefficients are significant at the 0.05 level with the exception of those indicated by *.

high (100.8%). Notably, those born in the US are significantly less likely to be suicides (35.1%), a contrast with the nonsignificant results for Asian American males. Asian American females do not share the Asian American male risk for certain regions of the country or the farm occupational category, and, apart from age, no other category is significantly related to suicide.

Native American males

Offering no support for Durkheim, none of the marital status categories achieves statistical significance for Native American males (Table 11.6). With the exception of age, the same is true for the other co-variates. Notably, the western region of the country, small city size, and the unemployed and farm occupational categories (analysis not shown) are not significant.

Native American females

Because the number of suicides among Native American females (table not shown) was only 40, resulting in empty cell problems, all categories other than marital status and age were eliminated from the model. The results, contrary to Durkheim, indicate that no marital status category is significantly related to suicide. Given the small sample and lack of multivariate results, the findings must be considered tentative. In the future as more data become available, we would suggest aggregating (individual) Native American female suicides over several years.

Discussion and summary

This study finds remarkably little support for Durkheim's theory of social integration. Durkheim predicts single people have the highest suicide odds ratios, followed by the divorced and widowed. That pattern applies to none of the ten sex and race/ethnic groups studied here. Even the less demanding notion that marriage provides more protection than the other marital status categories is not supported with any subgroup. More generously still, of the 30 comparisons between marriage and the other categories, only eight support Durkheim. Of these, six apply to divorce/separation. Overall, Durkheim's predictions about divorce are correct 60% of the time, 20% for widows and 0% for singles. By racial/ethnic group, Durkheim's predictions are best for whites and Asian Americans (3 out of 8), followed by African Americans and Hispanics (1 out of 8) and Native Americans (0).

Specifically, while Durkheim views single status as the most risky one for suicide, this study generally shows opposite or non-significant results. White males, all males (table not shown), black males, and Hispanic males and females who are single are less likely to commit suicide than the married. The result for all females (table not shown), white females, black females,

Table 11.6 Risks of suicide by marital status and other co-variates – Native American males

Co-variate	*Odds* *b*	*Ratio*
Marital status		
Married		1.000
Single	−0.014*	0.984
Widowed	0.333*	1.390
Divorced	0.179*	1.189
Education		
Graduate/prof.degree		1.000
Less than high school	0.133*	1.139
High school graduate	0.053*	1.053
Some college	−0.109*	0.891
Age		
65 years and over		1.000
15–24 years	6.337	561.747
25–34 years	4.504	89.964
35–44 years	3.627	37.452
45–64 years	1.411	4.102
Immigration status		
Foreign born		1.000
Born in the USA	0.825*	2.284
City size of residence		
Fewer than 100,000		1.000
Over 1 million	0.042*	1.042
500,000–1 million	−0.053*	0.949
250,000–499,999	−0.216*	0.797
100,000–249,999	−0.459*	0.633
Region of country		
Northeast		1.000
West	0.602*	1.823
Midwest	0.136*	1.144
South	0.189*	1.215
Intercept	−6.767*	
Model chi-square	556.555*	
Degrees of freedom	24	
Number of Native American male suicides	184	
Number of observations	1990	

Note: coefficients are age adjusted. All coefficients are significant at the 0.05 level with the exception of those indicated by *.

Asian American males and females, and Native American males and females, show non-significant results for singles. In not one category is single status significantly related to suicide risk in the expected positive direction.

The most encouraging results for Durkheim are those concerning the divorced. White males and females, African American females, Hispanic females and Asian American males and females show significantly positive results for divorce as predicted by Durkheim. The exceptions are for black, Hispanic and Native American males and females, all not significant.

Finally, the results for widow status indicate support for Durkheim only among white and Asian American males. At the same time, white and Hispanic females who are widows are significantly protected from suicide compared to those married.

Beyond Durkheim's *Suicide*, this study uncovers new patterns in the risk of suicide mortality. Most importantly, we have shown that single status is of greater benefit than marriage for white, black and Hispanic males. Less unexpectedly, white and Hispanic women similarly benefit from widow status. Unemployment is significantly related to suicide in the positive direction for only one group, white females. Finally, African American males and females, Hispanic males and females and Asian American females who are foreign born are at increased risk of suicide.

We have also suggested alternative theoretical explanations to those of Durkheim. First, the differences in suicide risk between males and females by marital status is striking and may point to a socialization effect. Such an effect may help to explain why, in contradiction to Durkheim, single white, black and Hispanic males are less likely to commit suicide than those who are married. Second, in addition to social integration, other social factors are likely to play a role in the loss of marriage through divorce and the death of a spouse. Specifically, divorce or widowhood involves the loss of an accustomed social role including status, prestige and legitimacy. Third, suicide risk differences between males and females with regard to widow status may suggest the effects of differential sex mortality on the formation of elder peer/support networks. Fourth, single African American males are more likely to be 'protected' from suicide because more of them are victims of homicide. Fifth, unlike white males, divorced/separated African American and Hispanic males may not be at increased risk for suicide, because for various social and economic reasons, including patterns of racism and discrimination, they may be better able to return to the peer groups they enjoyed as singles.

Without further study, however, it is essential in our opinion that we not be too hasty in overturning Durkheim's theory. It is possible that social integration may be related to suicide in ways current methods in sociology have been unable to reveal. This is not a disingenuous attempt to explain away results that are discomforting, but a call for more research. For example, there is good reason to believe that many single people have stronger and more social attachments than some married. In addition, it is not unreasonable to think that for some people widow status is associated with greater social involvement. And, of course, for many people divorce is the starting point for social attachments that will prove to be far more salubrious than their unhappy marriages. While the present research is an individual-level study, many of the independent-level variables we would like to investigate are nowhere available. Indeed, until we collect original data by surveying people to determine the role of social bonds in their lives (either by large scale Framingham-like studies or ones which focus on an experimental group of those who have made life-threatening suicide attempts), we will not know if Durkheim's fundamental idea is correct. That is: how many close friends do you have? How often do you see your relatives? How meaningful to you are your relationships with others? Do you have strong ties to others at your workplace? Do you actively participate in groups such as community or charity associations, religious organizations, recreational sports teams or other group activities such as bird watching? How often does your spouse make him or herself available to you in a supportive way? In times of need, do you feel you have others you can rely on?

In addition, suicide has been linked by competent researchers in medicine, psychiatry and psychology to a host of variables that can only be obtained directly from individuals or individual histories (e.g. medical records, psychological autopsies): affective disorders, notably bipolar illness, schizophrenia, inherited predisposition to affective illness, substance abuse, low levels in cerebrospinal fluid of 5-hydroxyindoleacetic and homovanillic acids, homosexuality, previous suicidal behavior, impulsiveness and aggressiveness. We submit that we will not be able to determine whether Durkheim is right until research also includes these variables. At the same time, from a theoretical perspective, we will not be able to go beyond Durkheim unless such research is done.

While we are not pessimistic that Durkheim's fundamental thesis will perform well in the kind of research outlined here, we are forced to admit that the present study provides little solace. Even the most encouraging results, those for divorce, are less meaningful when we consider the variables that are left out. Given the large sample and methods used, there is no question that for some groups (e.g. white males and females, Asian American males and females) the Durkheim-favourable divorce results are quite robust and are telling us something, but without additional study with the theory and variables mentioned here, we will not know what that is. It is a reasonable possibility that the divorce–suicide relationship will be rejected when other variables are controlled or that alternative social factors might emerge if they were investigated.

In the final analysis, perhaps, the importance of this research is that it continues to point us in the direction of the individual as the appropriate unit of analysis in the study of suicide. One hundred years later, Durkheim's compelling notion that social bonds are a crucial factor in morbidity and mortality is far too important for us to subscribe to his insistence that we focus on aggregations and aggregate-level variables.

Note

Direct correspondence to K. D. Breault, 4010 Dorcas Dr., Nashville, TN 37215–2211. Email: kbreault@compuserve.com. Fax: 615–648–7382. The authors contributed equally to the paper. This paper would not have been possible without the many helpful advances and criticisms of suicide researchers in sociology. We are especially indebted to Jack Gibbs, Chris Girard, Walter Gove, David Lester, Bernice Pescosolido, David Philips, Whitney Pope, Steven Stack and Ira Wasserman.

Bibliography

Breault, K. D. (1986) 'Suicide in America: A Test of Durkheim's Theory of Religious and Family Integration, 1933–1980', *American Journal of Sociology* 92:628–56.

(1994) 'Was Durkheim Right? A Critical Survey of the Empirical Literature on *Le Suicide*', in D. Lester (ed.) *Emile Durkheim:* Le Suicide *100 Years Later*, Philadelphia: The Charles Press.

(1997) 'A *Le Suicide* Commemorative: Toward a New Appreciation and Direction for Research', *Meetings of the American Sociological Association* August, 1997.

Chatters, L. M., Taylor, R. J. and Jackson, J. (1985) 'Size and Composition of the Informal Helper Networks of Elderly Blacks', *Journal of Gerontology* 40:605–14.

Duncan, G. J. and Hoffman, S. D. (1985) 'Economic Consequences of Marital Instability', in D. M. and T. Smeeding (eds) *Horizontal Equity, Uncertainty and Economic Well-Being*, Chicago: University of Chicago Press.

Gerstel, N. (1988) 'Divorce and Kin Ties: The Importance of Gender', *Journal of Marriage and the Family* 50:209–19.

Gibbs, J. P. (1969) 'Marital Status and Suicide in the United States: A Special Test of the Status Integration Theory', *American Journal of Sociology* 74:521–33.

(1994) 'Durkheim's Heavy Hand in the Sociological Study of Suicide', in D. Lester (ed.) *Emile Durkheim:* Le Suicide *100 Years Later*, Philadelphia: The Charles Press.

Girard, C. (1988) 'Church Membership and Suicide Reconsidered', *American Journal of Sociology* 93:1471–8.

Goldney, R. D. (1981) 'Parental Loss and Reported Childhood Stress in Young Women Who Commit Suicide', *Acta Psychiatrica Scandanavica* 64:34–59.

Gove, W. R. (1972) 'Sex, Marital Status and Suicide', *Journal of Health and Social Behavior* 13:204–13.

(1973) 'Sex, Marital Status and Mortality', *American Journal of Sociology* 79:45–67.

Gove, W. R. and Shin, H.-C. (1989) 'The Psychological Well-being of Divorced and Widowed Men and Women: An Empirical Analysis', *Journal of Family Issues* 10:122–44.

Gove, W. R. and Tudor, J. F. (1973) 'Adult Sex Roles and Mental Illness', *American Journal of Sociology* 78:1–24.

Health Care Financing Administration (1998) *International Classification of Diseases, 9th Revision, Clinical Modification 5th Edition*, Washington, DC: Health Care Financing Administration.

Helsing, K. J., Moysen, S. and Comstock, G. W. (1981) 'Factors Associated with Mortality after Widowhood', *Journal of Public Health* 71:802–9.

Humphrey, J. (1977) 'Social Loss', *Diseases of the Nervous System* 38:157–60.

Kobrin, F. E. and Hendershot, G. E. (1977) 'Do Family Ties Reduce Mortality?', *Journal of Marriage and the Family* 39:737–45.

Kposowa, A. J., Singh, G. K. and Breault, K. D. (1994) 'The Effects of Marital Status and Social Isolation on Adult Male Homicides in the United States: Evidence from the National Longitudinal Mortality Study', *Journal of Quantitative Criminology* 10:277–89.

Kposowa, A. J., Breault, K. D. and Singh, G. K. (1995) 'White Male Suicide in the United States: A Multivariate Individual-level Analysis', *Social Forces* 74:315–23.

Lester, D. (1993) *Patterns of Suicide and Homicide in America*, Commack, NY: Nova Science Publishers.

(ed.) (1994) *Emile Durkheim:* Le Suicide *100 Years Later*, Philadelphia: The Charles Press.

Moksony, F. (1994) 'The Whole, Its Parts and the Level of Analysis: Durkheim and the Macrosociological Study of Suicide', in D. Lester (ed.) *Emile Durkheim:* Le Suicide *100 Years Later*, Philadelphia: The Charles Press.

National Center for Health Statistics (1994) *Public Use Data Tape Documentation: Mortality Detail*, Hyattsville, MD: Department of Health and Human Services.

Norton, A. J. and Moorman, J. E. (1987) 'Current Trends in American Marriage and Divorce', *Journal of Marriage and the Family* 49:3–14.

Pescosolido, B. A. (1994) 'Bringing Durkheim into the Twenty-first Century: A Network Approach to Unsolved Issues in the Sociology of Suicide', in D. Lester (ed.) *Emile Durkheim:* Le Suicide *100 Years Later*, Philadelphia: The Charles Press.

Pescosolido, B. A. and Georgianna, S. (1989) 'Durkheim, Suicide, and Religion: Toward a Network Theory of Suicide', *American Journal of Sociology* 54:33–48.

Pescosolido, B. A. and Mendelsohn, R. (1986) 'Social Causation or Social Construction of Suicide?', *American Sociological Review* 51:80–100.

Pope, W. (1976) *Durkheim's* Suicide*: A Classic Analyzed*, Chicago: University of Chicago Press.

Rico-Velasco, J. and Mynko, L. (1973) 'Suicide and Marital Status: A Changing Relationship?', *Journal of Marriage and the Family* 35:239–44.

Robins, L. N., West, P. A. and Murphy, G. E. (1977) 'The High Rate of Suicide in Older White Men: A Study Testing Ten Hypotheses', *Social Psychiatry* 12:1–20.

Ross, C. E., Mirowsky, J. and Goldsteen, K. (1990) 'The Impact of the Family on Health: The Decade in Review', *Journal of Marriage and the Family* 52:1059–78.

Shafi, M., Carrigan, S., Whittinghall, J. R. and Derrick, A. (1985) 'Psychological Autopsy of Completed Suicide in Children and Adolescents', *American Journal of Psychiatry* 142:1061–4.

Stack, S. (1982) 'Suicide: A Decade Review of the Sociological Literature', *Deviant Behavior* 4:41–66.

(1985) 'The Effect of Domestic/Religious Individualism on Suicide, 1954–78', *Journal of Marriage and the Family* 47:431–47.

(1990) 'New Micro-level Data on the Impact of Divorce on Suicide, 1959–1980: A Test of Two Theories', *Journal of Marriage and the Family* 52:119–27.

Stack, S. and Wasserman, I. (1993) 'Marital Status, Alcohol Consumption and Suicide: An Analysis of National Data', *Journal of Marriage and the Family* 55:1018–24.

Teicher, J. D. and Jacobs, J. (1966) 'Adolescents Who Attempt Suicide: Preliminary Findings', *American Journal of Psychiatry* 122:1248–57.

Thorlindsson, T. and Bjarnason, T. (1998) 'Modeling Durkheim on the Micro Level: A Study of Youth Suicidality', *American Sociological Review* 63:94–110.

van Poppel, F. and Day, L. (1996) 'A Test of Durkheim's Theory of Suicide – Without Committing the "Ecological Fallacy"', *American Sociological Review* 61:500–7.

Wasserman, I. (1983) 'Political Business Cycles, Presidential Elections, and Suicide and Mortality Patterns', *American Sociological Review* 48:711–20.

(1984) 'A Longitudinal Analysis of the Linkage between Suicide, Unemployment, and Marital Dissolution', *Journal of Marriage and the Family* 46:853–9.

Wilson, W. J. (1987) *The Truly Disadvantaged*, Chicago: University of Chicago Press.

12

TEACHING DURKHEIM'S *SUICIDE*

A symposium

Christie Davies and Mark Neal, John Varty, Geoffrey Walford, Robert Alun Jones and William Ramp

Teaching Durkheim's *Suicide*: an unsurpassed exercise in the use of the sociological imagination

Christie Davies and Mark Neal

Durkheim's *Suicide* remains an invaluable teaching resource, not only for conveying comparative and historical knowledge about suicide rates, but for instilling in students an appreciation of important analytical issues in social research. This contribution discusses the use of Durkheim's *Suicide* in the teaching of comparative sociology and social analysis, and identifies the key strengths and weaknesses of the work which keep it relevant and useful today.

Our observations are based upon our experience of running a course on Durkheim's *Suicide* within a wider Introduction to Sociology unit at the University of Reading, UK. The course has been running for fifteen years, and student numbers have grown now to an enrolment of over four hundred. The 'Durkheim' section consists of seven lectures, with corresponding seminar classes. Appraisals of the course have been consistently excellent and indicate that students are left with a clear understanding of the nature, importance and implications of Durkheim's work.

The lectures begin with an outline of Durkheim's main empirical findings, presented not in tabular form on an overhead projector, but as a series of 'greater' and 'lesser' statements such as:

peacetime suicide rates > wartime suicide rates
rates among Protestants > Roman Catholics > Jews

These are presented simultaneously on the board and as a pre-distributed handout which the students annotate as the lecture proceeds.

The overriding emphasis here is on the elegance of Durkheim's models, which reduce over twenty different empirical statements about suicide to four variables and two dimensions, with the related but distinct concepts of egoism and anomie being the most important for an understanding of European data (Durkheim's work necessarily having been Eurocentric). The clarity of Durkheim's analysis is in marked contrast to his later rivals' sprawling classifications of the different types of suicide by motive, method and meaning. Indeed, some of these analyses resemble Lewis Carroll's 'perfect map' with its scale of 1:1 – so large and fine-grained as to be completely useless. In considering the appropriate 'pitch' of analysis, the point is thus made that models that are too close to descriptions are neither illuminating nor proper models. We thus stress again Durkheim's great achievement in teasing out egoism and anomie, altruism and fatalism from the complex data facing him.

Only when these points are established, elaborated and understood do we introduce the notion that all is not well with the categories of altruistic and fatalistic suicide. In discussing these flaws, it is important to stress, however, that those who wish to abandon Durkheim's framework and merge the analytically separate egoism and anomie are not merely misguided but wrong empirically.

This leads naturally to another of Durkheim's triumphs: his development of a theory that transcends common sense and transcends any attempt to extend otherwise valid work by psychiatrists and psychologists to explain relative suicide rates. Much social science is devoted to proving the obvious, such as the better health enjoyed by privileged individuals in a particular society relative to those who are destitute. By contrast there is nothing obvious or expected about Durkheim, however vital and significant his work seems to those who have mastered it. From comparisons with psychological and psychiatric data, it becomes clear just how right Durkheim was to stress that suicide rates are social facts, to be explained in terms of other social factors. Psychologists rightly stress the close links between suicide and depression, but most depressed persons do not commit suicide. It is for social reasons that depressed people (and others) in Denmark or Hungary are much more likely to kill themselves than depressed persons in Spain or Greece – not because they are more depressed, nor because depression is more common in the former countries. Likewise the incidence of depression among women is higher than among men, yet the male suicide rate is generally higher, and much higher than the female rate in all European countries. Egoism and anomie can now be shown to be the mediating social variables in each case. Thus modern data about psychological and psychiatric states, far from undermining Durkheim's approach, confirm the value of his emphasis on social facts.

Perhaps Durkheim's greatest triumph has been over those psychoanalysts who studied the relative suicide rates of the Scandinavian countries and concluded that the much lower suicide rate among Norwegians lay in the healthy relationship between mother and child, free from the clingingness of the Danes, and the coldness of the liberated Swedes. Unfortunately for this theory the Norwegian suicide rate rose sharply towards the general Scandinavian level after the Norwegians discovered oil and experienced an economic boom. Such a development could not be explained from within the socially static world of psychoanalysis where patterns of family relations with young children do not and cannot change rapidly.

By contrast, the change was exactly what was predicted by Durkheim's theory of anomie, with the suicide rate rising in booms (contrary to everyday belief) as well as in slumps when there are disruptive changes in incomes, economic expectations and patterns of economic social life.

Here then is a further strength of Durkheim's work – it can generate falsifiable predictions that can be tested, though care must be taken about the significance of a group's position within a social and cultural order. Farmers in many countries have very high suicide rates because they may be socially as well as geographically isolated, and are today, in England at least, more strongly enmeshed in the uncertainties of commercial and political society than were Durkheim's nineteenth-century French peasants.

Students are next shown how Durkheim's concept of anomie has been used to explain social facts other than suicide. We thus introduce Robert Merton's attempt to explain why cheating, crime and drug addiction are much more widespread in the United States than in Europe. We stress the point that his model is essentially a comparative one – though Merton himself did not always seem to have been aware of the importance of this. Students are thus shown how, without this comparative contrast, Merton's observations and analysis would not make sense.

Durkheim's *Suicide* is thus used to illustrate several key themes in sociological theory and analysis: the importance of social facts, accuracy and elegance; how the comparative method can be used to test truth-claims – especially contested ones; and the importance of prediction and falsifiability in the social sciences. Only from a masterpiece could all these themes be extracted.

Durkheim's *Suicide* is, however, a flawed masterpiece, and these flaws are important and useful in teaching students about the difficulties of doing social research. There are obvious problems with Durkheim's approach, but most of these problems are to be found throughout sociology, particularly concerning the nature and practice of definition, calculation, meaning and measurement. The measurement of even relative suicide rates is problematic; but then, as we point out to the students, so is the measurement of relative gross natural products, crime rates or the proportion of Presbyterians in the population. Even census data are shaped by social and measurement procedures, as with the exaggerated proportion of the Welsh population able to speak Welsh in the last census, or the age distribution of the Soviet male population in 1940. Durkheim is subjected to a demand for a level of rigour that would be unrealistic today, let alone in the 1890s.

Equally absurd is the anti-Durkheimian claim that suicide rates are meaningless because they are an aggregate of acts that had widely different meanings for the very varied people who took their own lives. So what? Some individuals buy Jaguar cars for aesthetic reasons, others for comfort, others to show off, and yet others out of veneration for Inspector Morse. None of these differing motives affects the validity of economists' analyses of the demand curve for Jaguars. There is, after all, a commonly understood and morally significant set of acts called 'suicide'. It is a reasonable category and one whose relative size can reasonably be linked empirically to other social variables. For admirers of Durkheim, we thus reach the high point of the lectures, the point at which his numerous critics are discussed and then dismissed and defeated.

Criticisms of the research do remain, of course. We have found such criticisms to be useful in that they provide the students with good examples of sceptical sociological reasoning. As we have argued elsewhere (see chapter 3), one area of weakness is Durkheim's discussion of altruistic and fatalistic suicides. The problem is not, as some claim, that these categories of suicide are rare – for as Asian data presented to the students show, they are not – but that they are indeterminate. Military altruistic suicides fall in wartime along with egoistic suicides, and cohesive religious sects can have either very high or very low rates of altruistic suicide. From this it can be seen that Durkheim's link between suicide and the social facts of social integration and social regulations can only make sense at the egoistic and anomic ends of the spectrum. At the altruistic and fatalistic ends, the content of regulation and the nature of integration – not just their intensity – becomes important, as indeed we might expect. If something is absent or weak it does not much matter what its nature is; if it is present and strong it clearly does.

Thus a tragic last act in which a part at least of Durkheim's edifice collapses succeeds the Durkheimian triumphalism that preceded it. Exposition has led to analysis, then to criticism and refutation leading to celebration and finally to further difficulties. This is clearly a lot more fun than following 'aims and objectives'.

At each stage, then, the unit seeks not only to teach Durkheim to first-year students but to introduce them to more general sociological questions that they will inevitably encounter in their later work. Durkheim's study, *Suicide*, though out of date, translated, fussy and at times moralistic, remains ideal for this purpose a hundred years on, for it is the basis of much of what we have argued about ever since.

Teaching Durkheim's *Suicide* in seminars

John Varty

I have taught seminars on Durkheim's *Suicide* in two first-year courses at Sussex University: one for sociology students and another for a mixture of social science students. In the sociology course *Suicide* crops up in a seminar on the debate between methodological individualists and their critics: the accompanying essay question asks whether society is anything more than the sum of its parts. Durkheim's *The Rules of Sociological Method* is on the reading list as a text opposed to individualist approaches to understanding society; *Suicide* is used as the specific example around which discussion is based. In the social science course, which has the theme 'Individual and society', there is a seminar on *The Rules of Sociological Method* and *Suicide*. In another seminar we look at *The Division of Labour*. In this course students are encouraged to read the classic texts themselves rather than rely on secondary commentaries. Both courses also feature a seminar based on Weber's essay on *verstehen*; students are expected to compare the two sociological approaches.

In the two courses *Suicide* is taken, much as Durkheim presented it, as an example of the method set out in the *Rules*. As these are courses for first-year students one dilemma I face is trying to avoid making things more complicated than they need be without oversimplifying matters and glossing over some of the details of Durkheim's account. I have, until now, skipped over the fact that, in *Suicide*, Durkheim 'reverses' his method as set out in the *Rules*, but I now feel that this is something worth drawing to the students' attention as it illustrates that Durkheim intended the *Rules* to be used in an imaginative not a rigid manner. At the same time it brings to notice one of the weakest points of *Suicide*: that Durkheim's 'aetiological classification' of suicide presupposes that his causal explanations of suicide are true (Lukes 1973:201).

It is common for seminars at Sussex to start with a short student presentation. I find that students have a clear understanding of why Durkheim chose suicide as a topic. They realize that Durkheim focused on social suicide rates, not individual cases. They are also able to summarize the basic details of the theory: the different forms of suicide; the different rates for Catholics, Protestants and Jews, married and unmarried; the influence of national crises, and more. Subsequent discussion can then turn to outlining and assessing Durkheim's explanations for these rates. Filling in the details of Durkheim's account and evaluating its plausibility seem to go easily hand in hand. Of the different forms of suicide I like to spend more time on anomic suicide. Students already have an idea what anomie means – normlessness – but I have to tease out why an absence of moral regulation might lead to higher levels of suicide. Furthermore they do not always realize that, for Durkheim, 'crises of prosperity' as well as 'crises of poverty' are potential causes of anomic suicide. The explanation for all of this can be found in the second section of the chapter on anomic suicide (Durkheim 1897a/t.1951a:246–54), but the basics of Durkheim's argument can be easily reconstructed – regardless of whether students have read or taken in this section – by asking a series of simple and often leading questions: can someone be happy if their needs are not met? Are there physical limits to human needs? If there are not, what can provide such limits? Once these points are understood it links in well to Durkheim's proposed solution that occupational groups will provide the necessary moral regulation of industry and thus determine levels of legitimate need. Then one could also complicate matters by asking whether anomic and egoistic suicide really are two separate forms of suicide. One could also refer to the discussion of anomie in the *Division of Labour*.

If time allowed, a discussion of the moral implications of suicide and an assessment of Durkheim's argument as to whether individuals have the right to take their own life would be valuable and could easily lead on to Durkheim's analysis of ethical individualism. One could also discuss whether Durkheim is right to suggest that suicide is a normal phenomenon, and whether it is possible to judge when suicide rates are pathological.

I find that students need no encouragement to assess *Suicide* critically. They tend to be quick to side with both Douglas' critique and his alternative 'Weberian' approach to studying suicide. What appears to be a more essential task for the tutor is to ensure that students do not dismiss Durkheim before they have positively engaged with the text. One way of ensuring this is suggested by Steve Taylor. It is to organize students into groups: one of which will argue for the Durkheimian approach to studying suicide, one in favour of Douglas' interpretive approach. Then the seminar group as a whole can assess the strengths and weaknesses of the different approaches; discuss which is the most interesting and enlightening; discuss whether the two approaches could be combined; and find out what, if anything, the two approaches neglect. On the final point, it might be possible to make a case that Durkheim should have developed further his fourth type of suicide – fatalistic suicide – and that he should have said more about, or at least provided stronger evidence for, the different psychological states – apathy, anger, etc. – that he thought accompanied the different forms of suicide. Taylor makes two other suggestions: students could, much as Atkinson (1978) does in his study, analyse the explanations found in newspaper accounts of suicide and compare them to academic and expert theories of suicide; a seminar could be set up to act out a coroner's inquiry in order to gain an understanding of how coroners come to make their verdicts (Taylor 1988:91–2).

Using *Suicide* in sociology and research methodology teaching

Geoffrey Walford

I have included at least a brief study of Durkheim's *Suicide* in my teaching for the last fifteen or more years. During that time I have taught Introductory Sociology and Introductory Research Methodology to undergraduates at Aston University and Research Methodology to postgraduate Masters and Doctoral students at Oxford University. The book has never formed a major part of my courses, but it has been a central illustrative example that I have used to encourage thought and to help inspire students.

Durkheim's *Suicide* needs little justification within any introductory undergraduate sociology teaching. It is, of course, a 'classic' text by one of the major founders of the discipline. But of far more importance to me is the fact that it focuses on such a fundamental example of the nature of sociological research and theorizing. Suicide is, by its very nature, an individual act – one of the most individual of acts that any person can commit. Yet sociology looks for and finds patterns within the statistics on suicide and is able to relate these patterns to other information on these individuals. Sociology finds that nationality, religion or marital status, for example, can be linked to overall patterns within suicide statistics. Within this one focus on the sociology of suicide, the nature of sociology can be discussed – and that is how I used Durkheim's work for many years within Introductory Sociology teaching.

I present students with *Suicide* very early in their course. Some may have had a knowledge of the work from A-level sociology courses, but most have no knowledge of either Durkheim or even that suicide might be an appropriate topic for sociology. My choice to use it early in the course means that not only does the text show the potential gains that sociology might make to understanding, it also illustrates the essence of what sociology is. My own way of doing this is to use a formulation of sociology simplified into theory, method, data and critique. These four elements and the inter-relationship between them provides the meat of two lectures, with *Suicide* as the central example.

The utility of *Suicide* for such a purpose will be obvious to readers of this present book. Durkheim develops and uses theory at several different levels. There are numerous examples of relatively straightforward hypotheses about, say, marital status and the suicide rates; here empirical, statistical data can be used to test 'common sense'. Then there are his theories of social integration and social regulation which seek to explain the statistical relationships found in data. Finally concepts such as anomie are used within these explanations but take on a wider life, moving beyond the study of suicide and inspiring a whole branch of research work on deviance and related areas.

Although *Suicide* is a complex book for new undergraduates, judicious selection of appropriate sections can give a wealth of understanding about the nature of theory, method and data.

As for the fourth of the set, Durkheim's *Suicide* itself has many examples of critique of the work of other researchers, but it also serves as an almost inexhaustible source of critique by others. Having shown the strengths of the work in the first lecture, in the second lecture I begin to introduce some of the sociological tools of critique. The secondary literature on *Suicide* is, of course, vast and a great deal of it is critical of one or many aspects of the theorizing, the methods used in analysis, or the data on which the analysis was based. My second lecture is never a 'hatchet job', but seeks to use *Suicide* to investigate problems of data, of analysis and of theorizing that are to be found not only in that book but in so much of today's sociological literature. I aim to show that any book – even those written by the founders of the discipline – has to be read critically. The claims, assertions and arguments put forward by researchers have to be recognized for what they are and appropriately tested. One of the advantages of taking *Suicide* as an example is that its critique shows some of the ways in which – at its best – sociology as a discipline has progressed. A century-old study can be shown to have much that is of merit, but also many problems that the author could not be expected to be able to recognize, let alone deal with. Thus, for example, while there are clear problems in parts of Durkheim's analysis where he commits the ecological fallacy, he cannot be faulted for not having recognized this (Pope 1976).

One of the most important areas that I always discuss is the nature of the data that Durkheim used. There has now been a great deal of work on the social construction of data; the studies that examined the construction of suicide statistics (e.g. Douglas 1967; Atkinson 1978) led this movement. We are now well aware of the human processes that are involved, not only in the act of suicide itself, but also in the processes undertaken by coroners and other officials in the procedures by which particular sudden deaths become classified as suicides, as well as in the ways that statistics on such deaths are collected and collated. Any lecturer can find some wonderful illustrations of the way sociological knowledge can become 'common knowledge' held by many – including those who are active in the production of the 'facts' on which that 'knowledge' is based. If coroners 'know' that lonely people are more likely to commit suicide, it is worth their considering the extent to which any victim of a sudden death was 'lonely'. The search for an explanation of an individual sudden death is informed by the 'common knowledge' about the nature of suicide, which is itself informed by data structured by very many similar searches for understanding.

This social construction of social statistics was the main focus in my use of *Suicide* within research methodology courses. I have used suicide as an example of the social construction of statistics in both undergraduate and postgraduate teaching. With such a vast array of official statistics easily available, it is important to consider why it is necessary to generate any more. This is not obvious. For example, in 1998, in one of several attacks on educational researchers, the Chief Inspector of Schools for England stated that the Office for Standards in Education (which he directs) collected such a vast amount of data on schools that there was no need for anyone else to collect any more. He appeared to believe that any questions about the nature of schools and schooling could be answered through that single, large data set. For him, data came before any theory or any detailed consideration of the methods of its generation.

Such ideas need to be challenged, and the work by Atkinson (1978) and others on how suicide statistics are constructed provides an admirable case study. Of course, students often argue that suicide is a very special case because of the impossibility of checking the classification of any sudden death with the individual involved. While this unique aspect needs to be acknowledged, most students also find that a consideration of school truancy figures, for example, raises practically all of the same problems.

Thus, over the years, *Suicide* has provided me with an excellent vehicle to introduce sociology to new undergraduates and to discuss a range of issues around data construction. This recognition of the social nature of data construction is at the centre of the way that I try to teach research methodology. To use *Suicide* as a first example is simply to show that sociology has developed and become a stronger discipline from the one that Durkheim was central to founding more than a century ago.

But I wish to raise one final point about the use of Durkheim's *Suicide* in teaching. It is 'common knowledge' that students are liable to commit suicide. The particular times of stress are in the first few weeks of leaving home and entering university and in the time around examinations. The truth of this common knowledge is not easy to untangle because there is often a high suicide rate for people aged about 18 to 22 which is the age at which most young people enter university. Moreover, the group that enters university is not a representative sample of 18- to 22-year-olds but is, in most countries, a highly selected group who may be more likely than others to commit suicide, with or without entry to university. But, whatever the truth of the common knowledge, it is certainly true that students do commit suicide at university and that there is a chance that the students in any sociology or research methodology class may know of suicides and actual people who have committed suicide. As sociologists, we may get excited by Durkheim's insights and by the quality of the theoretical and empirical debate, but students may be more concerned with the facts of the death of someone they knew. As university teachers we need to be aware of these possibilities. In one year when two students had committed suicide in the first few weeks of term, I cut the section on *Suicide* from my course.

Teaching Durkheim's *Suicide*: text and context

Robert Alun Jones

One of the greatest obstacles we face in teaching Durkheim's *Suicide*, or any other 'classic text' in the history of social theory, is what I have come to call 'interpretive essentialism'. Briefly, our students are convinced that there is something that *Suicide* is 'Really About', that it contains certain meanings and/or truths, shrouded in a cryptic code that the professoriate alone can decipher. This in turn encourages our dangerously flattering self-image as academic priests dispensing the intellectual sacraments, and the related notion that education is a matter of passively receiving these sacraments in the liturgical setting of the classroom.

As a pragmatist, I try to counteract this essentialism by insisting on three principles: first, that meaning is always a matter of context; second, that a text thus has as many meanings as there are contexts within which it might be placed; and third, that the question of which contexts we privilege, and thus of how the text is to be used, will always depend on our own interests and purposes. Any text, in sum, can be changed by being contextually redescribed, and thus the notion of a text having an 'essential meaning' is incoherent.

Suicide illustrates these principles particularly well – i.e. it can be placed in many different contexts, yields a variety of redescriptions and meanings, and serves numerous and sometimes quite divergent interests and purposes. Sometimes this simply means reading *Suicide* in the light of one of Durkheim's other works. Most obviously, perhaps, *Suicide* can be read as the implementation (or non-implementation) of the principles laid out in Durkheim's *Rules of Sociological Method* just two years earlier, thus illuminating the practical difficulties of defining, classifying, comparing and explaining social facts (Durkheim 1895a/t.1982a:50–163). *Suicide*'s discussion of the 'duality of human nature' – the social superimposed on the physical – might be usefully related to the parallel discussion in *The Division of Labour* (Durkheim 1893b/t.1984a), relating the personal, individual conscience to its collective counterpart, and providing the psychological infrastructure for the distinction between organic and mechanical solidarity (Durkheim 1897a/t.1951a:213). The recent discovery of André Lalande's notes from Durkheim's 1883–4 lecture course at the Lycée de Sens, with their a-sociological insistence that altruism is a basic feature of human nature rather than the product of socialization, affords a sharp contrast with the aggressively sociological treatment of altruism in *Suicide* (Durkheim 1897a/t.1951a:217–40; 1996a). And one might equally compare the discussion of the 'contagiousness' of suicide with that of the sacred, as developed in *The Elementary Forms of the Religious Life* (Durkheim 1912a/t.1915d:131–3).

A second form of contextualization sets the arguments of *Suicide* within the framework of other writers. The most obvious candidate here is Jean-Gabriel Tarde (1903, 1969), whose appeal to psychological theories of imitation as an explanation for suicide inspired some of the most querulous passages in Durkheim's 1897 classic. Douglas Challenger (1994:177–90) has encouraged us to see Durkheim's distinction between normal and pathological social facts within the context of Aristotle's political and moral philosophy. And Durkheim's (1897a/t.1951a:247–8) discussion of anomic suicide, with its insistence that happiness becomes possible only when our needs are sufficiently proportioned to our means, can be temporally contextualized by referring students back to Rousseau's *Discourse on the Origin of Inequality* (1994), and forward to the functional theory of stratification advanced by Kingsley Davis and Wilbert Moore (1945).

A third kind of contextualization emphasizes the social and political milieu of the Third Republic. In the most general sense, of course, all of Durkheim's work can be understood as an effort to provide a theoretical justification for the commitment of individual citizens to their sometimes precarious social order. But *Suicide*, published at the height of the Dreyfus Affair, is especially illuminated by setting it against the background of the *fin-de-siècle*'s most volatile debate over the nature of political duty and obligation. Durkheim's treatment of egoism and anomie – implicitly a critique, not unlike Rousseau's, of the rising bourgeoisie – can be set off against the backdrop of the shallow prosperities of the Second Empire; and in the face of the 'pathological' increase of anomic suicide resulting from such economic crises, Durkheim's preferred reform – increasing the political, economic, and especially moral authority of occupational groups – might be set within the larger history of the advocacy of administrative decentralization in French politics (Durkheim 1897a/t.1951a:390–1).

My earlier efforts to encourage this kind of historical contextualization were frequently conjoined with attacks on more 'presentist' – and therefore more anachronistic – accounts of Durkheim's works (see, for example, Jones 1977). More recently, however, I have come to recognize 'historicist' and 'presentist' reconstructions of classic texts as simply two more contexts within which such texts might usefully be placed. Richard Rorty, for example, has suggested that we see the history of ideas as a series of 'conversations' that we imagine, either between ourselves and the classic writers of the past, or among the classic writers themselves. In the first type of conversation, we try to imagine and then converse with an 'ideally reasonable and educable Durkheim' – e.g. the Durkheim who shares our 'disciplinary matrix' and speaks our language, and who thus might be brought to admit that his 'aetiological' classification of types of suicide presupposes the causal explanations he eventually proposes for them (see Lukes 1972:31). The purpose of such 'rational reconstructions', Rorty (1984:51) tells us, is reassurance or self-justification, namely our quite reasonable and natural desire to see the history of sociological theory as 'a long conversational interchange' in a fairly stable idiom, and thus to assure ourselves that 'there has been rational progress in the course of recorded history', and that 'we differ from our ancestors on grounds which our ancestors could be led to accept'. Such reconstructions are apt to be anachronistic, of course, but so long as this anachronism is self-conscious, it seems quite harmless; and in any case, reconstructions of this type comprise the vast proportion of statements made by sociological theorists about works like Durkheim's *Suicide*.

There is also a second, more genuinely 'historical' type of reconstruction. Here we are less interested in the Durkheim who might be led to converse with us than with imagined conversations between Durkheim and his contemporaries, in their own language rather than ours. The Durkheim who emerges from this account is not 'one of us', not a 'participant in the same disciplinary matrix', and thus fails to supply us with what Quentin Skinner (1984:197–8, 202; Jones 1998:115) has aptly called 'our usual and carefully contrived pleasures of recognition'. The special value of these more genuinely historical reconstructions thus lies, not in reassurance or self-justification, but in self-knowledge or self-awareness, in the recognition that there have been other idioms, other vocabularies, some of them quite powerful, but all subject to the contingencies of a particular history, biography, language and/or social structure. For students to learn this from the study of Durkheim's *Suicide* is to learn something, not only about the past, but also about themselves. Like 'rational' reconstructions, of course, such historical accounts provide another context in which *Suicide* might be placed.

Finally, something should be said about the specific institutional contexts within which we find ourselves. For these in turn alter the contexts in which we place Durkheim's *Suicide*, and thus its meanings. When I taught 'Introduction to Sociology', for example, I described *Suicide* as an instance of what C. Wright Mills called the 'sociological imagination', namely the counter-intuitive explanation of a seemingly unpredictable, psychological phenomenon in purely sociological terms. Teaching 'Introduction to Sociological Theory' – a step higher in our curriculum – I redescribed *Suicide* as an example of how sociological theorists sometimes resolve problems of definition, classification, observation, comparison and explanation. In 'Classical Social Theory' – a required graduate course focused primarily on Marx, Durkheim and Weber – I compared and contrasted Durkheim's concept of anomie with the Marxian notion of alienation, and Durkheim's emphasis on social facts with Weber's preoccupation with the meaningful orientation of social actors. And in a graduate seminar devoted exclusively to Durkheim, *Suicide* was redescribed within the larger context of his complete work, so that the growing influence of Rousseau, for example, could be traced throughout, and the early, limited conception of the 'anomic division of labour' could be sharply contrasted with the later, fuller development of the concept of anomie in *Suicide*.

Several years ago, after leaving sociology for religious studies, I found that the power and plasticity of *Suicide* impressed me still more. In an introductory lecture of 'World Religions', for example, I have used Durkheim's explanation of the variations of suicide rates among Protestants, Catholics and Jews to show students how religions work subliminally, beneath the level of the believer's consciousness, independent of creed or doctrine. And in a course titled 'The Secular Mind' – a history of western religious thought from the Enlightenment to the present – I have used *Suicide* to illuminate Durkheim's insistence, in opposition to both atheism and orthodoxy, that no religion is false, for all religious beliefs and practices express and correspond to something real.

Suicide, in short, is like all texts in that its meaning can change according to how it is redescribed and contextualized; but like very few texts, *Suicide* has been redescribed in ways that have served our interests and purposes in a variety of extremely productive ways. It is from this, rather than any essential, 'hidden' meaning, that its status as a classic derives.

Introducing Durkheim: the perils of theoretical pedagogy

William Ramp

To develop a full picture of Durkheim's place in North American undergraduate sociology curricula would be a quixotically ambitious if interesting exercise, involving a detailed survey of course offerings and of the different contexts (disciplinary, theoretical, substantive) in which Durkheim's name might be invoked. Such a study, moreover, would aim at a moving target: it itself would no doubt provoke reflection and thus introduce further change into the situations examined.

On a less ambitious scale, though, certain patterns can be identified and certain things said in a preliminary and limited way, on the basis of personal experience in teaching Durkheimian theory, searching for resources for such teaching, and conversing with colleagues and students. The remarks that follow stem from my own experience, and in particular my encounters with presentations of Durkheim to be found in selected, mass-market introductory sociology texts.

My sense is that the Durkheim of many of these texts – all too often the only Durkheim many undergraduates meet – is one constructed in the cutting-edge scholarship of a few generations ago, and sadly distanced from the creative uses made of Durkheimian sociology in scholarship today. This distancing, to foretell my conclusion, is not simply a matter of 'lag' or laziness, but something embedded in the state of the discipline itself.

The reception initially accorded Durkheim by American sociologists was often sceptical, as evidenced by the first full-length study of his work, by C. E. Gehlke, in 1915 (see also Small 1901–2). The fact that Durkheim later became a major presence in North American sociology is primarily a result of the work of theorists who reinterpreted his work in light of the emerging concerns of what came to be known as American structural functionalism. Interestingly, the new popularity of Durkheimian sociology stemmed in part from its reinterpretation as a solution to an issue in terms of which it had earlier been construed as a problem. A major concern of American sociological theory before and after Talcott Parsons was the reconciliation of individual agency and social determinism (MacDougall 1912; Allport 1925; Alpert 1939; see also Hinkle 1960). Durkheim was initially condemned for resolving this dichotomy (falsely) in terms of a 'group mind' theory. Parsons' recasting of the issue, in terms of a sociological version of the problem of order, used Durkheim as a means to conceptualize, as being central, the role of norms and values. They were first used in the construction of actors' choices of means and ends and ultimately in the integration of social, cultural and personality systems (Parsons 1935, 1949[1937], 1951).

Parsons, and especially Robert Merton, saw in Durkheimian sociology an example of a necessary conjunction of good, middle-range theory with a clear focus on the resolution of empirical problems. Thus Durkheim became for them a harbinger of the theoretical and methodological progress that would eventually put sociology in its own way on a par with other sciences (see Parsons 1938; Merton 1957[1948], 1967; see also Hinkle 1960).

In the light of these concerns, Durkheim's *Suicide* became an icon: a milestone in the evolution of theoretically informed empirical research, and in the integration of a theory of personal agency with a theoretical description of the larger systems with which agency could be seen to intersect (see, e.g. Selvin 1965; Merton 1957c[1938]).

Today, North American sociology can in no way be described as dominated by structural functionalism of the Parsonian or any other school. Indeed, 'functionalism' has long been a straw man for those who would seek to distinguish their work from it. But Durkheim has been popularly identified with functionalism ever since: one famous early attack on the epistemology and methodology associated with functionalism was couched in the form of an extended critique of the premises and conclusion of Durkheim's *Suicide* (Douglas 1967).

Today, when attempting to survey the discipline, North American introductory sociology texts are faced with a particular problem: the reaction against functionalism did not give rise to any one pretender to theoretical dominance. Rather, a number of different approaches to sociology, some indigenous and some imported, vie with each other.

George Ritzer attempted in his 1975 study, *Sociology: a Multiple-paradigm Science*, to apply Thomas Kuhn's analysis of paradigm-building in the natural sciences to sociology. Ritzer argued that sociology is characterized by three different paradigms, which he characterized in terms of their respective concentration on 'social facts', 'social definition' and 'social behaviour'. He argued for a kind of pluralistic coexistence of these paradigms; much as if they might constitute a kind of analogue at the level of social theory for a renewed, pluralistic commonwealth in American society. At the same time, he argued that Durkheim, Weber and other classical theorists were distinguished by their ability to cross paradigmatic boundaries (see also Ritzer and Bell 1981).

Ritzer condemned a tendency in American sociology to make certain perspectival distinctions in sociological theory and research. In particular, he argued that the so-called 'functionalist' and 'social conflict' perspective had much in common with each other and did not constitute distinct paradigms. But in a sense, the pluralism implicit in Ritzer's approach to the discipline parallels that present in the presentation of sociology in many undergraduate texts, while his warnings about the insufficiency of perspectival labels such as 'functionalism' and 'conflict theory' have been ignored. Such texts still often divide sociology into different perspectives, approaches or traditions; these are often distinguished along a 'micro–macro' axis (e.g. Hagedorn 1994:11–20), or carved into a three-way distinction between 'functionalist', 'interactionist' and 'social conflict' theories (see Kendall *et al.* 1997:24–33; Schaefer *et al.* 1996:11–14). While these distinctions are at odds with the paradigms Ritzer identifies, they do, perhaps, reflect a practical assessment of the manner in which sociologists have often grouped themselves. Such phenomena can legitimately be identified, as they are by Collins (1985), as 'traditions'. But Collins deftly illustrates the multiple fecundity of Marx, Weber and Durkheim for several different strains of twentieth-century sociology, and Ritzer, in placing Durkheimian sociology within the 'social facts' paradigm, makes it clear that he is to some extent using Durkheim as a straw man. These subtleties progressively fade from view in the characterizations made in introductory texts, and the latter do not always make their own exercises in reduction so explicit. At worst, the contributions of Marx, Weber and Durkheim may be effectively rewritten to fit their respective slots, and elements of each that do not fit edited out. Thus, for example, 'functionalist' aspects of Marx's analysis of capitalism may be downplayed, while Marx's emphasis on the centrality of social contradiction may be reworked into a softer version focused on 'inequality', and 'conflict' between unequal interest groups (a focus that begins to sound suspiciously Weberian, and certainly owes more to Dahrendorf than Marx!). Weber, on the other hand, is often written out of the 'conflict' approach and made to reside in an 'interactionist' slot, while Durkheim, of course, is made father to Parsons, Merton and Davis within functionalism.

In a sample of recent introductory texts to hand, the Durkheim presented is still for the most part the Durkheim of Parsons, Merton and Alpert. *Suicide* is often given prominent mention as an early attempt to test theories of social integration and regulation by rigorous empirical investigation (e.g.

Hagedorn 1994:5–6; Hale 1995:129–31; Kendall *et al.* 1997:41, 43–50; Schaefer *et al.* 1996:6–7). Its value is seen to lie in the dramatic way in which it presents evidence that is both compelling and counterintuitive – especially in a cultural context in which suicide is primarily characterized in terms of personal motivation and individual psychopathology. The other two of Durkheim's works that rate frequent mention are *The Division of Labour in Society*, and *The Elementary Forms of the Religious Life*, and are used to demonstrate how social systems can be seen to be organized functionally in terms of different types of solidarity, and how religion serves integrative and other functions in social life (e.g. Hagedorn 1994:404–5; Hale 1995:124–39; Kendall *et al.* 1997:17–18, 576–7).

These ways of characterizing Durkheim are all, in their own ways, still valid, and can still be used to pedagogical advantage, especially where (as in the better texts), concrete contemporary examples are used as exercises to which a 'Durkheimian' approach may be applied. For example, Brym (1995:1.4–1.7) demonstrates the continuing power of *Suicide* as an example of the counterintuitive power of sociological research. He specifically points to its ability to lead us to question explanations of social phenomena that reduce them to the individual or personal. Again, Hale refers to Collins' work on questions of the role of social energy and excess in Durkheim's sociology of religion (Hale 1995:137). Hornsby (in Kivisto 1998:63–106) applies a Durkheimian analysis of community to an innovative study of electronic gatherings on the Internet, and in so doing makes note of Durkheim's unique emphasis on the importance of emotions in social life and his apprehensiveness about the overdevelopment of the modern state relative to secondary social institutions (Hornsby 1998:81).

Aside from such developments, however, the continuing characterization of Durkheim as a 'functionalist' is a straitjacket. Its continuing currency in many popular texts means that those of us who want to present a different Durkheim must continue to teach against the grain of many available resources. Few, if any introductory texts, for example, link Durkheimian sociology to the interactionist tradition by pointing out (as does Collins) how heavily Durkheimian is Goffman's discussion of interaction ritual. Nor does Durkheim's discussion of industrial anomie or the forced division of labour get him classified as a 'conflict theorist', despite the fact that a Durkheimian theory of class conflict is definitely possible. Often, the assignation of authors to different 'perspectives', 'approaches' or 'traditions' as identified in introductory texts seems to be based on characterizations of authors' supposed intents. But as Pearce (1989) has demonstrated, a body of theoretical work can be read productively even against the grain of its purported intent.

What versions of Durkheim, present in contemporary scholarship, might one hope to find in future introductory treatments? Here is my own (quite biased) list of favourites:

1 Durkheimian approaches to the sociological analysis of identity and embodiment, both personal and collective: e.g. extensions of Mauss' work on the category of the person, or of the work of Hertz on regeneration and expiation; Pearce's discussion of the constitution of the 'juridical subject'; explorations of Durkheim's many suggestions about the role of religion in the constitution of identity, embodiment and emotional life, as in Mellor and Shilling (1997), Meštrović (1997) and Mellor (1998).
2 Durkheimian approaches to the analysis of culture in terms of mutuality, limit and transgression: e.g. Victor Turner's studies of liminality (and extensions of it: see Alexander 1990); Goffman's studies of interactional order; the anthropological heritage of Mauss and Hertz.
3 An 'interactional' Durkheim, focusing on parallels between Durkheim's and Mead's discussion of language and symbol, or Durkheimian elements in Goffman's discussions of interaction ritual, as proposed by Collins.
4 Durkheimian approaches to issues of social inequality, justice and conflict: I am thinking here not only of obvious references from *The Division of Labour*, but also to Durkheim's discussions of the nature of property, the concept of inheritance and the idea of justice in *Professional Ethics and Civic Morals*. One might also point to the themes of reciprocity and conflict developed in Mauss' essay, 'The Gift', which in itself would make a wonderful undergraduate pedagogical tool. The work of Gane *et al.* (Gane 1992) and Pearce, among others, would provide useful material for such study.
5 Durkheim's contribution to the moral, as well as sociological analysis of modernity, e.g. as discussed in work by Cladis (1989), Hawkins (1998) and Watts Miller (1996), among others.
6 Comparisons (with attention to historical and discursive contexts, as in, e.g. Corrigan and Sayer's *The Great Arch*, 1985) between Durkheim's sociological characterizations of the modern state and modern citizenship, and contemporaneous discussions of similar issues, such as that found in M. P. Follett's *The New State* (1918).[1]
7 Durkheim's contribution to discussions of the moral and political grounds of social science enquiry. Specifically, here, *The Rules of Sociological Method* deserves attention as a manifesto concerning the place of sociology in human affairs as much as it does for its methodological and epistemological statements.

Each of the above approaches to Durkheim has been the subject of interesting scholarship, both recently and of long standing. But for that scholarship to break the barriers separating it from introductory surveys of the discipline, something has to change: the impulse to carve up sociology into competing (or complementary) approaches or perspectives. Whatever the usefulness of these distinctions,[2] they cripple the efficacy of Durkheim as a resource for undergraduate sociology students. Done well, accounts of Durkheim as part of a 'functionalist' tradition can be relatively sensitive to the complexity of his thought, though within relatively narrow limits. Done badly, they can reduce him to little more than a caricature; one easily forgotten or (depending on one's preferences) dismissed.

Unfortunately, the impulse to distinguish remains strong, and for good reason. First, it still reflects (whether or not accurately) a reality in the discipline: sociologists find themselves isolated from each other by different theoretical preferences, political stances and substantive concerns. (Ironically, of course, this was a situation Durkheim himself referred to in a discussion of anomie in the sciences.) Yet the pedagogical impulse in introductory texts is still, and understandably, somehow to produce a comprehensive picture of sociology that makes sense. The political ideals of democratic pluralism (and the commercial desire to sell textbooks acceptable to a wide range of academic consumers) make the identification of 'traditions' and 'perspectives' an easy option to adopt as a convenient map to a fractured terrain.

But to repeat, the problem is that the map gets mistaken for the terrain, and the caricatures are taken for the real thing. Durkheim becomes a pen sketch of a functionalist pioneer. If there is any way in which it still makes sense to teach classical theory, this kind of approach ultimately will make it wither. I would suggest that the continued vitality of Durkheim scholarship today, as with that of Weber, Marx or Simmel, lies in two things. First, Durkheim addressed a crucial historical turning-point: the advent of modern, global industrial capitalism, and of modern culture. His resonance, in that sense, is historically specific, and if he is to be taught or engaged with effectively today, it has to be in terms of a discussion of the extent to which we are now living in a similar time of transition. But second, Durkheim's work still provides openings to new and unexpected avenues of theory and research. It is not easily sewn up: it contains innumerable loose ends which continue to provoke argument and incite new ways of looking at the social world. It is productive in its very contradictions. But it is precisely such loose ends and contradictions which get tidied up and forgotten in a 'perspectives' or 'approaches' model of theoretical pedagogy.

In short, then, the way Durkheim is taught at the introductory undergraduate level is closely linked to issues in the definition of sociology itself, as a discipline and an enterprise. Given Durkheim's own concern with the disciplinary status of sociology, would it not be appropriate to use his work today to open up discussion, between ourselves and with our students, as to what we are about, theoretically, methodologically, historically and morally?

Notes

1 I am indebted to H. T. Wilson for bringing this specific comparison to my attention.

2 One might suggest that such distinctions are more appropriate as topics for discourse analyses of the history and politics of sociological inquiry, than as theoretical resources in their own right.

Bibliography

Alexander, J. (ed.) (1990) *Durkheimian Sociology: Cultural Studies*, Cambridge: Cambridge University Press.

Allport, F. H. (1925) 'The Group Fallacy in Relation to Social Science', *Journal of Abnormal and Social Psychology* 19:60–73.

Alpert, H. (1939) 'Emile Durkheim and Sociologismic Psychology', *American Journal of Sociology* 45:64–70.

Atkinson, J. (1978) *Discovering Suicide*, London: Macmillan.

Brym, R. J. (1995) *New Society: Sociology for the 21st Century*, Toronto: Harcourt Brace.

Challenger, D. F. (1994) *Durkheim through the Lens of Aristotle: Durkheimian, Postmodernist, and Communitarian Responses to the Enlightenment*, Lanham, MD: Rowman and Littlefield.

Cladis, M. (1989) 'Durkheim's Communitarian Defense of Liberalism', *Soundings* 72:2–3.

Collins, R. (1985) *Three Sociological Traditions*, New York: Oxford University Press.

Corrigan, P. and Sayer, D. (1985) *The Great Arch: English State Formation as Cultural Revolution*, Oxford: Blackwell.

Davis, K. and Moore, W. (1945) 'Some Principles of Stratification', *American Sociological Review* 10:242–9.

Douglas, J. (1967) *The Social Meanings of Suicide*, Princeton, NJ: Princeton University Press.

Durkheim, E. (1996a) *Cours de philosophie fait au Lycée de Sens*, Paris, Bibliothèque de la Sorbonne, MS# 2351.

—(1893b/t.1984a) by W. D. Halls, *The Division of Labour in Society*, with an introduction by L. Coser, London and Basingstoke: Macmillan.

—(1895a/t.1982a) by W. D. Halls, *The Rules of Sociological Method*, London: Macmillan.

(1897a) *Le Suicide: étude de sociologie*, Paris: Alcan.

—(t.1951a) by J. A. Spaulding and G. Simpson, *Suicide: A Study in Sociology*, edited with an introduction by G. Simpson, Glencoe, IL: Free Press (London: Routledge and Kegan Paul, 1952).

—(1912a/t.1915d) by J. W. Swain, *The Elementary Forms of the Religious Life: A Study in Religious Sociology*, London: Allen and Unwin (New York: Macmillan).

—(1950a/t.1957a) by C. Brookfield, *Professional Ethics and Civic Morals*, London: Routledge and Kegan Paul.

Ellwood, C. A. (1925) 'The Relations of Sociology and Social Psychology', *Journal of Abnormal Psychology and Social Psychology* 19.

Follett, M. P. (1918) *The New State. Group Organization and the Solution of Popular Government*, London: Longmans Green.

Gane, M. (ed.) (1992) *The Radical Sociology of Durkheim and Mauss*, London: Routledge.

Gehlke, C. E. (1968[1915]) *Emile Durkheim's Contribution to Sociological Theory*, New York: AMS Press.

Hale, S. (1995) *Controversies in Sociology: A Canadian Introduction*, 2nd edition, Toronto: Copp Clark.

Hagedorn, R. (1994) *Sociology*, 5th edition, Toronto: Harcourt Brace and Co. (Canada).

Hawkins, M. (1998) 'Durkheim's Sociology and Theories of Degeneration', unpublished ms. based on presentations to the conference 'Le Malaise sociale: Durkheim et la fin de siècle', Maison Française, Oxford, 23 March 1996, and to the Political Theory Seminar, University of Hull, 5 December 1997.

Hinkle, R. C. (1960) 'Durkheim and American Sociology', in K. H. Wolff (ed.) *Emile Durkheim, 1858–1917*, Columbus: Ohio State University Press.

Hornsby, A. M. (1998) 'Surfing the Net for Community: A Durkheimian Analysis of Electronic Gatherings', in P. Kivisto (ed.) *Illuminating Social Life: Classical and Contemporary Theory Revisited*, Thousand Oaks, CA: Pine Forge Press.

Jones, R. A. (1977) 'On Understanding a Sociological Classic', *American Journal of Sociology* 83(2):279–319.

Jones, R. A. (1998) 'Ironists and Metaphysicians: Reflections on Sociology and Its History', in N. K. Denzin (ed.) *Cultural Studies: A Research Volume*, New York: JAI Press.

Kendall, D., Murray, J. L. and Linden, R. (1997) *Sociology in Our Times*, 1st Canadian edition, Scarborough, Ontario: ITP/Nelson.

Kivisto, P. (ed.) (1998) *Illuminating Social Life: Classical and Contemporary Theory Revisited*, Thousand Oaks, CA: Pine Forge Press (Sage).

Lukes, S. M. (1972) *Emile Durkheim. His Life and Work: A Historical and Critical Study*, New York: Harper and Row.

(1973) *Emile Durkheim. His Life and Work: A Historical and Critical Study*, Harmondsworth: Penguin.

MacDougall, R. (1912) 'The Social Basis of Individuality', *American Journal of Sociology* 18:1–20.

Mauss, M. (1925/t.1990) by I. Cunnison, *The Gift: Forms and Functions of Exchange in Archaic Societies*, with an introduction by E. E. Evans-Pritchard, London and Henley: Routledge and Kegan Paul.

Mellor, P. A. and Shilling, C. (1997) *Re-forming the Body: Religion, Community and Modernity*, London: Sage.

Mellor, P. A. (1998) 'Sacred Contagion and Social Vitality: Collective Effervescence in *Les Formes elémentaires de la vie religieuse*', *Durkheimian Studies/Etudes Durkheimiennes* 4:87–114.

Merton, R. K. (1957[1948]) 'The Bearing of Empirical Research on Sociological Theory', in R. K. Merton, *Social Theory and Social Structure*, Glencoe, IL: Free Press.

(1957b) 'The Bearing of Sociological Theory on Empirical Research', in R. K. Merton, *Social Theory and Social Structure*, Glencoe, IL: Free Press.

(1957c[1938]) 'Social Structure and Anomie', in R. K. Merton, *Social Theory and Social Structure*, Glencoe, IL: Free Press.

(1967) 'On the History and Systematics of Sociological Theory', in R. K. Merton, *On Sociological Theory*, New York: Free Press.

Meštrović, S. (1997) *Postemotional Society*, London: Sage.

Parsons, T. (1935) 'The Place of Ultimate Values in Social Theory', *International Journal of Ethics* 45:282–316.

(1938) 'The Role of Theory in Social Research', *American Sociological Review* 3:13–20.

(1949[1937]) *The Structure of Social Action*, New York: Free Press.

(1951) *The Social System*, Glencoe, IL: Free Press.

Pearce, F. (1989) *The Radical Durkheim*, London: Unwin Hyman.

Pope, W. (1976) *Durkheim's* Suicide*: A Classic Analysed*, Chicago: University of Chicago Press.

Ritzer, G. (1975) *Sociology: A Multiple-paradigm Science*, Boston: Allyn and Bacon.

Ritzer, G. and Bell, R. (1981) 'Emile Durkheim: Exemplar for an Integrated Sociological Paradigm?', *Social Forces* 59:966–95.

Rorty, R. (1984) 'The Historiography of Philosophy: Four Genres', in R. Rorty, J. Schneewind and Q. Skinner (eds) *Philosophy in History*, Cambridge: Cambridge University Press.

Rousseau, J. J. (1994) *Discourse on the Origin and Foundations of Inequality among Men*, translated by F. Philip, Oxford and New York: Oxford University Press.

Schaefer, R. T., Lamm, R. P., Biles, P. and Wilson, S. J. (1996) *Sociology: An Introduction*, 1st Canadian edition, Toronto: McGraw-Hill Ryerson.

Selvin, H. (1965) 'Durkheim's *Suicide*: Thoughts on a Methodological Classic', in R. A. Nisbet (ed.) *Emile Durkheim. With Selected Essays*, Englewood Cliffs, NJ: Prentice-Hall.

Skinner, Q. (1984) 'The Idea of Negative Liberty: Philosophical and Historical Perspectives', in Rorty, R., Schneewind, J. and Skinner, Q. (eds) *Philosophy in History: Essays on the Historiography of Philosophy*, Cambridge: Cambridge University Press.

Small, A. (1901–2) Review of E. Durkheim, *De la division du travail social*, *American Journal of Sociology* 7:566–8.

Tarde, G. (1903) *The Laws of Imitation*, translated by E. C. Parsons, New York: Holt.

(1969) 'Sociology, Social Psychology, and Sociologism', in T. N. Clark (ed.) *On Communication and Social Influence*, Chicago: University of Chicago Press.

Taylor, S. (1982) *Durkheim and the Study of Suicide*, London: Macmillan.

(1988) *Suicide*, London: Longman.

Watts Miller, W. (1996) *Durkheim, Morals and Modernity*, London: UCL Press.

INDEX

For Product Safety Concerns and Information please contact our EU representative GPSR@taylorandfrancis.com
Taylor & Francis Verlag GmbH, Kaufingerstraße 24, 80331 München, Germany

www.ingramcontent.com/pod-product-compliance
Ingram Content Group UK Ltd.
Pitfield, Milton Keynes, MK11 3LW, UK
UKHW021303190926
475701UK00009B/628
* 9 7 8 1 1 3 8 0 0 7 3 0 7 *